PRACTISING COMMUNITY-BASED PARTICIPATORY RESEARCH

Practising Community-Based Participatory Research

Stories of Engagement, Empowerment, and Mobilization

EDITED BY SHAUNA MacKINNON

PURICH
BOOKS

Purich Books, an imprint of UBC Press
2029 West Mall
Vancouver, BC, V6T 1Z2
www.purichbooks.ca

26 25 24 23 22 21 20 19 18   5 4 3 2 1

Printed in Canada on FSC-certified ancient-forest-free paper
(100% post-consumer recycled) that is processed chlorine- and acid-free.

Library and Archives Canada Cataloguing in Publication

Practising community-based participatory research: stories of engagement,
empowerment, and mobilization / edited by Shauna MacKinnon.

Includes bibliographical references and index.
Issued in print and electronic formats.
ISBN 978-0-7748-8010-7 (hardcover). – ISBN 978-0-7748-8011-4 (softcover).
ISBN 978-0-7748-8012-1 (PDF). – ISBN 978-0-7748-8013-8 (EPUB).
ISBN 978-0-7748-8014-5 (Kindle)

1. Communities – Research – Manitoba – Case studies. 2. Participant
observation – Manitoba – Case studies. I. MacKinnon, Shauna, editor

HM756.P73 2018   307.072'07127   C2017-907822-4
                                                        C2017-907823-2

Canada

UBC Press gratefully acknowledges the financial support
for our publishing program of the Government of Canada
(through the Canada Book Fund), the Canada Council for the Arts,
and the British Columbia Arts Council.

This book has been published with the help of a grant from the
Canadian Federation for the Humanities and Social Sciences,
through the Awards to Scholarly Publications Program, using funds provided
by the Social Sciences and Humanities Research Council of Canada.

Printed and bound in Canada by Friesens
Set in Univers Condensed and Minion by Artegraphica Design Co. Ltd.
Copy editor: Deborah Kerr
Proofreader: Judith Earnshaw
Indexer: Judy Dunlop

Contents

PART 2: WALKING BESIDE

PART 3: DETOURS

    Together / 179
    CAROLE O'BRIEN

11 Preserving the History of Aboriginal Institutional Development
    in Winnipeg: Research Driven by the Community / 193
    JOHN LOXLEY and EVELYN PETERS

12 Breaking Barriers, Building Bridges: Challenging Racial, Spatial,
    and Generational Divides in the City / 213
    SHAUNA MacKINNON, CLAIRE FRIESEN, and CAROLE O'BRIEN

13 Reclaiming the Talk: Popular Theatre and Historical
    Testimonies as First Nation Women's Empowerment in Hollow
    Water, Manitoba / 231
    DORIS DIFARNECIO

    Conclusion: Possibility, Promise, and Policy Change / 246
    SHAUNA MacKINNON

    Appendix: MRA Reports and Related Publication and Knowledge
    Mobilization Tools / 252

    Contributors / 256

    Index / 258

Preface

The idea for this book came to me as I reflected on my several years of conducting research in Winnipeg's inner city. It occurred to me that we – researchers, activists, community-based organizations, and local residents – have learned a great deal about doing research collaboratively and using it to advocate for change. After I spoke with colleagues about sharing our experiences, we decided to compile this collection of research stories. Our aim is quite simple: we hope that this book will be useful to anyone who is interested in conducting research as a means to social justice.

Most of the chapters discuss past and current Manitoba Research Alliance (MRA) projects. The MRA is a consortium of academics, community researchers, and community-based organizations. It has been awarded three consecutive multi-year research grants through the Social Sciences and Humanities Research Council (SSHRC), beginning in 2003. The projects discussed in this book were funded through two of these grants, including a five-year Community University Research Alliance Grant (2007–11) and a seven-year Partnership Grant (2012–18). Although the MRA involves researchers from three Manitoba universities (University of Manitoba, University of Winnipeg, and the University College of the North), research grants awarded to the MRA are administered through a community-based non-profit research institute, the Canadian Centre for Policy Alternatives–Manitoba, which makes our approach somewhat unique. The centre is one of very few non-academic research institutes to receive SSHRC grants, and this has been key to our success. Administering the grant at the community level has been particularly conducive to the community-based participatory research (CBPR) model that we employ because we are on the front lines, working with community organizations daily, responding to emerging issues and concerns. In 2013, the Community Campus Partnerships for Health gave the MRA an award for excellence in community-engaged research, describing our CBPR model as one that "communities should aspire to." The model is grounded in meaningful community partnerships that engage participants as much as they wish and at every stage of the research. As one of our community partners noted, it is "research that belongs to us."

We believe that the length and depth of the Manitoba Research Alliance's involvement in the community, and the value the community extracts from collaborating with us, make our experience (and hence our book) unique. We believe that our approach is distinctive in that the MRA is situated within the community, rather than at an academic institution. This is an important factor in establishing meaningful, long-term, trusting relationships with community partners, especially those who have long been the subjects of research but who have exerted little control over it. The governance structure of the MRA, in which university and community partners are equals, ensures that researchers are accountable to the partners both throughout and beyond the life of a project. The MRA does not dissolve as an entity once a project is completed, mainly because it is driven by a community-based, community-led collaboration that will persist beyond the scope of a single research grant.

Many of our research ideas have come directly from our community partners; they tell us what topics need to be studied and why. We work together to design research frameworks and arrive at appropriate methods. Building capacity is an important objective of the MRA. Where possible, we choose community researchers, whom we then hire and train as research assistants. We publish our findings in various widely disseminated forms to ensure accessibility. As mentioned throughout this book, our community partners often use our research to advocate for improved government policy and programs that better address the needs of the individuals and families whom they serve.

The research described in this book is a small sample of the MRA's work. Projects were selected to demonstrate the breadth of experiences of those involved and the many different methods used. Our aim here is to present a particular way of doing research. The chapters do not provide detailed results of the various projects: the focus is on the *process* of doing CBPR. The authors explain how their projects took root and developed in collaboration with community partners. They talk about how their research has been used for program development and policy advocacy. And they show how partnerships with the community drove the research agenda and how the community used the findings.

Several years have elapsed since the MRA began this journey in 2002. We have learned many valuable lessons and have benefitted greatly from the experience. We believe that this symbiotic relationship between researchers and community organizations nurtures our understanding of the complex poverty and social exclusion afflicting Winnipeg's inner city and Manitoba's Indigenous groups, and it helps them convey their needs and wisdom to policy makers who control the resources that they require.

Acronyms

CBO	community-based organization
CBPR	community-based participatory research
CCPA	Canadian Centre for Policy Alternatives
CCPA–MB	Canadian Centre for Policy Alternatives–Manitoba
CD	community development
CEDA	Community Education Development Association
CLOUT	Community Led Organizations United Together
CMHC	Canada Mortgage and Housing Corporation
IMFC	Indian and Metis Friendship Centre
LSP	Lord Selkirk Park
MRA	Manitoba Research Alliance
NDP	New Democratic Party
NECRC	North End Community Renewal Corporation
OCAP	ownership, control, access, and possession
PAR	participatory action research
PR	participatory research
RCAP	Royal Commission on Aboriginal Peoples
R2H	Right to Housing Coalition
SIC	State of the Inner City
SPSWs	student parent support workers
SSHRC	Social Sciences and Humanities Research Council
TRC	Truth and Reconciliation Commission of Canada
YFC	Youth for Christ

PRACTISING COMMUNITY-BASED PARTICIPATORY RESEARCH

Introduction
"Research That Belongs to Us"

SHAUNA MacKINNON

Although this book deals with research methods, it isn't a typical research methods text. It is best described as a collection of stories about doing community-based participatory research (CBPR) with an eye toward social justice. Throughout the book, the authors discuss the impetus for their research, how it came to be implemented, and how communities and policy advocates are using it to effect change. They believe that individuals and communities who are excluded from and/or negatively affected by public policy have much to contribute to policy dialogue. However, though their experiences and insights are invaluable to social science researchers, many have come to distrust researchers, and for good reason. For example, Smith (1999) chronicles how Western forms of knowledge have been used as tools of colonization. In Canada, we have seen the deeply damaging effects of misguided research and public policies, which gave us Indian residential schools (TRC 2015) and the Sixties Scoop (Johnston 1983). For Indigenous people and others who have been socially and economically excluded, a deep distrust in research is understandable – they have seen little evidence of its value and much evidence of its harm.

All the research described in this volume was conducted with organizations and individuals who work and live in socially and economically marginalized Manitoba communities. Many chapters focus on Indigenous communities. Manitoba has a very large and growing Indigenous population, which measures poorly against a host of social and economic indicators (Fernandez, MacKinnon, and Silver 2015). As highlighted throughout the book, colonial policies and systemic racism continue to leave a trail of trauma. The authors recognize that if we are to engage with marginalized communities, particularly Indigenous ones, to shift the policy discourse in a meaningful way, our starting point must be the establishment of trusting relationships in which research is guided by communities and all contributors are recognized for their strengths.

Although Manitoba forms the backdrop for the stories included here, the issues they address are not unique to the province. They occur in urban centres and rural and Indigenous communities throughout North America and beyond. The research methods and the policy solutions that are put forward here can be used – probably are being used – in communities everywhere. We believe our stories will be informative to scholars and community practitioners who wish to undertake research that is sensitive to the negative effects that "outsider" research has had for many communities.

CBPR Defined

A vast literature describes research models and methods that, to varying degrees, are participatory and action-oriented. The idea of involving communities in the research process is not new. For example, in the 1930s, Kurt Lewin suggested engaging "minority groups" in "action research" as a means to "overcome the forces of exploitation and colonialization" (Adelman 1993, 8). Reason and Bradbury (2001, 2) note that action research is about "working towards practical outcomes, and also about creating new forms of understanding." Some commentators suggest that action research has a "conservative influence" on community-based research, failing to acknowledge class conflict (Strand et al. 2003), whereas others trace its evolution to Marxist theories and Freirian pedagogies that emphasize the need to move beyond the generation of knowledge to action – praxis. Gramsci's theory of the organic intellectual also lends itself well to participatory research practice (Reason and Bradbury 2001, 3).

Participatory research (PR), participatory action research (PAR), and CBPR are similar in that they value engaging non-researchers in the research process. This can vary from minimal participation in design and implementation to full involvement throughout. Green et al. (2003, 419) describe PAR as "systematic inquiry, with the collaboration of those affected by the issue being studied, for purposes of education and taking action or effecting social change." Although PAR is not limited to research with marginalized and oppressed communities, many researchers who work in this context and with transformative aims do employ it (Gatenby and Humphries 2000; Khanlou and Peter 2005; Mertens 2008). PAR has also been called a "process and a goal" that entails collaboration and the incorporation of local knowledge; eclectic, diverse, and case-oriented, it involves emergent processes that link scientific understanding to orientation (Greenwood, Whyte, and Harkavy 1993).

Engaging marginalized communities in research has become quite common in the health field, and the term CBPR is most often used there. As Israel et al. (2005, 8–9) explain, health-related CBPR is guided by certain principles: acknowledging community as a unity of identity; building on strengths and resources with the community; facilitating collaborative, equitable partnerships in all phases of the research, involving an empowering and power-sharing process that attends to social inequalities; fostering co-learning and capacity building among all partners; integrating and achieving a balance between knowledge generation and intervention for mutual benefit; focusing on the local relevance of public health problems and on ecological perspectives that attend to the multiple determinants of health; involving systems development using a cyclical and iterative process disseminating results to all partners and involving them in the distribution; involving a long-term process and commitment to sustainability. Since it has become increasingly clear that health outcomes are determined by social and economic factors, it makes sense that CBPR focused on public policy has emerged as a common practice.

Although the participatory nature of action research, PAR, and CBPR does differ from project to project, all three models are designed to be more inclusive than their traditional counterparts and to conduct research that builds capacity. However, some models are rooted in an understanding of oppression. For example, in the 1960s Paulo Freire asserted that the oppressed should be engaged in education connected with research and action as a means to emancipation and social justice. In *Pedagogy of the Oppressed* (2006, 65), Freire states that a critical stage in their emancipation is an understanding of their oppression, leading to an active role in their liberation. A methodology that enables participants to have a voice and be empowered through their storytelling is also consistent with Indigenous research methodologies. As Smith (1999, 127) writes, "community action approaches [to research] assume that people know and can reflect on their own lives." This is especially important for the Manitoba Reseach Alliance (MRA), given the significant number of Indigenous people who participate in our research. Developing a research paradigm that acknowledges the importance of cultural identity and the role of colonization and oppression in shaping lives can contribute to consciousness raising, empowerment, renewed cultural identity, individual emancipation, and movement toward systemic transformation. Social science researchers who are schooled in Western research methods and are interested in systemic transformation have some work to do. As Guba and Lincoln state, social science research "needs emancipation from hearing only the voices of Western Europe, emancipation from generations of silence, and emancipation from seeing the world in one colour" (quoted in Chilisa 2012, 3).

Although there are similarities among the participatory approaches described above, levels of engagement and ownership differ, and not all approaches move from research to action. Because CBPR has become increasingly popular in recent years, we believe that researchers must clearly articulate what it means to them. It entails much more than simply undertaking research in a community. We have heard far too often of incidents in which a university researcher asks a community-based organization for a letter of support, claiming that his or her project is grounded in community-based research, even though the organization itself has had no input or awareness of the project. A university colleague once asked me, "How do I find a community organization that would like to work with me on my research?" She seemed surprised when I explained that in my experience, the best CBPR unfolds in the opposite direction – the community brings an idea to a researcher with whom it has established a relationship of trust. The researcher then works with the community to move its ideas forward in a way that is meaningful to it. My colleague's somewhat superficial understanding of CBPR is not uncommon. Nor should it be surprising, given the context in which university researchers currently operate. In the age of neoliberalism and corporatization of universities, research for the sake of expanding knowledge is devalued, and the emphasis shifts to that which responds to market needs (Brownlee 2015). In part, the trend toward university-community collaborations has emerged due to necessity, as funding agencies increasingly prioritize research that involves partnerships beyond the academy.

The blossoming interest in CBPR is also due in part to the intense pressure on universities to demonstrate that they are not merely ivory towers, detached from the world. It also reflects community concerns with situations in which outside experts have done research *on* communities rather than collaborating *with* them and recognizing their expertise. Learning from their negative experiences, some communities now refuse to participate in research unless they are accorded greater control and something useful is left behind. In addition, many researchers are genuinely interested in CBPR but don't know how and where to begin.

It is also the case that the structures in place to finance research are based on the Western paradigm. This presents a dilemma for both universities and community researchers who wish to pursue egalitarian approaches that value diverse forms of knowledge. Although research-granting bodies are increasingly encouraging "community collaboration," requirements and models of practice remain hierarchical in design, placing higher value in academic credentials than in organic and Indigenous knowledge (Chilisa 2012).

Our Approach to CBPR

The approach outlined by Strand et al. (2003) aligns well with what we do. It is influenced by the idea of praxis and by "popular education models that emphasize the involvement of people in educating themselves for social change." Strand et al. (ibid., 4) move beyond more conservative action research approaches to participatory models that "emphasize the involvement of people in doing their own research for social change." Such models entail collaboration between academic researchers and community members and the validation of multiple forms of knowledge, methods, and dissemination practices, with the goal of working for social justice. We are guided by Indigenous researchers who remind us that Western ways of knowing do not have primacy over Indigenous ways of knowing or the knowledge that comes with lived experience (Chilisa 2012; Smith 1999; Wilson 2008).

We also aspire to the approach of Mertens (2008, 5), which pushes beyond the participatory notion of research toward what she describes as a "transformative" research paradigm that challenges oppressive social structures, embraces inclusion, establishes trusting relationships with communities, and disseminates findings broadly and in diverse ways that support social justice aims. Like the models described above, the CBPR presented in this book intends to move beyond the generation of knowledge to that which empowers and mobilizes communities to engage in public policy change. CBPR means different things to different people. For us, it is conducted *with* communities, but it doesn't stop there. It is guided by the belief that communities can use research to advocate for policy change in hopes of creating a more equitable world.

Many of the research stories told in this book are more accurately described as *community-driven* rather than community-based, because the research ideas and methods were identified by people in communities where social and economic injustices are experienced daily (see Chapters 1, 2, 11, and 12). Working alongside trained researchers, they sought to explore and expose issues as well as propose and advocate for public policy solutions to improve social and economic conditions in their communities. For us, CBPR relationships that move from research to action and/ or that produce tools for use by communities best reflect the spirit of social-justice-focused CBPR.

The Importance of Trusting Relationships

The relationships chronicled in this book have developed due to mutual trust between researchers and community members. These take time to nurture. In many cases, community partners determined which methods would best suit the needs and objectives of the research project. In all cases, findings were disseminated widely and in accessible forms. In some instances, researchers continued to be involved in moving research to action through public policies and program development (see Chapters 4, 5, and 12).

Through the stories of researchers and their community partners, this book provides rich insights into the possibilities of conducting CBPR while also reflecting on some associated challenges and realities. One challenge is the process of writing up the results. Very few service providers and activists are particularly interested in this task. They want to drive the process and ensure that their opinions are reflected in it, but most are happy to leave the writing to university researchers. For example, in the case of the chapters co-authored by myself, my community partners drove the research and were fully engaged in the writing in that they reviewed and commented on various revisions and gave final approval to be included as co-authors. But they did not take the lead on the writing. This process succeeded largely because we had built trusting relationships with each other and because each person's contribution was respected. The reality is that the stories in this book would not have been written had researchers not taken the initiative. We think this division of labour makes sense, as writing is one of the skills that researchers bring to the work. Our community partners are service providers and activists who have many abilities, but they are not academics, and most are not writers. They are busy doing the work that we write about. They want their stories to be told, and we have negotiated a way to do this respectfully, accurately, and as collaboratively as possible.

Power and Privilege

Although we have made every effort to be participatory and inclusive, it is also true that those who hold the pen or shoot the video wield a certain amount of power over the process, and we need to be mindful of this. As Carole O'Brien points out in Chapter 10, even when we do our best to follow the lead of our community partners and engage them throughout the research process, they typically do not see every frame of film or every word transcribed. If only for practical reasons, we make certain choices in determining which words and images are important. Indeed, our trusting relationships with our partners have allowed us to take some liberties, but we must acknowledge that we have not completely eliminated power and privilege from our process.

How the Book Is Organized

The stories presented in this book are organized in three parts, followed by a concluding chapter.

Part 1 is titled "We're in It for the Long Haul." Every story in this section is an example of research partnerships that evolved over several years, most of which continue. They show that university researchers can remain engaged with their community partners, using their findings to advocate for policy change.

The second part is titled "Walking Beside." The stories here, which have more clearly defined beginnings and endings, typically involve emerging researchers who were either students or recent graduates when they conducted their studies. The projects were important to them and to the communities with whom they worked. The students acquired a better understanding of what it meant to conduct research *with* communities. For example, reflecting years later on her participatory action research with sex trade workers (Chapter 8), Maya Seshia notes a number of things she would do differently to further engage the women, not only in naming the issues, but also in developing a plan of action toward policy change. Although the authors of these chapters did not remain involved beyond the project, they walked alongside their partners, benefitting from "the best combination of experiential and intellectual learning" (Strand et al. 2003, 10) while also bringing knowledge, policy advocacy tools, and new skills to the community.

Part 3 of the book is titled "Detours." It focuses on research that took roads less travelled, using less typical methods and approaches. These case studies are important because they demonstrate how being open to new ways of gathering and disseminating knowledge can have a powerful impact. MRA researchers have learned of the importance of using tools and methods that extend beyond the traditional formula, which emphasizes research design, gathering and analyzing data, and writing a report for academic publication. Although MRA researchers do this too, our community partners have taught us to be more broadminded. They have taught us to be open to innovative ideas and methods, and to concentrate more on what is useful to the community than on our own personal interests and expectations. Some of our best, most effective, and far-reaching work has been atypical research. This is particularly important when working with Indigenous communities for which Western methods have been deeply damaging. Our community partners, especially those who are Indigenous, remind us of the harm done by outside researchers. The Indigenous people and communities with whom we work will not tolerate this situation and are keenly aware of the principles of ownership, control, access, and possession (OCAP) that are now firmly entrenched in Canada's Tri-Council Policy Statement: Ethical Conduct for Research Involving Humans. Nonetheless, research remains dominated by Western methods, and so we continue to follow the lead of our Indigenous partners if they choose to explore differing ways of knowing and telling.

Because of its natural alignment with OCAP, CBPR has become a typical model for research with Indigenous communities. However, it transcends this application because it operates from a basic level of respect for "multiple sources of knowledge and methods of discovery and dissemination" (Strand et al. 2003, 8). It creates a level playing field by removing researchers as "the experts," positioning them as possessing expertise that is valuable but no more and no less than the expertise of others.

The Conclusion, subtitled "Possibility, Promise, and Policy Change," brings us back to the beginning – reflecting further on "what we do and why we do it," and the broader unintended benefits of community-based research as a means of transforming public policy and effecting social change.

For readers who are currently doing CBPR, we hope you will find comfort and familiarity with our stories and perhaps take away a fresh new idea or two. For those who are new to CBPR but are intrigued by its possibilities, we hope our enthusiasm will inspire you. And for those who aren't convinced of its value, we hope that this book will change your mind.

REFERENCES

Adelman, Clem. 1993. "Kurt Lewin and the Origins of Action Research." *Educational Action Research* 1 (1): 7–24.

Brownlee, Jamie. 2015. *Academia Inc.: How Corporatization Is Transforming Universities.* Halifax: Fernwood.

Chilisa, Bagele. 2012. *Indigenous Research Methodologies.* Thousand Oaks: Sage.

Fernandez, Lynne, Shauna MacKinnon, and Jim Silver, eds. 2015. *The Social Determinants of Health in Manitoba.* Winnipeg: Canadian Centre for Policy Alternatives–Manitoba.

Freire, Paulo. 2006. *Pedagogy of the Oppressed.* 30th anniversary edition. New York: Continuum.

Gatenby, Bev, and Maria Humphries. 2000. "Feminist Participatory Action Research: Methodological and Ethical Issues." *Women's Studies International Forum* 23 (1): 89–105.

Green, Lawrence W., M. Anne George, Mark Daniel, C. James Frankish, Carol P. Herbert, William R. Bowie, and Michel O'Neill. 2003. "Appendix C: Guidelines for Participatory Research in Health Promotion." In *Community-Based Participatory Research for Health,* ed. Meredith Minkler and Nina Wallerstein. San Francisco: Jossey-Bass.

Greenwood, Davydd, William Foote Whyte, and Ira Harkavy. 1993. "Participatory Action Research as a Process and as a Goal." *Human Relations* 46 (2): 175–92.

Israel, Barbara A., Eugenia Eng, Amy J. Schulz, and Edith A. Pareker, eds. 2005. *Methods in Community-Based Participatory Research for Health.* San Francisco: Jossey-Bass.

Johnston, Patrick. 1983. *Native Children and the Child Welfare System.* Toronto: James Lorimer and the Canadian Council on Social Development.

Khanlou, Nazilla, and Elizabeth Peter. 2005. "Participatory Action Research: Considerations for Ethical Review." *Social Science and Medicine* 60 (10): 2333–40.

Mertens, Donna. 2008. *Transformative Research and Evaluation.* New York: Guilford Press.

Reason, Peter, and Hilary Bradbury, eds. 2001. *Handbook of Action Research: Participative Inquiry and Practice.* London: Sage.

Smith, Linda Tuhiwai. 1999. *Decolonizing Methodologies: Research and Indigenous Peoples.* New York: Zed Books.

Strand, Kerry, Sam Marullo, Nick Cutforth, Randy Stoecker, and Patrick Donahue. 2003. *Community-Based Research and Higher Education.* San Francisco: Jossey-Bass.

TRC (Truth and Reconciliation Canada). 2015. *Honouring the Truth, Reconciling for the Future: Summary of the Final Report of the Truth and Reconciliation Commission of Canada.* Winnipeg: Truth and Reconciliation Commission of Canada.

Wilson, Shawn. 2008. *Research Is Ceremony: Indigenous Research Methods.* Halifax: Fernwood.

PART 1

WE'RE IN IT FOR THE LONG HAUL

1

It's All about Relationships
The State of the Inner City Report Project

SHAUNA MacKINNON

In 2005, researchers with the Canadian Centre for Policy Alternatives–
Manitoba (CCPA–MB) began a journey with Winnipeg inner-city organizations that evolved into a multi-year research collaboration. Since then,
several hundred individuals from diverse backgrounds and experiences
have been involved in the State of the Inner City (SIC) Report project in
various ways. This chapter discusses the origins of the SIC Report, the
community-driven research model in which it is grounded, and some of
the resulting benefits as participants become increasingly informed and
are able to connect their personal troubles with structural and political
realities. It also notes some of the difficulties of doing research with community capacity building that also aims to effect public policy change, and
why the project endures despite the challenges.

The SIC project encourages its community partners to take the driver's
seat while also emphasizing the need to generate tools with which to advocate for policy change. For this reason, SIC researchers and community
participants often describe the project as community-based research with
a political edge. Although CCPA–MB, university, and community-based
researchers continue to handle the core scholarly investigation and writing,
the model moves beyond research that engages community to being
directed by community for community use. As one of the community
partners explains, "We tell the researchers what the issues are and what
research we think we need. They come back to us with some ideas and
together we make it happen ... I feel like I'm driving it."[1]

Before the advent of the SIC project, the CCPA–MB had been engaged in community collaborative research for many years and had developed a reputation for conducting research on issues of importance to the inner city. It had established a significant level of trust, making it possible to explore new ways of undertaking research in response to shared interests and concerns. And so, the SIC project was born.

Why a State of the Inner City Report?

The inner-city communities that are the focus of the SIC project have a long history of struggle (Silver 2006). Although pockets of poverty exist across Winnipeg, it is concentrated in the inner city. As discussed in Chapter 12, Winnipeg has long been divided by race and class, with the inner city generally perceived as a dangerous and hopeless place.

An increasing number of new immigrants, especially refugees, are adding to the diversity and complexity of the area (Ghorayshi 2010), but it has become very much an Indigenous space. Winnipeg has a large and fast-growing Indigenous population, the highest among Canada's census metropolitan areas, which is particularly concentrated in the inner city. Indeed, in some inner-city census tracts, upward of 50 percent of residents identify as Indigenous (Silver 2015). This group fares poorly in comparison with the non-Indigenous population on several social and economic indicators (Fernandez, MacKinnon, and Silver 2015), and it is therefore a priority of SIC project research.

The expansion of Winnipeg's Indigenous population is due in part to the relatively high birth rates of urban Indigenous people, but it also arises because many Indigenous people move to the city in search of education and employment. Many congregate in the inner city, where residents generally experience low incomes, high rates of unemployment and single parenthood, low levels of educational attainment, housing insecurity, and dependency on state assistance. Indigenous people often gravitate to the inner city because family and friends from their home communities already live there. All too often, they become trapped in a cycle of poverty; caught up in oppressive systems, they can sometimes lose hope. But though despair is evident in the inner city, community-based organizations have refused to give up, and a strong spirit of hope, reclaiming of cultures, neighbour-hood revitalization, and community building exists there.

The SIC Project and Manitoba Politics

For decades, political power in Manitoba has alternated between the right-leaning Progressive Conservatives and the left-leaning New Democrats (NDP). After spending ten years out of office, an NDP government won the provincial election of 1999. As inner-city neighbourhoods consistently vote for NDP candidates and are thus best off when that party holds power, this development was positive.

Social investment in the inner city has always depended on the political landscape, most crucially on the ideological orientation of the provincial government, and the new NDP administration was committed to supporting work in the area. In 2000, it introduced an initiative called Neighbourhoods Alive! This gave a much-needed injection of support for inner-city community development. At first, it was limited to funds for community projects, but in response to advocacy efforts, it soon expanded to include multi-year core funding for neighbourhood renewal groups in targeted districts.

Also in 2000, the federal, provincial, and municipal governments showed an interest in providing at least some investment in the inner city, and a tripartite funding agreement saw some support for inner-city community building.[2] In addition, the federal Liberal government contributed to inner-city development through various project funds during the later 1990s and through tripartite agreements in the early 2000s, though much of this funding was eliminated after the Harper Conservatives unseated the Liberals in 2006.

Though far from perfect, the NDP government was instrumental in boosting the energy, enthusiasm, capacity, and creativity of the inner city. After it took power, inner-city organizations enjoyed a better financial situation than was the case throughout the 1990s. The SIC project resulted from earlier research with community groups and an awareness that much of the work being done was possible only because the political climate was favourable.

Knowing that this would eventually change, as indeed it did in 2016 when the provincial Conservatives resoundingly defeated the NDP in the election of that year, we felt it important to document the work. Our intent was to help organizations in the future, should governments show less interest in supporting their efforts. Thus, the SIC project was a form of insurance; it evolved from the belief that documenting inner-city stories would furnish organizations with proof that their work was making a difference and could help justify ongoing government support for inner-city development.

The Values That Guide Us

From the outset, the SIC project was driven by the values that guide community development work in the inner city. It aims to contribute to the capacity-building efforts in which our community-based partners are engaged. For this reason, *how* we do our research is as critical as *what* we do. We believe that the story of the inner city is best told by those who live and work there and that policy prescriptions should be rooted in their experiences.

A sense of community ownership is a central benefit of the SIC project, but there are many others. The project gives voice to people who are otherwise not heard and provides tools that they can use to advocate for their goals. It highlights the achievements of community-based organizations (CBOs), which is important because poverty is often hidden and because governments change and are not always appreciative of, or ideologically sympathetic to, the benefits that adequately financed CBOs can bring to community. CBOs do not have research capacity and are overwhelmed with day-to-day work. The SIC project can help with research that they identify as necessary. Individuals who are hired and trained as research assistants gain new skills, and as discussed later in this chapter, the experience has been transformative for some.

The scale of participation and the solidarity that CBOs demonstrate through their involvement in the SIC project inspire governments to pay attention. Approximately two hundred people attend annual SIC celebrations, including policy makers and funders who have come to know and respect that the SIC is important to inner-city development.

Beginnings: Building Relationships

The CCPA–MB introduced the idea of generating an annual SIC Report at a 2005 meeting that was attended by representatives from several inner-city groups. Most had some familiarity with the CCPA–MB's work and its researchers. It had a long history of advocacy on inner-city issues and had thus established trusting relationships with many inner-city activists and service providers.

This didn't mean that everyone at the meeting accepted the idea of a SIC Report without comment. Indigenous participants raised concerns, noting the historically damaging effects of research conducted by outsiders. But the extant relationships with the CCPA–MB convinced even the most skeptical Indigenous inner-city activists that their concerns would be respected and that they would have a central role in guiding the project forward.

From this point, we began to shape a project that would be subject to principles established by our community partners. There were several reasons for producing the SIC Report. First, it would attract public attention to the many developments, both negative and positive, that were occurring in the inner city and would thus prompt a wide-ranging conversation about the area. Many Winnipeggers associated the inner city solely with hopelessness and violence, and most knew very little about its positive community-led work or the many beneficial results that this produced. Presenting the inner city in a good light could begin to dispel myths, quash stereotypes, and break down racial and spatial divides. Given this, we decided to underscore the positive work being done, to share knowledge about and celebrate those strategies and interventions that were working well. Of course, this didn't entail ignoring the many problems, but we wanted to draw attention to a great many remarkably innovative and effective initiatives that were transforming people's lives. The project would also be guided by the belief that much more could be done and that communities could not solve their ongoing problems alone. It would expose continuing challenges and gaps in service, and would make connections with public policy by assessing its failings and proposing solutions. This approach would be common to all SIC Reports.

After lively discussion, we agreed that bringing the lived experience of inner-city activists, service providers, and residents together with the skills of researchers could help achieve the aim of influencing public policy through community-based policy-oriented research. And so, our journey began.

Strengthening Relationships: Participation in Research Design

Since the first SIC Report appeared in 2005, many individuals have been involved in projects, experimenting with a variety of research methods including journals, photo-voice, film, interviews, sharing circles, and focus groups. Our commitment to community-partner-driven research has sometimes pushed researchers out of their comfort zones, as we try to adapt to the creative and sometimes unconventional ideas and methods of our partners. This can be a challenge, but it has produced some highly engaging and community-empowering projects.

Participants in our various studies have ranged in age from as young as eight in the project titled "Is Participation Having an Impact?" (MacKinnon et al. 2008) to an eighty-year-old Indigenous Elder who shared her knowledge with young people in the project titled "Breaking Barriers, Building Bridges" (see Chapter 12). Although our community partners direct our work, the process is no less rigorous than other research. We obtain ethics approval through the University of Winnipeg Ethics Review Board, and various drafts are reviewed and modified prior to publication.

We begin each project early in the calendar year by gathering new and existing inner-city CBO partners and researchers to discuss current challenges and issues. Our meetings are normally held over lunch, and a meal is always provided to demonstrate our respect to participants for taking time out of their busy schedules. A core group has been involved since the first SIC Report, with new faces coming to the table every year. This is mainly due to staff turnover in community organizations, as long-time activists and service providers move on to other projects. This has produced some challenges in terms of consistency, but the project's overarching principles have generally kept things on track. The SIC process enables participants to take time away from day-to-day work to think about broad issues and to engage in research that improves the social and economic conditions that prevent far too many inner-city residents from realizing their full potential.

Through a process that typically involves a series of meetings, participants choose a topic or theme that will define the research for each year. The sense of ownership is established at this stage because the community determines the focus. This is not to say that the researchers and the project coordinator play no role here. The coordinator ensures that the goal of bringing the community voice to the policy environment is always observed. Community participants, who tend to be service providers rather than researchers, writers, and policy wonks, often want to concentrate on telling stories. These are always central to the SIC, but it is the coordinator's job to ensure that the research moves beyond them.

Because attendance at meetings is fluid, maintaining a focus can sometimes be difficult. This makes it especially important for the coordinator to listen attentively for common themes and ideas that arise at meetings and to make suggestions based on the broader vision of the SIC. So, whereas the community defines the project's focus, the coordinator helps to direct it and can bring knowledge and context to the discussion.

The SIC has always been viewed as a capacity-building project. University students are commonly involved as research assistants and are supervised by experienced university and community researchers. Inner-city residents have often been trained and employed to conduct interviews and help with transcription. However, the initial emphasis on hiring and training residents has been lost to some extent. This is partly due to the enormous amount of time and resources that are required to fully engage them. Some would say that the SIC has deviated from its original goal of full participation and might suggest that its organizers should assess if and how it could return to its participatory, capacity-building roots.

Notwithstanding the challenges and imperfections, interest in the SIC remains robust, as does the idea of bringing people together to discuss issues for potential research and to engage in that research. Some community partners take an active role in developing research tools and contributing to research design and implementation, whereas others choose to be more minimally involved. Regardless, all are viewed as "the experts" in that they are working on the front lines and best know the issues and obstacles. They are encouraged to participate in policy-focused dialogue and identify ways that governments and other funders can better respond. All partners are given the opportunity to review draft reports and provide input into final publications.

Defining and Measuring Outcomes

Among the most important outcomes of the SIC project are the intangible contributions to the lives of participants and to community-led advocacy efforts. The more tangible "deliverables" (as our funders like to call them) consist of the many publications and ancillary tools generated by the project. To date, twelve annual SIC Reports, two videos, and many summary documents have been produced, all designed to be accessible to residents and program participants.

The reports have been widely disseminated to policy makers, CBOs, and the broader community. They have been downloaded from the CCPA–MB website more than 100,000 times. The videos are available on YouTube, and we regularly use them as educational tools at academic conferences, invited lectures, and government professional development events. As noted, each and every report includes public policy recommendations to address the social and economic challenges that it explores. This is a central component of our work because it responds to our community partners' interest in research that will make a difference in the lives of inner-city residents.

The research materials are used by organizations as educational tools and can sometimes make their way to unexpected places. For example, in the 2006 SIC Report titled *Inner City Refugee Women: Lessons for Public Policy,* we explored the challenges of refugee women, primarily from Africa, as they struggled to adapt to inner-city life. They discussed the tension they experienced – feeling gratitude for the refuge that Canada provides but also learning to accept that it is not the paradise they had hoped for. Their interviews revealed that they continue to deal with many obstacles. When the project was completed, the Somali women who had guided it and worked as research assistants asked if we could translate the summary document (which we call "research for communities") into Arabic. We did so, assuming that the intended readership consisted of refugees who spoke Arabic as a first language. However, when we presented the translated document to the women, we learned that the summaries would be sent to their families in Somalia. The women were proud of the work they had done and wanted their relatives to see it. But more interestingly, they referred to the overwhelming pressure to send money back home. Their families typically believed that life in Canada came with wealth and stability, and tended not to understand that refugees often struggle financially. Unable to help their families as much as they would like, the women felt guilty. Sharing their research might show their relatives that life in Canada, though better in many respects, was complicated and sometimes very difficult. If their families understood this, the pressure to help financially might decrease. For us, this was a pivotal lesson in the value of fully engaging communities in the research process. We would not have thought that what seemed a simple gesture (translating a short document) could have this transformative impact on the women's lives.

Since its inception, the SIC project has taught us a great deal, and we have developed a specific kind of expertise in conducting community-driven research that is focused on public policy. But maintaining a fully participatory model has also been difficult. Projects that entail the highest level of participation, from design through to implementation, have prioritized hiring and training local residents, many of whom have complicated lives. Some community researchers do move smoothly through their projects, embracing newfound skills and developing confidence along the way, but others need more support and encouragement, which can be extremely time consuming and resource intensive. These researchers sometimes drop out of a project due to unforeseen circumstances, which means that we must scramble to fill in the gaps. We acknowledge that our model is by no means perfect, but the challenges and trade-offs that inevitably occur in highly participatory research projects are dwarfed by the benefits to individuals, organizations, and communities. However, they can be difficult to maintain. After completing the fifth SIC Report, we were concerned that we had run out of steam – that the project had reached its full potential and that it was time to move on to something else. Our partners disagreed. Many told us that their engagement in the SIC marked the first time that they found research to be of direct value to them, and they believed the exercise to be worth continuing. And so, we continued.

The Indigenous Context and Influence

It is notable that the majority of SIC participants have been women and that Indigenous women in particular played a leadership role during the early years of the project's development. Because so many Indigenous people live in inner-city neighbourhoods, our partner organizations provide services to a high number of them. Some organizations have built their programming around anti-oppressive theoretical frameworks, and many integrate strong Indigenous cultural components into their programs. Given the intergenerational trauma resulting from measures such as residential schools and the Sixties Scoop, teaching participants about the effects of colonization and oppression is fundamental to their transformative goals.

The demographics of the inner city led us to agree very early in the SIC process that our framework would need to consider the historical context of the Indigenous experience. Many of our community partners know all too well that healing from the damage caused by colonization and oppression is slow and painful work. Furthermore, oppression through racism, sexism, and classism remains systemic, which means that healing occurs in a context of ongoing injury. For this reason, we grounded our research in an understanding of colonial systemic forces. Taking this step was crucial because, as Indigenous scholar Linda Tuhiwai Smith (2006, 153) notes, governments and social agencies have failed to connect Indigenous problems with the historical experience of Indigenous people. Decolonizing research is essential in the reframing of issues to acknowledge history.

Colonization had, and has, a considerable impact in Manitoba. Indigenous Manitoba researcher Michael Anthony Hart (2002, 27) describes the deep damage caused by internalized colonization: "Aboriginal people start to believe that we are incapable of learning and that the colonizers' degrading images and beliefs about Aboriginal people and our ways of being are true." Reversing this damage is a critical step toward transformation, and it is central to program models of many inner-city CBOs. We have ensured that our projects are designed with this in mind. Careful attention is given to all aspects of the process, including identification of projects, research design, and data analysis. We aim for a process that remains true to the inclusive, empowering, anti-oppressive, and transformative objectives of our partner CBOs. But attaining this is no small feat. Engaging inner-city residents in the process requires us to understand the controlling relationships that marginalized individuals often experience (Keys et al. 2004). For example, many of our community researchers and interviewees live under the watchful eye of state agencies, including social assistance, child welfare authorities, and the criminal justice system, all of which exert significant control over their daily lives. This has implications for research because it complicates the process of establishing trust with such individuals. Yet trust is essential if they are to feel safe to fully share their stories and be empowered through the process.

Our community researchers have been extremely important in this regard, as they bring a sensitivity to the interview process that can come only from shared experience. We have learned that if research acknowledges the importance of cultural identity and the ways in which colonization and oppression shape lives, it can contribute to consciousness raising, empowerment, reclaimed cultural identity, individual emancipation, and ultimately, transformative change. Broadening community involvement in the process, building egalitarian relationships with participants through ongoing collaboration, hiring and training researchers, sharing findings in various forms, and requesting feedback from participants are important elements of our research design. Learning to take direction is fundamental, which we discovered very early. For example, the first SIC Report looked at inner-city housing because the community told us that this issue was especially pressing. We know that safe, reliable housing is a fundamental social determinant of health and well-being. We also know that children who lack it have difficulties in school (Waterston, Grueger, and Samson 2015). The theme of housing has remained constant in our research and is arguably the policy area where we have had the greatest impact. CBOs regularly use SIC housing research to advocate for policy change, and they have played an important role in steering the provincial government toward a renewed investment in social housing (see Chapters 4 and 5 in this volume).

In the second year of the SIC project, our community partners expressed an interest in examining the difficult-to-measure outcomes for individuals and families who used community-based programs (see Chapter 2). This theme emerged because they were frustrated with the reporting demands of their funders. In the third year, we worked with our partners to develop a research model to gather information about the experiences of inner-city residents who used various community-based programs. Their input was critical to the design that subsequently evolved, and the project provided significant insight into the benefits of participation for individuals, their families, and the broader community (MacKinnon et al. 2008). This initial research had a transformative effect on evaluation discourse in the inner city. Indigenous methods of evaluation were explored and integrated into evaluation conducted by the CEDA Pathways program (see Chapter 3). More recently, the Indigenous Learning Circle, an inner-city collaborative led by Indigenous women, has endeavoured to develop an Indigenous evaluation framework and guiding principles (MacKinnon forthcoming).

In the seventh SIC Report, titled *Neoliberalism: What a Difference a Theory Makes* (CCPA–MB 2011), our community partners took the research to a deeper level, choosing to focus on neoliberalism, which has prompted the scaling back of public support and worsened the poverty and inequality that deeply affects their communities. The process that produced it reflected their politicization, as they began to consider the limitations of community development work in the absence of strong state support. As we gathered to discuss a research focus for the report, long-time community-based service providers remarked that despite their best efforts, they often seemed to be taking one step forward and two steps back. This was a transformative moment for the group. It enabled us to connect the neoliberal economic policies that had evolved during the past thirty years with the declining public investment in income supports, social housing, affordable childcare, and postsecondary education. Neoliberalism was a new concept to many of our partners, and understanding its meaning helped them to make sense of their daily realities. This was important for researchers as well – it reminded us of the extent to which neoliberal policies keep communities busy and distract them from the real source of social and economic oppression (Incite! 2007; Schram 2015; Shragge 2013).

As Smith (2006, 147) emphasizes, decolonizing research requires that "intervention is directed at changing institutions which deal with indigenous peoples and not at changing indigenous peoples to fit the structures." Understanding the impact of neoliberal economic policies and the interrelationship with continued colonial policies and systemic racism is essential to our understanding of problems as structural and our crafting of policies aimed at changing systems and structures rather than the individuals whom they oppress. We are not interested in scrutinizing the failings of inner-city residents. Rather, we examine the context in which they live, how community development activities contribute to their lives, how state policies have failed, and how the policies might be changed to address the issues that the research has highlighted.

Research Methods Emerge through Participation

In employing a transformative research model that emphasizes community participation and the generation of knowledge for social change (Mertens 2007), we encourage our community partners to select the methods that fit their research objectives. In our model, outside researchers provide information about various methods and tools, and they assist in identifying methods that might be most effective. Although we use both quantitative and qualitative methods, the chosen method will ultimately allow us to tell the story that community members isolate as significant while also engaging the community in the data-gathering process and analysis. We feel this to be important as it provides a capacity-building component that can have lasting benefit for the community (Mora and Diaz 2004). Whereas quantitative data can be useful, they are insufficient for our aims. Our Indigenous research partners have made it very clear that stories have the most meaning for them (MacKinnon et al. 2008). In one discussion about methods, the director of a CBO advocated for qualitative research as a means to understand "more than just numbers." She pointed out that "funders just want to know how many women we are providing service to and the outcomes of that service. What they don't take into consideration is the broader effects of these women's healing – the changes that result for their children, their families, and the broader community" (MacKinnon et al. 2008, 6).

We have come to appreciate that though quantitative data can be useful, they do not capture the richness that stories provide or the experiences and perceptions of those who are most affected by policy. Nor do quantitative data fully capture the impact of the structural forces that are at the root of poverty and social exclusion.

Stories and Transformative Research

Westwood (1991, 83) emphasizes the value of narratives to transformative research. She states that such research offers those who are involved not merely a voice "but a speaking position through the narrative mode."

Research that focuses solely on quantitative methods cannot provide a potentially empowering experience for interviewees, and the depth of knowledge that transpires through hearing the voices of the "researched" will be lost.

The idea of giving voice to the oppressed as a necessary stage of emancipation and transformation was central to Freire's classic work *Pedagogy of the Oppressed* (2006, 88), which notes that "if it is in speaking their word that people, by naming their world, transform it, dialogue imposes itself as the way in which they achieve significance as human beings." From an anti-oppressive/decolonization perspective, dialogue is an essential precursor of action and reflection, or praxis. To be transformative, the messages exposed through dialogue must be situated within broader conditions (poverty, colonization) to draw a connection to structural problems. If individuals are to move from self-awareness to empowerment, researchers must "redefine informants to be those *with* whom they study, and redefine their own activities far beyond the production of a document describing events experienced, recorded, and analyzed" (LeCompte 1993, 14, emphasis in original). Our research is guided by the awareness that historical conditions, systemic racism, and contemporary social and economic realities can be exposed through narratives. When conducted through a critical framework, narrative research can be an appropriate methodology to complement quantitative measures, to ensure that in our efforts to quantify through numbers and statistics, we don't lose sight of cause and context.

The Benefits: Individual, Community, and Policy Impact

As outlined above, the SIC Report has broad, overarching benefits. A central purpose was to document the diverse but interconnected developments and learning that were taking place in Winnipeg's inner city during a period of relatively significant political support for community-based initiatives. Organizations that receive state support are vulnerable. This is confirmed by the developments of the 1990s, when Manitoba's Conservative government made deep cuts to community-based work, a trend that the federal Conservatives followed in later years. After having a relatively supportive NDP government for sixteen years, Manitoba returned the

Progressive Conservatives to power in 2016, and community-based organizations braced for change. The hope is that research demonstrating the effectiveness of community development work will provide organizations with important evidence to justify continued state support.

SIC research is also beneficial to community groups that can become preoccupied with their individual mandates. All too often, they are forced to chase project funds to finance their work and are then consumed with demonstrating "success" to their funders. They can easily drift away from collective and social justice efforts (Shragge 2013; Incite! 2007). The SIC project brings them together to share their experiences, successes, and challenges. It also provides an opportunity to move beyond service to policy change.

One such example of policy impact is in the area of housing. As noted, housing has been a constant theme for SIC, and community groups use its quantitative and qualitative findings when they advocate for policy change and renewed investment in social housing. Advocacy efforts aligned with our research have contributed to a shift in provincial policy, with significant investment in the repair of social housing after several years of neglect as well as in new supply (see Chapters 4 and 5 in this volume).

Another example of research that may have contributed to a policy shift, albeit a very slow one, is related to income supports. The 2009 SIC Report was titled *It Takes All Day to Be Poor* (CCPA–MB 2009), a phrase coined by Josie Hill, who was then the executive director of Ma Mawi Wi Chi Itata Centre, a CBO that provides services to Indigenous children and families. During one of our meetings, Josie expressed frustration that people seemed to have little understanding of how complex life can be for the poor. She referred to women who transported their children on top of a wagonload of laundry as they made the trek to a laundromat several blocks away. She noted that women and children can spend hours at the welfare office, waiting to see a worker whom they can't reach by phone – sometimes because they themselves don't have a phone and sometimes because the worker doesn't pick up, and a message can't be left because the voicemail is full. Josie said, "What people don't seem to understand is that it can take all day to be poor." Heads nodded, people sighed in agreement, and the focus of the 2009 SIC was chosen. Telling this story would help to dispel the common myths that lead to blaming the poor for their own predicament and to inadequate income security policies. From there, we developed an innovative method: we hired and trained a community researcher to meet regularly with individuals living in poverty who kept a journal of their experiences over several months. Since then, the phrase "it takes all day to be poor" has been broadly used by anti-poverty activists in Winnipeg. Like the housing-related and other research, this project contributed to policy change. In 2015, the Province of Manitoba increased income supports for housing through its RentAssist program and before leaving office in 2016, the NDP government indicated that it was in the process of developing increased income support to address rising food prices and food insecurity. Whether the current government will pursue this objective remains to be seen.

In this chapter, I have provided a few examples of how community organizations are using the SIC to identify issues, propose solutions, and advocate for policy change. In the spirit of building capacity, the SIC has also aided many individuals. Those who have participated as community researchers and those who have told their stories in interviews, focus groups, sharing circles, and other projects have benefitted in various ways. Our commitment to hiring and training local residents as research associates proved beneficial for the individuals themselves. University students who have been involved with a SIC project have gone on to undertake master's and PhD programs, and others have gone on to work in CBOs. Although we provide community researchers with guidance, they are at liberty to exercise their creativity. For example, an inner-city social work student was trained as a research assistant for the housing-related 2008 report (CCPA–MB 2008). After graduating, she was hired as the principal researcher for the 2009 report (CCPA–MB 2009) and was given the freedom to implement a general idea discussed at a community meeting – using journaling to capture the day-to-day experiences of people living in poverty.

Others have benefitted in far more profound ways than we could have imagined. For example, in the report titled *Is Participation Having an Impact?* Nancy, an inner-city resident who was hired and trained as a research assistant, stated that "participating in this project gave me my voice back" (MacKinnon et al. 2008, 42). Another inner-city resident, a refugee from Somalia, trained as a research assistant. She later returned to university and is now a practising social worker.

Reflection: Challenges and Realities Moving Forward

In 2017, the SIC project celebrated twelve years. CBOs remain committed to the idea of the SIC Report for the same reasons that inspired them in 2005 – because it enables them to come together to identify and investigate issues of shared concern, to suggest policy solutions, and to use the tools that are produced to advocate improved policies and programs. They have seen the benefits of engaging in a process that emphasizes building egalitarian relationships through ongoing collaboration, hiring and training community researchers, and sharing findings in various forms. In many ways, the SIC has become part of the development process in Winnipeg's inner city. One challenge in moving forward will be assessing how it has evolved and where it might go. Although inner-city CBOs still embrace the concept of a SIC, their involvement has waned in recent years due to the demands of doing CBPR and the difficulty in obtaining the necessary resources to engage local residents with minimal experience and complex lives. This may be the new reality of the SIC, but it would be useful for researchers and partners to look back at the twelve-year-old partnership and establish where it might go and how it might get there.

Celebration

Regardless of where the SIC goes, it has changed the way that many inner-city residents view research, and this is cause for celebration. Since 2005, an important component of the project has been to bring the inner-city community together to celebrate and share its research. Traditionally, in December, everyone gathers at the Circle of Life Thunderbird House, a sacred Indigenous meeting place in the centre of town. We profile our work and tell our stories; we share food, hugs, laughter, and sometimes tears. And we leave knowing that in a few months, we will reassemble to begin the process for the next year. Though the release of the report is the impetus for our gathering each December, it is really the shared love of our community, our pride in the work that we do, and our appreciation for the tireless, dedicated people who do it that bring us together. For those of us who are primarily researchers, great satisfaction comes from knowing that our research is useful to the community. In the words of a long-time community leader who previously dismissed research because, as she said, "we have been researched to death," the SIC Report is important because it is "research that belongs to us."

NOTES

1 Statement made by Diane Roussin, past executive director of the Ma Mawi Wi Chi Itata Centre (date unknown). This was cited in the MRA's application for a SSHRC partnership grant.
2 There is a history of tripartite agreements between the three levels of government. To varying degrees, they have provided at least nominal support to inner-city revitalization.

REFERENCES

CCPA–MB (Canadian Centre for Policy Alternatives–Manitoba). 2008. *Getting Our Housing in Order: State of the Inner City Report, 2008.* Winnipeg: CCPA–MB.

–. 2009. *It Takes All Day to Be Poor: State of the Inner City Report, 2009.* Winnipeg: CCPA–MB.

–. 2011. *Neoliberalism: What a Difference a Theory Makes – State of the Inner City Report, 2011,* 20–36. Winnipeg: Canadian Centre for Policy Alternatives–Manitoba.

Fernandez, Lynne, Shauna MacKinnon, and Jim Silver, eds. 2015. *The Social Determinants of Health in Manitoba.* Winnipeg: Canadian Centre for Policy Alternatives–Manitoba.

Freire, Paulo. 2006. *Pedagogy of the Oppressed.* 30th anniversary edition. New York: Continuum.

Ghorayshi, Parvin. 2010. "Diversity and Interculturalism: Learning from Winnipeg's Inner City." *Canadian Journal of Urban Research* 19 (1): 89–104.

Hart, Michael Anthony. 2002. *Seeking Mino-Pimatisiwin: An Aboriginal Approach to Helping.* Halifax: Fernwood.

Incite! Women of Color against Violence. 2007. *The Revolution Will Not Be Funded.* New York: South End Press.

Keys, Christopher B., Susan McMahon, Bernadette Sanchez, Lorna London, and Jaleel Abjul-Adil. 2004. "Culturally Anchored Research: Exemplars for Community Psychology." In *Participatory Community Research: Theories and Methods in Action,* ed. Leonard A. Jason, Christopher B. Keys, Yolanda Suarez-Balcazar, Rene R. Taylor, and Margaret I. Davis, 177–98. Washington, DC: American Psychological Association.

LeCompte, Margaret D. 1993. "A Framework for Hearing Silence: What Does Telling Stories Mean When We Are Supposed to Be Doing Science?" In *Naming Silenced Lives: Personal Narratives and Processes of Educational Change*, ed. Daniel McLauglin and William G. Tierney, 9–27. New York: Routledge.

MacKinnon, Shauna. 2014. "It's More Than a Collection of Stories." In *Community, Research and Social Change: State of the Inner City Report, 2014*, 3–17. Winnipeg: CCPA–MB.

–. Forthcoming. "Integrating Indigenous Ways of Knowing into Community-Based Evaluation." In *Seeking Equity and Inclusion in Canadian Municipalities*, ed. C. Andrews, F. Klodawsky, and J. Siltanen. Montreal and Kingston: McGill-Queen's University Press.

MacKinnon, Shauna, et al. 2008. *Is Participation Having an Impact? Measuring Progress in Winnipeg's Inner City through the Voices of Community-Based Program Participants*. Winnipeg: CCPA–MB.

Mertens, Donna. 2007. "Transformative Paradigm: Mixed Methods and Social Justice." *Journal of Mixed Methods Research* 1 (3): 212–25.

Mora, Juana, and David Diaz. 2004. *Latino Social Policy: A Participatory Research Model*. New York: Haworth Press.

Schram, Sanford. 2015. *The Return of Ordinary Capitalism: Neoliberalism, Precarity, Occupy*. New York: Oxford.

Shragge, Eric. 2013. *Activism and Social Change: Lessons for Community Organizing*. 2nd ed. Toronto: University of Toronto Press.

Silver, Jim. 2006. *In Their Own Voices: Building Urban Aboriginal Communities*. Halifax: Fernwood.

–. 2015. "Spatially Concentrated, Racialized Poverty as a Social Determinant of Health." In *The Social Determinants of Health in Manitoba*, ed. Lynne Fernandez, Shauna MacKinnon, and Jim Silver, 227–40. Winnipeg: Canadian Centre for Policy Alternatives–Manitoba.

Smith, Linda Tuhiwai. 2006. *Decolonizing Methodologies: Research and Indigenous Peoples*. New York: Zed Books.

Waterston, Sarah, Barbara Grueger, and Lindy Samson. 2015. "Housing Need in Canada: Healthy Lives Start at Home." *Paediatrics and Child Health* 20 (7): 1–7. http://search.proquest.com/docview/1724022516?accountid=15067.

Westwood, Sally. 1991. "Power/Knowledge: The Politics of Transformative Research." *Convergence* 24 (3): 79–86.

2

Community Collaborative Research Partnerships
Together We Have CLOUT

SHAUNA MacKINNON
with JOSIE HILL and DIANE ROUSSIN

This chapter tells the story of a 2006 project titled "Is Participation Having an Impact?," which was part of an ongoing collaborative relationship between a Winnipeg coalition named Community Led Organizations United Together (CLOUT) and researchers associated with the Canadian Centre for Policy Alternatives–Manitoba (CCPA–MB) (MacKinnon et al. 2008). CLOUT and the researchers began working together during that year, and their relationship evolved into much more than a research partnership. The project solidified their connection and inspired them to continue working together. Later, the affiliation broadened to include researchers from the Manitoba Research Alliance (MRA), a community-university collaboration, after two CLOUT members joined the MRA steering committee. Since that time, CLOUT and the MRA have collaborated on several projects. In addition to producing original research with CLOUT, MRA researchers provide ongoing support to CLOUT members. This entails supplying them with information to aid their policy advocacy and helping them to tell their story in innovative ways. For example, researchers, in collaboration with CCPA–MB, produced a film in 2011 for CLOUT that profiles its collaborative model (see Chapter 10 in this volume).[1] Although the association between CLOUT and researchers centres on research, it has become much more than that. It is built on trust and respect, and the knowledge that the researchers will make every effort to provide CLOUT with the support that it needs.

The three authors of this chapter have been closely involved in this partnership. Shauna was the director of the CCPA–MB and a co-investigator with the MRA. Diane was a past executive director of Ma Mawi Wi Chi Itata Centre in Winnipeg. And Josie, who was the founder of CLOUT, also was a past director of Ma Mawi Wi Chi Itata Centre.

About CLOUT

The CLOUT coalition formed in 2003, when a group of executive directors from nine community-based organizations with shared values and complementary mandates realized that working collectively would make them stronger and more effective. The nine groups, all of which provide services to individuals and families in Winnipeg's inner city, are Andrews Street Family Centre, Community Education Development Association, Ma Mawi Wi Chi Itata Centre, Native Women's Transition Centre, Ndiniwemaaganag Endaawad, North End Women's Resource Centre, Rossbrook House, Wahbung Abinoojiiag, and Wolseley Family Place. CLOUT's stated mission is to "work towards an integrated community led approach to service delivery that ensures community needs and aspirations are supported through neighbourhood based capacity building solutions."[2]

CLOUT organizations aim to provide non-judgmental services based on respect and openness. They pride themselves on treating everyone who accesses their services as if they were guests in their home. They prioritize hiring from within their communities, offering choices in programming and taking direction for their policies and programs from the communities they serve.

The Research Partnership

Although MRA researchers had worked with individual CLOUT organizations before 2006, that year marked the beginning of a more formal partnership with the coalition. Central to this association was a commitment to conduct research in a manner that contributed to CLOUT's goals, which are to

- share knowledge and best practices regarding how to support children, youth, and families in an urban environment
- become partners in the process of change – ensuring that sustainable solutions focused on early intervention, prevention, and support are in place for children, families, and neighbourhoods

- support service delivery partners in creating a system that works for families, building communities from the grassroots up and reducing the need for costly crisis-oriented services
- increase individual and family capacities for self-care through strength-based supports and services at the community level
- share opportunities for decision making and involvement with community members through local community economic development and community development principles
- celebrate the many successes occurring at the neighbourhood and community level through the support of community-led service providers.

Our partnership began with a conversation between two of the co-authors of this chapter, Josie Hill and Shauna MacKinnon, who spoke together early in 2006, soon after the first State of the Inner City Report was released (see Chapter 1). Josie had represented Ma Mawi Wi Chi Itata Centre in that project and was interested in exploring other research possibilities connected with but distinct from the report. She suggested that CLOUT members might have some ideas for research.

Shortly afterward, Josie invited Shauna to attend a CLOUT meeting. This gathering proved very lively, and Shauna was struck by its collaborative and respectful nature. Everyone at the meeting was female.[3] They clearly had a strong bond, and though they represented independent organizations, they always emphasized the collective. References to "we," "us," and "our community" were the norm. Rarely were the words "me," "I," and "my" used. The women were very supportive of and comfortable with each other. They seemed to view their organizations as contributing equally to the overall benefit of the community – none more so than the others.

A research idea quickly germinated at this meeting. The women expressed their frustration with the reporting requirements of their funders, including governments and philanthropic agencies. They themselves were interested in providing services to improve the lives of their program participants, their families, and the broader community, but the funders concentrated on narrowly defined quantifiable outcomes. The women felt pressured to demonstrate that their groups had achieved these outcomes.

They talked about the latest buzzwords they were hearing from funders – "evidence-based" research and evaluation – and questioned exactly what that meant. Who decided what evidence was useful and for whom? Much of the evidence came from research on non-Indigenous experiences, and they wondered why it was automatically assumed to be transferable to the inner city, which has a very large Indigenous population.

We met somewhat regularly over several months, exploring how we might develop a project to address their concerns, with the overall intent of demonstrating to the funders that outcomes can take various forms and are sometimes difficult to measure. Applying a participatory action research approach, we worked to hone a research question and a methodology that would best fit with CLOUT's objectives. At this stage, Shauna's role was to provide information about various methods and tools, and to support CLOUT in deciding how to proceed. Importantly, CLOUT wanted to ensure that community members would be engaged in the process, not only as subjects, but also as research assistants. This fit with its philosophy that capacity building should be integrated into everything it did. This included hiring and training local residents as much as possible.

Several questions arose as we tossed around ideas about how to build a project. The CLOUT members asked, What is an outcome? How do we measure outcomes? What are we measuring, and who determines what needs to be measured? Their discussions about evidence-based research centred on what they understood as constituting evidence versus what government policy makers accepted as evidence. They maintained that they too were interested in understanding outcomes, but they felt that the current emphasis on quantifiable outcomes didn't capture the experience of their program participants in a meaningful way.

After much discussion, the group chose a fairly simple methodology: the best way to understand outcomes was simply to ask the individuals who used CLOUT programs for their opinions. From there, we formulated the questions that would guide the interviews with program users. As the researcher, Shauna created a draft interview guide that included questions proposed by CLOUT members during the discussions. The group met again, revising until the interview guide was finalized (MacKinnon et al. 2008).

Research through an Indigenous Lens

Because a high proportion of CLOUT program users are Indigenous, we quickly agreed that we needed to recognize the historical context of the Indigenous experience in Canada. Indigenous people continue to suffer the damaging intergenerational effects of colonization. Misguided policies that systematically removed Indigenous children from their families, whether through residential schools or the Sixties Scoop,[4] have left a painful legacy that spans generations. Healing from the damage caused by colonization and oppression is slow and painful. Further, oppression through racism, sexism, and classism is systemic, which must also be taken into account.

Education, with an awareness of systemic forces, is an essential first step toward individual healing and empowerment. CLOUT wanted to ensure that researchers were mindful of this throughout the process. Through its work on the front lines, CLOUT sees first-hand the long-lasting effects of racism and oppression that Paulo Freire (2006, 63) presents as so deeply internalized. He notes, "So often do they hear that they are good for nothing, know nothing and are incapable of learning anything – that they are sick, lazy and unproductive – that in the end they become convinced of their own unfitness." Alfred (2009, 59) describes the intensely destructive impact of colonial oppression, particularly the psychological effects that perpetuate this damage:

> Once a group of people have been assaulted in a genocidal fashion, there are sociological ramifications. With the victim's complete loss of power comes despair, and the psyche reacts by internalizing what appears to be genuine power – the power of the oppressor ... At this point, the self-worth of the individual and/or group has sunk to a level of despair tantamount to self-hatred. This self-hatred can be either internalized or externalized.

CLOUT believes that reversing the damage of colonization is a first step in the transformation process. Thus, its program participants are given an opportunity to learn about oppression and colonization so that they can proudly reclaim their Indigenous identities and move forward. But for many, the journey is long, and outcomes are not always easy to measure. Therefore, it was essential that the research project, from design through to analysis, was rooted in an understanding of the profound effects of colonization. To ensure that community researchers, the majority of whom were Indigenous, possessed this understanding, a well-respected Indigenous teacher assisted us in our training. We believe that his teachings contributed to the quality of interviews and provided knowledge to community researchers that was consistent with our capacity-building objectives.

Ownership, Control, Access, and Possession Principles

Early in our process, we discussed control of the research. We talked about the principles of ownership, control, access, and possession (OCAP), and about how these might apply to our work. The OCAP principles (FNIGC 2014) have been adopted in *Canada's Tri-Council Policy Statement: Ethical Conduct for Research Involving Humans*.[5] The tri-council consists of the Canadian Institutes of Health Research, the Natural Sciences and Engineering Research Council of Canada, and the Social Sciences and Humanities Research Council of Canada. The OCAP principles were initially instituted in the First Nations and Inuit Regional Longitudinal Health Survey in 1998 and were later integrated into the Tri-Council Policy Statement, where they were subsequently amended in response to concerns raised by First Nations, Inuit, and Metis groups. Chapter 9 of the 2010 Tri-Council Policy Statement, titled "Research Involving the First Nations, Inuit and Métis People of Canada," provides specific guidelines to ensure that research complies with the OCAP principles.

Our partnership also respected the OCAP principles of ownership, access, and possession. Although CLOUT is not an Indigenous organization per se, some of its member groups are, and most are led by Indigenous women. The majority of the individuals and families that CLOUT organizations serve are Indigenous. CLOUT is very aware that research has the potential to be oppressive and destructive, as noted in the *Report of the Royal Commission on Aboriginal Peoples* (RCAP 1996).

We believe that the gathering of information in Indigenous communities and its subsequent use have been inherently political. In the past, research has been damaging to Indigenous people because they have not been consulted regarding the kinds of research conducted, the type of information gathered, the manner in which it is collected, and how it is used. This has led to harmful policies and practices, and to a deep mistrust. Because data gathering has frequently been imposed by outside authorities, it has met with resistance (NAHO 2007, 3).

The OCAP principles and the destructive legacy they were designed to address have been important in guiding our work. We understand that the community retains ownership of the research. We also believe that both community and academic partners have a role to play in presenting research outcomes and in doing so through various means. For example, CLOUT has agreed that the Canadian Centre for Policy Alternatives– Manitoba will publish and disseminate its research. Researchers are mindful that CLOUT is an equal partner in the process, bringing important skills and experience to the mix. So, when they are asked to present project findings, it is always made clear that a CLOUT representative must also be invited. This has sometimes proved challenging for event organizers if their policies and budgets are limited to supporting a single presenter per project. In one case, Shauna was invited to present CLOUT research at a symposium and was informed that though two presenters were welcome, the funding covered just one. She consulted with colleagues at CLOUT, and the group agreed that if funding were not available for both Shauna and a CLOUT representative, neither would attend. The group felt that both the community and the academic perspective were required, and neither Shauna nor the CLOUT representative was qualified to provide both. This created a dilemma for the conference organizers, especially since their symposium focused on research partnerships between the community and academia. In the end, they found a way to accommodate us and agreed to revisit their policy for future events. We saw this as an important step forward for the way in which conferences that claim to profile community-university collaborations deal with community-based participatory research (CBPR).

The Making of "Is Participation Having an Impact?"

Research Design

In keeping with the central values of CBPR, we pay careful attention to process, instrument design, and data analysis. We ensure that the process remains as true as possible to our inclusive, empowering, and transformative objectives. We know that research plays a limited role in the day-to-day realities of the individuals and families who use CLOUT programs, but we believe it can contribute to CLOUT goals if it is designed to engage community members.

In their participatory research approach, Keys et al. (2004) emphasize the need to consider the controlling relationships that marginalized individuals often experience. Individuals and families who use CLOUT programs are typically involved with numerous state agencies that exert significant power over their lives. As we designed our project, our conversations often centred on oppressive systems, including child welfare, criminal justice, income assistance, public housing, and others. These discussions reminded us of the importance of establishing trust with research participants and seeing that they were well informed about the scope and limitations of the project. It also reminded us of our responsibility to ensure that they were safe to share their stories and wouldn't be penalized by the state as a result. We tried to be mindful of these dynamics throughout the "Is Participation Having an Impact?" study. We tried to be conscientious about broadening community involvement in the process, building egalitarian relationships with participants through ongoing collaboration, hiring and training community researchers, sharing findings in various forms, and requesting feedback from participants. We wanted our project to be as participatory as possible, which entailed involving CLOUT members in the selection of research methods. We discussed using quantitative versus qualitative methods or a combination of both. We agreed that the process was as important as the outcome, and this meant choosing methods that would engage local residents – to be hired and trained where possible - in the data-gathering process and analysis. This was important to ensure a capacity-building component that would have lasting benefit for the community (Mora and Diaz 2004).

In the process of identifying research areas that might be of interest to community-based organizations (CBOs), we discussed the use of indicators to measure progress. The question "How do we measure?" evolved into an exploration of what was being measured and who determined what needed to be measured. After much discussion, we concluded that the best way to determine progress and outcomes was fairly simple – we would interview CLOUT program users, asking them if and how their participation had made a difference to them. Inner-city CBOs are constantly under pressure to demonstrate to funding institutions that their programs are having an impact on the lives of participants. Funders are looking for "evidence" of effectiveness. For the most part, they want quantitative measures that can reveal how many participants found work, returned to school, and so on. Organizations argue that these expectations are often unrealistic, given that participants are subject to the deep and damaging effects of colonization and oppression, and that subtle yet important gains also need be identified. Quantifiable measures tell only part of the story.

CLOUT felt it ironic that funding agencies expressed an interest in "building capacity" and "social capital" but overlooked the felt experience of individual participants when they measured progress. CLOUT members believed that this needed to change. They were pleased that their funders were beginning to understand the importance of community and individual capacity building, but they also believed they had some catching up to do with regard to how they measured these more subjective goals. For example, assessing whether capacity has been built is far more difficult than determining whether a participant has found paid employment.

Accepting building capacity as a goal meant that we would need to use subjective measures, placing a greater value on outcomes as they related to participants' personal goals, rather than the goals of funding agencies. For many people, involvement in a CLOUT program was an important outcome in its own right. We agreed that regardless of the outcomes that agencies and funders wanted to measure, people engaged in programs for their own reasons and had valuable insights to share through their stories. Their perceptions of what involvement in the CLOUT programs meant to them, their families, their neighbourhoods, and their broader communities were critical to the measurement of whether progress was being made. Listening to their stories was the best way of understanding outcomes, an approach that is consistent with Indigenous research. As Smith (1999, 127) notes, "community action approaches [to research] assume that people know and can reflect on their own lives."

In *Pedagogy of the Oppressed,* Freire (2006, 65) states that a critical stage in the emancipation of the oppressed is an understanding of their oppression, leading to an active role in their liberation. This is particularly pertinent to our research, given the intergenerational trauma of colonial measures such as residential schools and the Sixties Scoop. Our research paradigm acknowledged the importance of understanding the harm caused by colonization and oppression, and the centrality of cultural reclamation in the healing process as an essential step toward both individual and systemic transformation. From there, the research instruments evolved in the context of a decolonization framework. Outcomes were not measured simply to please funders. The process itself was part of the outcome. As one inner-city development worker notes, "the process is the product, I think, like it's a journey not a destination" (Silver 2006, 150). This can pose challenges for funding institutions that seek linear, quantifiable outcomes. But by increasing awareness of the effects of colonization, CBOs hope that funders will recognize that reversing the damage of colonization requires mainstream institutions to change their policies, programs, and measurement methods to better reflect the needs of colonized people. It is also worth noting that much of the work performed by CBOs is necessary *because* of the harm wrought by the very institutions that fund them, and therefore it is ironic that institutions continue to expect CBOs to demonstrate their effectiveness on mainstream institutional terms. We are also acutely aware that much of what CBOs manage to achieve is *in spite* of public policies and programs, which are commonly inadequate at best and damaging at worst. Although CBOs can do their best to help individuals adapt, increase awareness, and advocate for their "clients," they have little control over the reality that housing is sorely lacking, social assistance incomes are inadequate, and access to good jobs, childcare, and training is limited. Unless public policy shifts considerably to address these issues, improvements in the economic and social well-being of the people whom CBOs serve will remain less than what is possible. Raising individual awareness of structural forces, so that people will better understand their oppression, is a critical first step toward transformation.

Gathering the Data

After obtaining ethics approval through the University of Winnipeg, the research assistants began to interview individuals who had used programs offered by the CLOUT organizations. We sought to interview a mix of people to include those who were engaged for various periods of time. All interviewees were given an orientation to ensure that they were fully informed regarding the objectives and intended use of the project. Although they were at liberty to review the findings before the research report was finalized, few did so. Ninety-one people were interviewed.

What We Learned

A full description of our analysis is given in MacKinnon et al. (2008) and MacKinnon and Stephens (2010). Because our community partners emphasized program design and delivery that were embedded in decolonization and anti-oppressive frameworks, our data analysis took shape through this lens. Within the context of the central research question, we were looking for a much deeper understanding of the impact of program use. We also wanted to know if and how it was reversing the harms of colonization and oppression, and whether it helped interviewees, their families, neighbourhoods, and the broader community to move forward. As colonization and oppression can profoundly erode the self-esteem, self-confidence, and hope of individuals, it can also lead to a weakening of collective social capital. Reversing the damage is slow but is essential to self-empowerment, emancipation, and community transformation.

To supplement our narrative inquiry, we integrated a series of questions to quantitatively measure improvement in social well-being (MacKinnon et al. 2008). Respondents reported improvements in physical (36.5 percent), mental (39.3 percent), and spiritual (40.7 percent) well-being, and 61.0 percent reported increased involvement in the community. Although this information proved useful, everyone agreed that the qualitative data were most valuable.

Participant-Identified Progress

Progress as identified by people who used the programs is captured under the following themes, which are also discussed in MacKinnon et al. (2008) and MacKinnon and Stephens (2010):

- empowerment and having a voice
- sense of purpose

- reclaiming culture
- meeting people
- new opportunities
- knowledge of resources
- parenting skills
- reciprocity and social capital
- feelings of safety
- caring and compassion
- overcoming addictions
- recreation and having a place to go
- sense of community and belonging.

Respondents also shared their views on what services were lacking and how these gaps might be filled. They talked about how their involvement in the various programs had contributed to their individual well-being, but the majority of interviews also revealed the broader benefits of participation. Many people said that they had moved from "client" to "volunteer" and expressed great pride in being able to help others in their community. Others spoke of the benefits to their children as they became better parents. Many mentioned their increasing interaction with others whose circumstances were similar and their relief in discovering they were not alone in their troubles.

Many pointed out that government systems – primarily welfare and child welfare – created significant stress in their lives, which suggested that structural change remained a challenge. However, many interviewees seemed to be aware that the failure of systems to respond adequately to their needs did not mean that they themselves were failures. Coupled with their willingness to discuss systemic issues, this speaks to a transformation from self-blame to an understanding of systemic oppression. Many people explained that they continued to struggle with inflexible and insensitive government systems, and that their use of CLOUT programs enabled them to better understand systemic problems and get help in manoeuvring through various government agencies. Nonetheless, there was little indication that attitudes were changing on a broader community level or that structural change was imminent. For most, the journey was one of individual healing and building relationships. Many of the

Indigenous participants were most focused on reclaiming their identities and understanding their culture. Staying safe and building positive relationships were important for youth. But these are all critical first steps toward broader social change.

Challenges and Design Limitations

Although CBPR and the use of narrative have many advantages as a means of doing research with transformative goals, there are also limitations. Because our research has multiple purposes – systematic research that is also community-owned and empowering – it can be a complicated process with risky outcomes. For example, because the process aimed to increase capacity and transfer knowledge, engaging local residents as research assistants who handled the interviewing was critical. Inevitably, this meant that some interviewers were inexperienced, which created challenges. They needed ongoing support and mentoring to ensure that they were sensitive to interviewees and were encouraging them to share information that would be useful for our analysis. The interview dynamics were somewhat inconsistent; some researchers withdrew midstream. But we saw definite improvement in the quality of interviews as researchers became comfortable with and increasingly knowledgeable about the process. Using experienced interviewers would have had its advantages, but we strongly believe that the trade-offs were important to achieving the project's capacity-building goal.

On final reflection, we wondered whether the project met the transformative objectives of CLOUT. Did it contribute to significant social change? Ostensibly, one could argue that it was generated in reaction to the demands of funding institutions and that its aims were narrowly directed and hardly transformative. Although this is partly true, we suggest that the project contributed to transformation on at least three levels. First, it demonstrated that progress could be much more broadly measured than is currently favoured. Thus, it could help funding institutions to understand and accept why CBOs resist their measurement instruments. The fact that CBOs are taking this stance and are developing their own models shows that transformation is already occurring. Second, hiring and training local residents to conduct interviews and assist with data analysis provided an important opportunity to raise awareness and develop capacity, potentially fuelling further interest in participatory action research and/or anti-oppressive practice. And third, the experience of "naming their world" could potentially be empowering for interviewees and might lead to praxis (Freire 2006).

Lessons Learned: It's All about Relationships

Working on this project and the ones that followed it taught us some valuable lessons about doing research together. First and foremost, we learned that CBPR isn't just about research. The link between researchers and CBOs must extend beyond the research relationship. Researchers should make themselves available to their community partners on an ongoing basis. As discussed in the Introduction of this volume, researchers have skills that can be useful to community organizations. They themselves benefit from their associations with CBOs, and it is their responsibility to make a long-term commitment to them. This is most likely to occur when researchers are deeply rooted in the community. In such instances, they often establish relationships with the people whom they hire and train to act as assistants.

One example of this is a research assistant named Nancy. She joined our team on the recommendation of Lucille Bruce, who was then the executive director of the Native Women's Transition Centre. Lucille got to know Nancy as a participant in a community mentorship program. Nancy had no experience in conducting research and was initially hesitant to get involved but agreed to give it a try after a bit of encouragement. I (Shauna) got to know her quite well during the several months of designing and implementing the "Is Participation Having an Impact?" study. Eventually, she shared her own story with me. A Sixties Scoop survivor, she had lived through some very challenging times and was committed to a personal healing journey when she joined the project. As I completed the writing phase of the study, I emailed Nancy, asking how she wanted to be identified in the report. Along with two other research assistants, she agreed to include her story in its pages. Asked to share how she became involved with the project and her thoughts about her participation, Nancy sent me the following email in October 2007:

> I really don't mind if you put my real name on the final report. Our people have been silent for way too long ... without a name or a face, which is known as an identity. I'm starting to know my culture and my identity, so without a name or a face, I am not complete or whole. I feel our government and/or other agencies could and will know the real facts. I feel too, we as people need to speak up, and let our voices be heard. I am speaking up for people who don't have a voice or they're afraid to speak up. I am giving you permission to put my real name on the final report. I want to thank you for giving me the chance to speak up, I have learned so much about human beings, including myself.

Receiving this letter was a powerful moment for me. At this point in the project, I was going through the motions of writing up the final report. To be honest, I was feeling somewhat detached from the findings, more focused on completing the work and meeting our deadline. Nancy's message stopped me in my tracks and brought me to tears. It was a reminder that despite the many challenges we encountered, our commitment to engage community members in a meaningful way was beneficial not only for our project, but also for the people involved, including Nancy and myself. This, I was reminded, is what CBPR is all about.

Nancy and I didn't manage to work together again. She went on to do other things in the community, but we remained in contact during the years following the study. She passed away from cancer in 2012. I think of her often.

A final important lesson learned is that the best research ideas are often identified by community partners and subsequently developed through a collaborative and mutually respectful relationship rooted in the belief that everyone brings important knowledge, skills, and experience to the table. Nobody is smarter than anyone else.

The project described in this chapter was made possible only because researchers and community partners spent many hours building mutual trust, discussing what they wanted to learn and how best to learn it. This relationship remains strong because we continue to take time to nurture it, based on shared social justice goals. Through our work, we have developed a mutual understanding and respect for what each of us knows and how best to use our collective knowledge in effecting social change.

NOTES

1 The film, directed by Carole O'Brien, is titled *Together We Have CLOUT.* See https://www.youtube.com/watch?v=rSmn7X2-Glw.
2 CLOUT mission statement (no date).
3 At this time, all of CLOUT's member organizations happened to be led by women. CLOUT does not have a women-only policy.
4 Extracting Indigenous children from their families, typically without consent, and placing them in non-Indigenous homes, often out of province and country, was common in Canada during the 1960s and 1970s. The term "Sixties Scoop," which applies to this practice, was coined in Johnston (1983).
5 Canadian Institutes of Health Research, Natural Sciences and Engineering Research Council of Canada, and Social Sciences and Humanities Research Council of Canada, *Tri-Council Policy Statement: Ethical Conduct for Research Involving Humans,* December 2014. See http://www.pre.ethics.gc.ca/pdf/eng/tcps2-2014/TCPS_2_FINAL_Web.pdf.

REFERENCES

Alfred, Taiaiake. 2009. *Peace, Power, Righteousness: An Indigenous Manifesto.* Don Mills: Oxford University Press.

FNIGC (First Nations Information Governance Centre). 2014. *OCAP Ownership, Control, Access and Possession.* http://fnigc.ca/ocap.html.

Freire, Paulo. 2006. *Pedagogy of the Oppressed.* 30th anniversary edition. New York: Continuum.

Johnston, Patrick. 1983. *Native Children and the Child Welfare System.* Toronto: James Lorimer and the Canadian Council on Social Development.

Keys, Christopher B., Susan McMahon, Bernadette Sanchez, Lorna London, and Jaleel Abjul-Adil. 2004. "Culturally Anchored Research: Exemplars for Community Psychology." In *Participatory Community Research: Theories and Methods in Action,* ed. Leonard A. Jason, Christopher B. Keys, Yolanda Suarez-Balcazar, Rene R. Taylor, and Margaret I. Davis, with Joseph A. Durlak, 177–98. Washington, DC: American Psychological Association.

MacKinnon, Shauna, et al. 2008. *Is Participation Having an Impact? Measuring Progress in Winnipeg's Inner City through the Voices of Community-Based Program Participants.* Winnipeg: Canadian Centre for Policy Alternatives–Manitoba.

MacKinnon, Shauna, and Sara Stephens. 2010. "Is Participation Having an Impact? Measuring Progress in Winnipeg's Inner City through the Voices of Community-Based Program Participants." *Journal of Social Work* 10 (3): 283–300.

Mora, Juana, and David Diaz. 2004. *Latino Social Policy: A Participatory Research Model.* New York: Haworth Press.

NAHO (National Aboriginal Health Organization). 2007. *OCAP Ownership, Control, Access and Possession*. Ottawa: NAHO.

RCAP (Royal Commission on Aboriginal Peoples). 1996. Ottawa: Royal Commission on Aboriginal Peoples.

Silver, Jim. 2006. *In Their Own Voices: Building Urban Aboriginal Communities*. Halifax: Fernwood.

Smith, Linda Tuhiwai. 1999. *Decolonizing Methodologies: Research and Indigenous Peoples*. New York: Zed Books.

3

Participatory Evaluation Research
The CEDA Pathways Story

SHAUNA MacKINNON, DARLENE KLYNE,
and JANET NOWATZKI

The Community Education Development Association Pathways to Education program (CEDA Pathways) is a community-based after-school program modelled on Pathways to Education Canada. Its goal is to provide at-risk youth with academic, social, financial, and emotional supports to help them finish high school and to encourage them to pursue post-secondary education. CEDA Pathways is not an Indigenous program, but the neighbourhoods that it serves have a large Indigenous population, so it formulates its programming in keeping with the teachings of the medicine wheel.

Evaluation is an important component of the Pathways to Education program, and CEDA Pathways wanted to develop an evaluation method that aligned with the Indigenous philosophies that guided it. To this end, Darlene Klyne, the program director at CEDA Pathways, called upon researcher Shauna MacKinnon to assist in developing an evaluation model that could capture the holistic nature of its programming. The two had worked together on previous projects. Janet Nowatzki later came on board as the quantitative researcher. In this chapter, Shauna, Darlene, and Janet describe the continued efforts to develop, implement, and refine a participatory evaluation model grounded in Indigenous values. We discuss our process of trying to create a comprehensive evaluation framework that satisfied the desire of funding agencies for quantifiable outcomes while also capturing more difficult to measure outcomes aligned with CEDA Pathways' desire to develop programming based on Indigenous values and beliefs.

CEDA Pathways

Located in the North End of Winnipeg, CEDA was established as a non-profit organization in 1979 to support parents and residents by bringing a community voice to the education system. It serves a large Indigenous population as well as a growing number of refugees. CEDA describes itself as "an association comprised of passionate, active community members who believe that all people have the right to education."[1] As explained on CEDA's website, it aims to achieve this by

- developing a welcoming culture and environment that reflects the community we serve
- exploring individual histories to foster self-identify, pride and self-empowerment
- employing staff that reflect the cultural diversity of the community we serve
- exploring and responding to systems of oppression
- developing mutually beneficial partnerships with community members, organizations, and government
- fostering multi-generational learning that includes grandmothers, caregivers, and extended families.

In 2010, CEDA entered into a partnership with Pathways to Education Canada, establishing Pathways to Education Winnipeg, an after-school program for students in the North End. The central mandate of Pathways to Education Canada (Pathways Canada) is to provide academic and mentoring supports as well as financial incentives to low-income students. Founded in 2001 in Toronto's Regent Park, it is a non-profit organization with a mandate to assist youth from low-income neighbourhoods across Canada to graduate from high school and transition into postsecondary education. This mandate is straightforward, and the success of its objectives, as it would seem, is easy to measure by assessing school attendance, credit accumulation, and graduation rates. However, program delivery and evaluation become far more complicated when viewed in a historical context and in recognition of multiple challenges, systemic barriers, and the complex realities of Indigenous youth in the North End.

Preventative, supportive education-related programs are much needed in North End neighbourhoods, which lie in what is known as the inner city of Winnipeg. The neighbourhoods served by CEDA Pathways are among the poorest in Canada. As is often the case in such areas, its high school completion rates are low in comparison with other parts of the city. As will be explained below, it is not coincidental that the inner city is home to a large and growing Indigenous population. Fully 21 percent of its residents identify as Indigenous, and in some neighbourhoods that Pathways serves, such as Lord Selkirk Park, more than 50 percent are Indigenous (see Chapter 4 in this volume). Indigenous people are also among the poorest and most marginalized inhabitants of the inner city – in 65 percent of their households, incomes fall below the low-income cut-off. Many Indigenous families have lived in poverty for generations and have little hope of escaping it. And though significant evidence indicates that education can help to improve social and economic outcomes for many Indigenous people, many others do not trust the education system. This is because the horrific experiences of colonial policies and programs such as Indian residential schools have left a lasting scar. There are few Indigenous families who have not been touched in some way by the devastating legacy of residential schools, as was recently documented by the Truth and Reconciliation Commission of Canada.

Like many organizations in the inner city, CEDA Pathways believes that improving the outcomes of urban Indigenous people requires that the damaging effects of residential schools and policies and programs designed to acculturate Indigenous people be tackled head on. It aims to do so by using decolonizing programming that assists Indigenous people in their journey toward self-sufficiency and self-determination. This necessitates providing students with an opportunity to learn about their history through Indigenous eyes and to reclaim their cultures and identities so that they can move forward with strength and pride.

Aligning Programming and Evaluation with Indigenous Values

The main objective of Pathways to Education Canada is to increase high school graduation rates in low-income communities. Thus, its evaluation focus is on measuring the degree to which programs are accomplishing this goal. However, this becomes more complicated in the case of CEDA Pathways because it views success in more holistic terms.

CEDA Pathways had decided early on that it would move beyond the Pathways Canada model to integrate teachings based on the medicine wheel. Guided by the wisdom of local Elders, parents, and community members, CEDA Pathways wanted students to develop spiritually, emotionally, and physically, as well as intellectually. CEDA Pathways staff continue to create programming aimed at the holistic development of students within this framework. While the central quantifiable objectives of Pathways Canada remain in place, the goals of CEDA Pathways are more broadly based on the belief that students cannot become whole without first understanding who they are in the context of their histories and cultures. CEDA Pathways encourages students to value their heritage so that they are well equipped to move forward from high school as proud Indigenous people and role models for future generations. The intent is to develop individuals who are not only successful in their own right, but are also leaders dedicated to giving back to their community. This model is consistent with the Indigenous value of collective responsibility, which is embedded in the teachings of the medicine wheel.

In keeping with the spirit of participatory program development, CEDA Pathways consulted early on with Elders and other Indigenous leaders, who made it very clear that programming aligned with medicine wheel teachings is required to address the historical, social, cultural, and individual barriers that are the reality for students. The importance of "healing the spirit first" is increasingly understood beyond the Indigenous community in Winnipeg, as we become more educated about our colonial past and the damage it has caused. The challenge then became how to evaluate this aspect of CEDA Pathways programming.

The holistic, Indigenous-centred approach to programming requires an evaluation method that is grounded in similar values. CEDA Pathways believes that evaluating progress must move beyond mainstream measures to capture an equally important objective of the programming – reclaiming identities as strong, proud Indigenous people. CEDA Pathways wanted to develop better aligned means of measuring success.

Just as program development aligned with Indigenous values requires consultation with community, so too should the generation of a means by which to measure progress. In 2010, Pathways Canada provided funding to CEDA Pathways to develop an evaluation framework. Through consultation with youth, Elders, and staff members, it created a model, one that would use sharing circles to evaluate progress through the voices of students, Elders, parents, teachers, program staff, and other key stakeholders.

It should be noted that though Pathways Canada did not reject the use of Indigenous evaluation methods, it continued to require quantifiable outcomes as measured by school credits earned, attendance, and graduation rates. Of course, CEDA Pathways complied with this stipulation. It was pleased that Pathways Canada was at least open to exploring new methods, and though it had not succeeded in moving entirely beyond Western methods, this was a good start.

Indigenous Foundations of Program and Evaluation Design

CEDA Pathways understands the long-term value of decolonization and reclaiming of identity and cultures as a critical form of learning that strengthens self-awareness and self-esteem, and that builds much-needed positive social networks. As McKenzie and Morrissette (2003) note, "cultural reconstruction" can provide an important source of strength in the development of self-identity. Education that focuses on academic success is incompatible with holistic approaches to learning based on the medicine wheel because it disregards the importance of cultural identity.

To adequately evaluate Indigenous, decolonizing programming, it is imperative to understand decolonization in practice. Decolonization is essentially the undoing of colonization. Providing exposure to Indigenous knowledge and cultures, informing students that colonial policies were designed to eliminate Indigenous cultures, and understanding the intergenerational damage caused by these policies can be life changing (MacKinnon 2015). It provides context for individual difficulties, and it furnishes participants with knowledge that can lead to a renewed sense of pride and strength that is critical for their life journey. The medicine wheel provides a basis from which students can begin to learn who they are, where they come from, and where they see themselves in the future and in the context of the broader community.

The Medicine Wheel

The medicine wheel is a common symbol in North American Indigenous cultures, where it often functions as a tool in the teaching of philosophies. Though the wheel is uniquely interpreted across differing tribes, its core values remain consistent. The medicine wheel is used to guide Indigenous teachings in the context of the four directions (east, south, west, north), with each direction representing a teaching in the circle of life. Teachings typically begin in the eastern quadrant, moving around the circle in a clockwise direction, and they encompass the spiritual, emotional, intellectual, and physical aspects of life. The directions often represent the various human races but can also stand for the seasons of the year, stages of life, elements of nature, and animals/ceremonial plants (Native Voices n.d.). Individuals are seen in the broader context of the environment and the community.

Diane Hill (1999) discusses a medicine-wheel-based learning process that is consistent with decolonizing methods of practice. In her interpretation, learning begins in the east, with *awareness*, which entails developing an understanding of one's self and the world. This is consistent with Indigenous teachings that emphasize understanding of identity in the context of the broader community to which individuals are responsible. Hill associates the south with *struggle*, typically that of changing negative life experiences to positive patterns of feeling and believing, which influence behaviour. This is consistent with teachings that stress knowing and understanding the past in order to move forward. To the west, learners embark on *building (mind and knowledge)* – integrating new positive life experiences into continuous patterns and developing a view of life that includes the strengths they have already acquired. In the north, they reach a stage of *preservation*, where they discover how to maintain the positive patterns and view of life as an ongoing system. This is consistent with Indigenous teachings that accentuate continuous learning, reflection, and giving back.

In their Circle of Courage model of learning and development, Brendtro, Brokenleg, and Van Bockern (2002) also employ the medicine

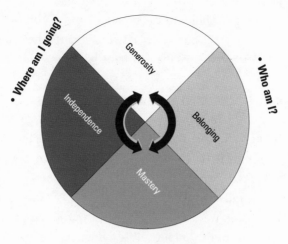

Where do I come from?

Evaluating CEDA Pathways using the medicine wheel.
Adapted from Brendtro, Brokenleg, and Van Bockern (2002).

wheel. Emphasizing the importance of self-esteem in the development process, they provide a framework based on "four bases of self-worth," which they situate within the four directions of the wheel. The east is associated with the universal *need for belonging*. The south is linked with opportunities for *mastery toward competency*. At the west, students learn to express *independence toward personal empowerment*. And in the north, they internalize the *pre-eminent value of generosity*.

The Circle of Courage model is built from Indigenous child-rearing philosophies that see self-worth as the essential ingredient in development. Brendtro, Brokenleg, and Van Bockern (2002) identify four bases of the development of self-worth found in traditional Indigenous educational practices and that also align with definitive work on self-concept in child-hood. In developing its programs, CEDA Pathways uses methods inspired by Hill (1999) and Brendtro, Brokenleg, and Van Bockern (2002), but it also listens to the wisdom of local Elders who stress an individual's ability to answer four key questions: Who am I? Where do I come from? Where am I going? What is my purpose in this life?

So, in addition to the quantifiable goal of graduating from high school, the primary goal of the CEDA Pathways program is the emotional, physical, spiritual, and intellectual development of young adults in the context of their responsibility to the broader community, including past and future generations. The diagram of the medicine wheel illustrates the way that CEDA Pathways uses the medicine wheel to guide its work.

The Role of Elders

The Pathways model is built from the premise that self-awareness, relationship building, encouragement, and guidance are constant themes throughout participants' time in the program. In Indigenous cultures, Elders play an essential role as educators, mentors, spiritual advisors, and counsellors, helping to guide youth into adulthood. CEDA Pathways has engaged Elders and continues to seek ways to integrate them into programming so that students have access to this important resource. As the program evolves, the hope is that Elders will have a formal place in its design, delivery, evaluation, and ongoing refinement. Although high school completion will remain an important goal, Elders and other Indigenous leaders will ensure that the lessons of the medicine wheel contribute to holistic development that responds to the physical, intellectual, spiritual, and mental needs of students in the context of families and communities, and in recognition of the historical, social, cultural, and individual barriers that continue to make life difficult for Indigenous people. The challenge remains – How do we measure progress aligned with this important aspect of CEDA Pathways?

Indigenous Evaluation in Context

The approach described in this chapter is consistent with the transformative evaluation framework of Donna Mertens (2009, 59), which stresses "methodological decisions made with a conscious awareness of contextual and historical factors, especially as they relate to discrimination and oppression." In keeping with Smith's (1999) criteria for Indigenous research methods, evaluation methods must be based on an ongoing relationship of trust between evaluators, programmers, and program users. This speaks to the need for the development and implementation of an evaluation framework that uses a participatory model. The wisdom and knowledge of Elders, program developers, students, and teachers should be used to generate a framework that makes sense to the program.

Though the effects of decolonizing pedagogy are sometimes invisible and difficult to measure, it can have a positive – even transformative – impact and can influence the education paths of individuals who are vulnerable to dropping out of school. Studies of Indigenous adults who participated in such learning in Winnipeg show that it helped many to regain their confidence and hope (MacKinnon and Stephens 2010). Many individuals who have dropped out of formal education and who have little hope for the future attribute their involvement in community-based programs as inspiring them to further their education as adults (ibid.; Silver 2006). This tells us that integrating similar methods into Pathways programming can encourage youth to remain in high school. But the value of such programming extends beyond this and is not easily measured by standard quantifiable methods. Our task – our challenge – was to explore and develop methods that would allow us to capture progress beyond that which can be quantified.

The Sharing Circle

Formal and informal discussions with Elders, students, staff members, community leaders, and others in the local community led us to explore the sharing circle as a model for holistic learning and evaluation. Sharing circles have long been part of Indigenous cultures as a means of learning, problem solving, and healing. From the beginning, CEDA Pathways has employed these circles to bond with students and to engage them in traditional teachings. Employing the circle to measure progress made sense because students were already familiar and comfortable with it. Using circles for evaluation evolved from the belief that learning and evaluation are intertwined processes. Allowing students to reflect on their own development while also assessing and contributing to program design can be empowering for them. It can tell us much about their progress and can help staff to improve the services that they provide. Just as students learn from their teachers/advisors, so too do teachers/advisors learn from them. It is also true that individuals become more committed to a program or process if they are fully engaged in it and believe that they can help to determine its nature. By definition, the sharing circle is participatory and thus leant itself to CEDA Pathways' interest in developing a participatory evaluation model.

Next, we explored how using the sharing circle might work in practice. The basic idea is that participation in regular circles with peers creates a safe environment for students to provide feedback and input into program refinement, while also reflecting on their progress.

Unique Features of the Sharing Circle Approach

It should be noted that the evaluation model described in this chapter is unique in two important ways: it was developed using a participatory process, and it diverges from the evidence-based approaches that have dominated evaluation research in recent years. As evaluation expert Lisbeth Schorr (2009) notes, focusing on evidence-based evaluation risks "losing programs that do not lend themselves to random-assignment evaluations because such programs feature multiple interactive components and significant front-line flexibility." Schorr also points out that the ability to be innovative is lost when we rely on evidence-based methods that have worked in the past or in other communities. Evidence-based evaluation does have some valid applications, but it is limited in what it can tell us. Nor does it fit well with Indigenous methods, because it is too linear and too often relies on concrete quantifiable objectives and measures. It also fails to consider that evidence is not always transferable, and it can disregard the importance of process. This is important to us because many Indigenous leaders have told us that process is as important as outcomes (MacKinnon and Stephens 2010). In this regard, the sharing circle can be useful because it is very much about process. It allows program participants and their teachers and advisors to work collaboratively and to support each other through a process of development that measures and celebrates "success" and "outcomes" in a holistic, encouraging, and positive manner.

CEDA Pathways students experience complex challenges. Solutions are equally complex, so assessing outcomes is more difficult than simply determining whether a person has obtained a high school diploma. From an Indigenous, decolonizing perspective, it is equally important to assess progress in other areas. This is consistent with the medicine wheel framework, which places equal value on intellectual, emotional, physical, and spiritual growth. It also aligns with priorities identified by local Elders, who tell us that success requires evolving individual and collective understanding of "who we are, where we come from, where we are going, and what our purpose is" (McNeil 2010).

Testing the Model: A Matter of Trust

Once we chose the sharing circle as a method of evaluation, the next step was to test it with a cohort of students. The kind of circle that we had in mind differed from what they were accustomed to. It resembled a focus group, as students and other participants would be asked to reflect on and respond to specific questions, albeit in an open-ended fashion. Ensuring the safety of the circle – what's said in the circle stays in the circle – was also a concern. We would need to use the knowledge gained there while simultaneously respecting the privacy and anonymity of participants and preventing harm (Chilisa 2012). We talked about who should lead the circle and how the researcher/evaluator would be involved. We acknowledged that there was an unavoidable power imbalance in the circle and wondered if this would prevent students from being honest. We had few answers to these questions.

Ultimately, we decided to test our model with a cohort of students and staff who already had well-established trusting relationships. We would simply explain to the students what we were doing and why, and would encourage them to participate while also giving them the option to decline. The students had been with CEDA Pathways for a year and were now in Grades 11 and 12. CEDA Pathways chose to integrate our evaluation circle into a two-day retreat at the Windy Hill Community Learning and Wellness Centre, which lies an hour's drive from Winnipeg. A facility owned by Ma Mawi Wi Chi Itata Centre, an Indigenous social service provider in Winnipeg, Windy Hill is often used by Indigenous and other groups for meetings and retreats. The nine students had been there before, and it was seen as a peaceful, spiritual environment in which they could reflect on their experiences. They welcomed the chance to spend time with staff at Windy Hill. Darlene advised them that the retreat would also comprise the evaluation and that we were interested in their thoughts about CEDA Pathways, including what they liked, what might be improved, and what their experience had taught them thus far. A half-day was set aside for the sharing circle, which would encompass staff, students, and Shauna as the researcher/evaluator. The students were informed that Shauna would participate for part of the day. We all drove out together and spent time socializing over lunch. This was important because it enabled the students to meet Shauna and observe her interaction with staff. The students clearly had affection and trust for staff, and were at ease with them, but they didn't know Shauna. Spending time together would allow them to decide whether they felt comfortable sharing in her presence. Lunch was casual and comfortable, leading to an easy transition into the circle.

As is customary, we opened the circle with a smudge ceremony. This was conducted by Darlene, who also led the circle itself. Smudge ceremonies involve burning sacred herbs in a bowl, which is then passed among participants so that they can brush the smoke over their body. Commonly referred to as smudging, this practice is a symbolic way of warding off bad spirits. When used at the beginning of a sharing circle, it creates a space in which safe and trusting sharing can occur. After completing the smudge, Darlene explained our intentions and outlined program evaluation and the means by which CEDA Pathways was currently obligated to demonstrate student progress. Today's circle would be used to evaluate both programs and student progress. Students and staff could share their thoughts and feelings about the program, good and bad, as honestly as they wished. CEDA Pathways was trying to find evaluation methods that were more aligned with Indigenous values, and the circle was a possible candidate for this. We would go around the circle as many times as needed, giving each student numerous chances to reflect and share. First, we would go around the circle once to allow students and staff to say whatever they pleased. We would go around the circle a second time, asking them to respond to specific questions as they wished. The purpose of this was to help us understand what CEDA Pathways meant to them and if and how it was contributing to their lives. Darlene explained that Shauna was joining the circle as an observer and a kind of "translator" for the purposes of evaluation. Shauna said she would respect the safety and privacy of the circle and promised not to divulge any identifying information. The participants agreed to the process, and Darlene started the circle by expressing her thoughts, concerns, and hopes for the students and the program. We went around the circle until everyone had a chance to speak.

Our short-term goal for this test run was to see whether students would openly and honestly answer specific questions when staff and an outside researcher were present. Although we were not completely surprised by their forthright responses, we were encouraged. The words of a community member came to mind as we listened to them: "There is something that happens in the circle; it's a powerful and empowering thing." This is the best way to describe what occurred that day. The circle was obviously a good way to engage the students in honest reflection about the program and their experiences with it. It is inspiring that people who are otherwise hesitant to speak out find comfort and courage in a circle. Our concern regarding a possible power imbalance dissipated. Students, staff, and the researcher became equals, sharing both positive and negative experiences as well as disclosing their fears and vulnerabilities. Participants seemed to trust in the process of the circle. When it ended, we felt confident in its potential as an effective evaluation tool.

After we left Windy Hill, we developed a comprehensive evaluation plan with sharing circles at the core and presented it to Pathways Canada for consideration, noting that it would require significant financial support. We suggested a longitudinal approach that included the implementation of sharing circles aligned with Indigenous programming throughout students' entire time in the program. We recommended that evaluation of their progress be built around the questions identified by Elders as critical to successful development (Who am I? Where do I come from? Where am I going? What is my purpose?) and the four central features of the Circle of Courage model. Indigenous-focused programming and evaluation circles would be led by Elders and a researcher would attend the circles to observe trends, themes, and progress aligned with program objectives. Programming would take place weekly, and evaluation circles would be conducted with small consistent membership groups at regular intervals throughout the year and throughout students' time in the program.

Implementing the Framework: Next Steps

Several months later, CEDA Pathways received funding to proceed with an evaluation. Funders concurred with the use of the sharing circle to collect qualitative data that could be brought together with quantitative data gathered by CEDA Pathways staff. However, we were unable to implement our comprehensive longitudinal model, because the funding did not extend to this and the deadline for completion was too tight, lying only months away. Thus, we proceeded with an adapted version of our model.

Because Indigenous-focused programming was not yet fully integrated, we could not align sharing circle content directly with programming. However, we did arrange for several cohorts of students to participate in a series of circles. Some were intended for specific age/grade cohorts, one was for girls, and another was for boys. Once again, students generously shared their time and openly talked about their experiences at CEDA Pathways as well as some of the challenges in their lives. They commonly described CEDA Pathways as "home" and "family," and some said that if not for CEDA Pathways, they would have nowhere safe to be after school.

They identified the emotional, physical, and spiritual support at CEDA Pathways as important to them, more so than the academic support. They often mentioned that they felt comfort in knowing that CEDA Pathways was always there for them after school, that a meal would be served, and that they could talk to staff about their day – like family. Interestingly, though the primary mandate of CEDA Pathways is the attainment of formal education, students rarely mentioned this as their reason for attendance, a fact that speaks to the complexity of their lives. Many live in families for whom poverty is deep and intergenerational. Many live in families that are struggling with addictions related to the intergenerational trauma imposed by residential schools and the Sixties Scoop (Alston-O'Connor 2010). Families often struggle with a host of challenges that impede their ability to provide stability and support, which CEDA Pathways offers. This is probably why students are so quick to describe CEDA Pathways as "family."

Using the sharing circle as a means of evaluation, we were able to capture this, showing not only that students were making progress, but also reminding us of how much they deal with in their daily lives. This was important because it reaffirmed that the standard tools of measurement were insufficient for programs such as CEDA Pathways. In our report to Pathways Canada, we reaffirmed the need to consider the complicated context of the students, reiterating that the quantifiable data could not capture the important progress that they were making.

In 2013, the relationship between CEDA Pathways and the researcher was put to the test when Pathways Canada requested a comprehensive evaluation of its programming. Pathways Canada accepted the use of the sharing circle model, but it expected that mainstream Western methods of data collection and analysis would also be employed. To satisfy this requirement while also remaining true to the CEDA Pathways approach, we used a participatory-strengths-based evaluation model. Staff developed the evaluation research questions and identified the stakeholders to be included in interviews, focus groups, and sharing circles.

CEDA Pathways had experienced many growing pains since opening its doors in 2010. The evaluation revealed some weaknesses in the program, which challenged it to assess its organizational structure and operations. However, our strengths-based participatory approach to evaluation provided a foundation to move forward in a positive and empowering way. The evaluation outlined concrete ideas put forward by CEDA Pathways management and staff. A year after its completion, CEDA Pathways made changes and has been strengthened as a result.

The evaluation revealed that CEDA Pathways had not fully integrated the cultural reclamation component into its programming. Pressures to conform to Pathways Canada's primary focus on credit accumulation and graduation rates distracted CEDA Pathways from systematically integrating this essential feature. The evaluation confirmed its importance and encouraged CEDA Pathways to make it a priority for future program development.

In the fall of 2013, the research team was called upon to further refine the initial evaluation framework, an exercise that was completed in the spring of 2014. Because the initial tool was developed through a participatory process that included a broad cross-section of stakeholders, minimal changes were required to refine the sharing circle model that was designed in 2011. CEDA Pathways is now formalizing its cultural reclamation programming and has an appropriate evaluation framework to assess progress. The next hurdle is accessing the necessary funding to conduct an evaluation exercise that is aligned with the programming.

Quantitative Methods and Indigenous Evaluation

Indigenous, transformative, participatory, and other alternative forms of evaluation tend to favour qualitative methods, but they do not exclude the use of quantitative measures. Quantitative evaluation at CEDA Pathways has required attention at each stage of the process. Simply taking measures determined by Pathways Canada and applying them to the Winnipeg context has resulted in distorted perceptions of the program, both internally and externally. CEDA Pathways students do not fare particularly well when assessed solely in terms of credit accumulation, school attendance, program participation, and high school completion within a prescribed period of time. Although CEDA Pathways continues to collect this information, it does not accurately reflect what occurs in the program itself, including the context of the students' lives and the relationships between staff and students. Understanding the broader context of the students' lives is imperative to any evaluation or analysis of the CEDA Pathways program. Students who live in the CEDA catchment area are exposed to many risk factors that have an impact on education outcomes, and Indigenous students in particular bear the brunt of the exposure. Qualitative interviews and sharing circles give glimpses of these realities. However, though these stories are powerful and important, they too fail to capture the full impact of poverty and racism on the community.

CEDA Pathways staff felt that a "snapshot" of exposure to various risk factors associated with high school graduation would help complete the picture of the complicated lives of Indigenous students. Such information would benefit program funders who were unfamiliar with the North End or the challenges that colonization has imposed on the lives of Indigenous people.

Starting with a descriptive list of indicators identified in earlier evaluation work (MacKinnon 2011), CEDA Pathways support workers created a set of factors that were relevant to the students. These included being Indigenous (racism), the education values of their parents, being the first in their family to complete high school, their connection to culture, housing stability, "healthy" families and home environment (feeling safe at home, exposure to addictions, and extra family responsibilities at home), self-esteem and self-worth, being bullied, experience of being in care, involvement in gangs and the criminal justice system, single-parent households, and exposure to incidents of suicide and tragic death. A survey was constructed based on the list of indicators and was administered one-on-one by student parent support workers (SPSWs) to a subset of Indigenous students in March 2013 as part of the evaluation process. Titled the Life Factors Survey (see the appendix on page 71), it provided greater context regarding the lives of students. Not only have program funders been given individual stories from qualitative data from sharing circles, they now have a better understanding of the breadth of these experiences.

Although useful information can be gathered from surveys, as was the case with the Life Factors Survey, they must be used with caution and sensitivity. An example of Western research methods, surveys are inherently impersonal and can make participants feel that they are being put under a microscope. Sensitivity in conducting a survey is as important as the phrasing of its questions, and trust between surveyor and participant is imperative. This was particularly the case for us. Many of our questions were personal and difficult, and we could not have asked them had trusting relationships not been established with the students. Asking difficult questions was necessary to demonstrate the challenges that students face. Importantly, the purpose of the survey was to give breadth to these challenges, not to assess each individual student's level of risk. CEDA Pathways staff were adamant that surveys be administered a few months into the program when relationships have been developed, that they be administered by a staff member with whom the participant had a relationship, and that they be used as minimally as possible. Ninety-five of 182 students agreed to complete the survey. The collected information shed some light on the context of CEDA Pathways Indigenous students. It affirmed what other research had shown – that colonialism had led to intergenerational trauma and complex challenges (TRC 2015). Increasing high school completion rates will require much more than academic supports and financial incentives (MacKinnon and Nowatzki 2013).

A key aspect of CEDA Pathways is nurturing trusting relationships and offering comprehensive supports that are focused on individual and family healing. Indeed, our success on this dimension has been a pivotal outcome of qualitative evaluations of the program. However, it is missed from standard quantitative measurement of the program.

The measure for student participation in the CEDA Pathways program has been attendance at tutoring and mentoring activities. In general, attendance is quite low, but this does not accurately reflect student involvement in the program. Many students develop strong relationships and receive substantial support from their SPSW outside of programming activities, and the type of contact varies from student to student. Benefits of the SPSW-student relationship are highlighted in qualitative evaluations as a key aspect of program success; however, funders continue to prefer quantitative measures. Because the needs of the students are broad, it is difficult to define categories of participation or access to the program; relationships are indeed difficult to quantify. Regardless, it is important that participation statistics somehow acknowledge the relationship and support component of the CEDA Pathways program. Otherwise, in the absence of an understanding of the students' lives, interpretation of program participation data can be skewed in a negative direction. Janet continues to work with staff to determine how to track student contact in a manner that is meaningful. Ideas under consideration include tracking daily time spent by SPSWs in various relationship-building and support activities with students and indicating in routine reports the level of contact between students and SPSWs. Both sharing circles and surveys may also be needed to fully assess how the program has helped students to overcome barriers and achieve positive educational outcomes.

Collection and Analysis of Educational Outcomes Data

CEDA Pathways has been able to more accurately demonstrate its effectiveness by adding measurements of both the students' lives and the relationship building and support that occurs in the program. It is also necessary to analyze standard educational outcomes data from an Indigenous perspective. In particular, the grouping of data and the measurements against which they are compared (baselines, standards, and goals) tend to be dictated by Eurocentric standards. Analysis has typically been framed by the expectation that a student enters Grade 9 at a certain age, progresses to the following grade each year, and completes high school in four years. The use of Eurocentric measurement standards merely highlights the effects of colonization and is not an appropriate way to evaluate the success of the CEDA Pathways program.

For many CEDA Pathways students, the educational journey does not follow a predictable linear timeline. Many cannot be classified easily in one grade, as they may simultaneously be taking courses at differing grade levels. On average, students spend a significant period out of school, either dropping out completely for a time or accumulating large numbers of absences. Other school interruptions are frequent as well, including switching schools mid-year or changing programs. This pattern resembles that of other low-income urban neighbourhoods (Wilson 2009). Measurement of student progress must therefore take into consideration diverse educational paths.

In consultation with CEDA Pathways staff, Janet made some adjustments to the analysis of educational outcomes data. First, although it is still necessary to group students by current grade level, analysis of CEDA Pathways data by this variable has not been rigid; the length of time a student remains in the program has also been considered in analyses. Additionally, supporting a student to return to school after time away or to become more highly engaged in school are program successes that are being tracked. The variety of program streams, including modified programming and adult education programs, is another important component of educational outcomes that needs to be included in analyses. Finally, as the program continues, looking at five-, six-, and seven-year high school completion rates will be more beneficial than focusing on four-year completion rates, given the non-linear paths of most students in the catchment area.

Quantitative measurement remains an important part of evaluation of the CEDA Pathways program. Because the program mandate is fundamentally connected with mainstream education objectives and measures of success, this is unlikely to change. However, we continue to be mindful of the limitations of narrowly used measures and try to educate governments and funding agencies regarding the realities of students' lives and the effects of colonialism, including the legacy of the residential school system, so that they are not forgotten when standard educational outcomes are examined. The failure to understand students' lives seriously affects the interpretation of any outcomes data. Counteracting this issue has required staff to collaborate and to think creatively. Measuring the breadth of exposure to educational risk factors among students, tracking and highlighting the importance of relationship development and support activities outside of formal programming, and making adjustments to the way in which educational outcomes are assessed have all helped to give a clearer picture of the success of CEDA Pathways.

Program Evaluation: Lessons for Practitioners and Policy Makers

CEDA Pathways has learned that programming focused on narrow quantifiable outcomes such as credit accumulation and graduation rates is insufficient for its students. So too are narrowly focused evaluation methods. Mainstream models of evaluation are insufficient because they do not effectively measure all that needs to be measured from a holistic Indigenous perspective. Narrow evaluation methods do not consider the damaging effects of colonial policies in the lives of CEDA Pathways students and their families. They don't consider the continued impact of systemic racism and the challenges that many Indigenous students face, which put academic learning low on their list of priorities.

We may have known this intuitively before we developed our evaluation framework, but engaging in that process allowed us to confirm that CEDA Pathways holistic values aligned with medicine wheel teachings require a customized Indigenous values-based method of evaluation. We learned this because we knew that we needed to seek out the wisdom of Elders and to trust in the experience of parents, staff, teachers, and students to design an evaluation method that would help us understand more than how many credits were accumulated and how often students attended class. As one student said in frustration with a school policy that marked students absent if they came late to class, "When a student is late for class, [teachers] don't know what went on the night before. They don't know if that student was awake all night because there was a party in their house and people were drinking, drugging and fighting. And they don't ask, they just mark us as absent."[2] Using the sharing circle model of evaluation gives us a deeper understanding of individual students' challenges and progress. But it has the added benefit of helping students to develop strong bonds with their peers and mentors because they know that they are not alone in their struggles. As students move through the CEDA Pathways program, exploring their development in the context of the medicine wheel, they will also engage in an evaluation method that allows them to assess their own progress, provide input into ongoing program design, and build relationships with their peers and mentors.

We should note that our evaluation model was difficult to develop and implement, and awkward to describe. This is because we continue to negotiate between two not always compatible worldviews of education and ways in which education outcomes are viewed and evaluated. Walking in both worlds can be problematic, but we believe we have found a way to gain valuable insights that can be used to improve policies and programs. However, if governments and other funders want programs such as CEDA Pathways to demonstrate, through evaluation, how they are making a difference in meaningful ways, they will need to fund the design and implementation of comprehensive evaluation models that tell the story of the journey – an often long and challenging one – for students with complicated lives.

APPENDIX: LIFE FACTORS SURVEY

1. Do your parents make sure that you get to school every day? If you don't go to school, do you get in trouble?

   [The intent of this question is to assess whether the student's education is a priority for his/her parents.]

2. Would you be the first person in your family to finish high school?
3. How do you feel about your Aboriginal heritage? Proud, don't care, or not proud?
4. Do you feel safe at home?
5. Does anyone in your home drink or use drugs?
6. Are there any responsibilities at home, such as taking care of younger brothers or sisters, which keep you away from school, homework, or other activities?
7. I have high self-esteem (circle response)

   Not very true of me [1 – 2 – 3 – 4 – 5 – 6 – 7] Very true of me

8. Have you ever been in foster care? How many homes have you been in? How has this experience been for you (positive, negative)?
9. How many different high schools have you attended? Why have you changed schools?

10. Have you ever felt bullied at school?
11. Have you ever been in trouble with the police?
12. How does having gangs in your community affect you? Have any of your friends or family members been involved in a gang?
13. Who lives in your home with you?
14. How has suicide in the community affected you? Do you know people who have committed suicide? (If yes, how many?)

NOTES

1 Excerpt from CEDA vision statement. The CEDA website is being redesigned and this vision statement will appear on the new website.
2 Personal communication with CEDA Pathways student, April 2011.

REFERENCES

Alston-O'Connor, Emily. 2010. "The Sixties Scoop: Implications for Social Workers and Social Work Education." *Critical Social Work* 11 (1). http://www1.uwindsor.ca/criticalsocialwork/the-sixties-scoop-implications-for-social-workers-and-social-work-education.

Brendtro, Larry K., Martin Brokenleg, and Steve Van Bockern. 2002. *Reclaiming Youth at Risk: Our Hope for the Future.* Bloomington: Solution Tree Press.

Chilisa, Bagele. 2012. *Indigenous Research Methodologies.* New York: Sage.

Hill, Diane L. 1999. "Holistic Learning: A Model of Education Based on Aboriginal Cultural Philosophy." Master's thesis, Saint Francis Xavier University, Nova Scotia.

MacKinnon, Shauna. 2011. "Predictive Indicators of Successful Education Attainment." Report for CEDA Pathways to Education, Winnipeg.

–. 2015. *Decolonizing Employment: Aboriginal Inclusion in Canada's Labour Market.* Winnipeg: University of Manitoba Press.

MacKinnon, Shauna, and Janet Nowatzki. 2013. "Evaluation of CEDA Pathways to Education: It's All about Relationships." Report for CEDA Pathways to Education, Winnipeg.

MacKinnon, Shauna, and Sara Stephens. 2010. "Is Participation Having an Impact? Measuring Progress in Winnipeg's Inner City through the Voices of Community-Based Program Participants." *Journal of Social Work* 10 (3): 283–300.

McKenzie, Brad, and Vern Morrissette. 2003. "Social Work Practice with Canadians of Indigenous Background: Guidelines for Respectful Social Work." In *Multicultural Social Work in Canada: Working with Diverse Ethno-racial Communities*, ed. Alean Al-Krenawi and John R. Graham, 251–82. Don Mills: Oxford University Press.

McNeil, Astrid. 2010. "Up-Next." Unpublished manuscript, Winnipeg.

Mertens, Donna. 2009. *Transformative Research and Evaluation.* New York: Guilford Press.

Native Voices. N.d. "Medicine Ways: Traditional Healers and Healing." https://www.nlm.nih.gov/nativevoices/exhibition/healing-ways/medicine-ways/medicine-wheel.html.

Schorr, Lisbeth. 2009. "To Judge What Will Best Help Society's Neediest, Let's Use a Broad Array of Evaluation Techniques." *Chronicle of Philanthropy,* December 2009. https://www.philanthropy.com/article/To-Judge-What-Will-Best-Help/174077.

Silver, Jim. 2006. *In Their Own Voices: Building Urban Aboriginal Communities.* Halifax: Fernwood.

Smith, Linda Tuhiwai. 1999. *Decolonizing Methodologies: Research and Indigenous Peoples.* New York: Zed Books.

TRC (Truth and Reconciliation Commission of Canada). 2015. *Honouring the Truth Reconciling for the Future. Summary of the Final Report of the Truth and Reconciliation Commission of Canada.* http://www.trc.ca/websites/trcinstitution/File/2015/Honouring_the_Truth_Reconciling_for_the_Future_July_23_2015.pdf.

Wilson, William J. 2009. *More Than Just Race: Being Black and Poor in the Inner City.* New York: W.W. Norton.

4

Community-Based Participatory Research in a Low-Income Public-Housing Project

JIM SILVER, JANICE GOODMAN,
CHEYENNE HENRY, and CAROLYN YOUNG

The four of us met on April 4, 2014, to talk about our work from 2005 to 2011 in Lord Selkirk Park (LSP) and to think about preparing this chapter. Although we see each other often because all of us are active in Winnipeg's North End, it isn't the same as the intensive years of working together in the Developments, as LSP is called by those who live there. We reflected on what we had achieved in that low-income public-housing complex and especially on how we did our work there, and ended up feeling that a great deal had been accomplished, so much in fact that Lord Selkirk Park could usefully be seen as a model for such work.

LSP is a large, 314-unit public-housing project in Winnipeg's North End. For decades, it was one of the city's most troubled neighbourhoods, plagued by high rates of poverty, unemployment, and crime. In the 1990s, half its units were boarded up, and many people referred to it as a "war zone." Indigenous street gang members who grew up there in the 1990s described remarkable scenes of violence and crime (Comack et al. 2013). In 2005, a woman from the neighbourhood said, "I'd like to just bulldoze this whole fricking place down, I hate it, I hate it, I hate what it's doing to families here" (CCPA–MB 2005, 27).

Today, LSP is a better place to live. We hope that a part of the reason for this is community development work, including the research in which we and others were involved.

We took various routes into LSP. From 1983 to 1988, Janice worked with CEDA (Community Education Development Association) as a community worker in David Livingstone, the elementary school in LSP. In

2005, she came back to LSP as the community development director at the North End Community Renewal Corporation (NECRC), a neighbourhood renewal body that works in eleven North End neighbourhoods. In 2004–05, NECRC secured National Crime Prevention Centre funding for a Comprehensive Community Initiative in LSP, and Janice directed the project. Cheyenne was hired by NECRC in 2005 as project coordinator for the then newly created Lord Selkirk Park Resource Centre, where a part of her job was community outreach. She had worked in community-based arts programming in the inner city and was already familiar with the Developments because she had relatives living there and often spent time there while growing up. Carolyn became part of the collective effort in LSP in 2007 when we started to work on developing a childcare centre, but she had run the R.B. Russell Infant Centre, just down the street from the Developments, since 1991, so she knew the area well. Jim had been doing community development work and community-based research in the inner city for about a decade when, in 2005, NECRC asked him to write a history of LSP, and he has stayed involved in LSP ever since.

A Bottom-Up Approach

Each of us came to our work in the Developments with a distinctly bottom-up, as opposed to top-down, understanding of how to do community development (CD). We did not assume that we had the answers to the area's problems. Rather, we were determined to listen to and be guided by its residents. When we arrived, we said, in effect, "We are not here to help you, but to work alongside you; will you join us?" Our research was always driven by this community-based approach to CD, and as a result it can accurately be described as community-based participatory research (CBPR), although we never employed that term.

The CBPR approach that we used is consistent with the Neechi Principles – a set of CD principles that emerged in Winnipeg's inner city in the early 1990s, arising primarily from the grassroots community-building efforts of urban Indigenous people. The Neechi Principles are derived from the convergence approach brought to Winnipeg by John Loxley (2010) via the work of Clive Thomas (1974). The convergence approach seeks to internalize economic linkages, so that economic benefits stay within a local community rather than being exported. In the 1980s, Loxley was involved with a Manitoba Metis Federation–sponsored training program that led to the development of several Indigenous-controlled institutions, including Neechi Foods and Payuk Housing Co-op, and that popularized the Neechi Principles. The principles, which guide much of the best CD work now being done in Winnipeg's inner city, include, among others, a commitment to hiring and purchasing locally so that wages and purchasing power stay in the community, investing locally to meet community needs rather than investing elsewhere where profits are likely to be higher, and building on existing strengths rather than relying upon outside skills. This approach focuses on mobilizing local resources and people to meet local needs, as does CBPR, which has been described as "a philosophy about how research should be conducted so that community needs are prioritized" (Sahota 2010, 1). As a result, there was a good fit between the Neechi Principles by which we operated and CBPR. As has been argued elsewhere, "the first indicator of goodness of fit is shared values. For a CBPR partnership to be successful, partners need a sense of shared standards and principles" (Andrews et al. 2010, 6). We shared a commitment to the values embodied in the Neechi Principles. We were also committed to action for changes that are identified by the community, to seeing the community through an asset-based rather than a deficit lens, and to holistic, transformative, and sustainable change, undertaken in ways that residents choose.

Overcoming Distrust and Cynicism

Finding out what residents wanted to do, and how research might be useful, was not easy. We soon learned the futility of pulling people together in a large group and asking what they wanted and needed. There was too much distrust in the community. People in this very distressed neighbourhood were closed, suspicious, and *very* cynical, and with good cause. They didn't believe that good things could happen in LSP. It has a long experience of people and organizations *saying* they would do things but not delivering, and of project-funded initiatives that quickly died once the short-term funding dried up.

What did work, slowly and patiently, was a combination of conceptually simple but practically challenging approaches. We did lots of one-on-one work, especially via the Lord Selkirk Park Resource Centre, which was the first thing that residents said they wanted and which opened in

two vacant units in the Developments in 2005. The creation of the resource centre is consistent with a CBPR methodology. We asked LSP
residents what their issues were and what *they* believed they needed. They
immediately told us that they wanted a safe space to meet, so we worked
with them to make that happen. From the beginning, the approach in the
resource centre was to provide a warm and inviting space, to listen, and
gradually to develop trusting relationships. Those who worked in the centre
were hired locally and knew from experience that it was all about slowly
and patiently building relationships and trust. At the same time, Cheyenne
did lots of door-to-door talking and networking with people and with
other community-based organizations (CBOs) in the neighbourhood. This
is classic, old-fashioned community organizing, and again, the point is
to take the time to develop relationships and build trust. We also did some
more formalized research, hiring local people to go door-to-door to talk
individually and at some length with people about their concerns and their
hopes and aspirations. In these ways, we gradually began to earn the trust
of the neighbourhood and to figure out how residents in the Developments saw the community and what they believed ought to be done. As
trust gradually emerged, they were encouraged to take ownership of what
was done at the resource centre and in the community.

This is an important aspect of a CBPR methodology. Local people need
to be involved, but in very low-income communities where they have long
experienced social exclusion and stigmatization, their participation cannot be secured quickly and easily. It requires that time be taken to develop
relationships and earn their trust.

We also created a Community Advisory Committee as a means of
pulling together on a regular basis all the many CBOs that worked in the
housing complex. This facilitated a sharing of information and helped us
to move out of the pre-existing silos and to respond to what the community
was telling us. For example, when residents said they wanted counsellors
at the resource centre, Cheyenne was easily able to connect with Mt. Carmel
Clinic, located just outside the Developments, to make the necessary
arrangements.

Another important part of developing relationships with, and earning
the trust of, the residents was the various community events that we
organized regularly. An example is the best yard contest, which started to

get people involved and created a sense of pride in the neighbourhood. We provided free soil and plants; residents did the work. In between larger activities, a great many smaller events and activities were organized, which had the effect of bringing residents and their children out of their units and into the broader community, contributing to a sense of togetherness and inspiring hope. All of these grassroots, face-to-face activities began gradually to shift attitudes, which had long been "I don't believe that will happen."

Another important reason for the change in attitudes was that we started to produce tangible results. As mentioned, the first of these was the Lord Selkirk Park Resource Centre. Then in 2007, after a great deal of work and much hard negotiating with the provincial government, we opened an adult learning centre (ALC) that offers the mature Grade 12 diploma, as well as a literacy program that ladders people who start from a lower educational level into the ALC.

Research played an important role in our work at this stage, as it did throughout. It revealed one of the genuine needs and aspirations in the community. Residents, single mothers especially, wanted to earn their Grade 12 and find a job because they were fed up with being on social assistance. They identified transport as a major barrier – taking children to daycare on the bus, catching another bus to get to school, and then doing the same on the way home each day was a real challenge. So, rather than suggesting that they leave LSP to attend school elsewhere, we brought the ALC to them by locating it in the Turtle Island Community Centre in the heart of the Developments. These same single mothers said that lack of childcare was a second major obstacle in their efforts to change their lives, so we began a long, hard struggle to establish a childcare centre in the Developments. It opened in January 2012. These were concrete and visible outcomes – the living proof that things really could change for the better.

A particularly important aspect of these achievements was what came to be called the "refresh." The provincial government used the fiscal stimulus dollars – the public funds rolled out as a response to the global economic crisis of 2008–09 – to renovate every single unit in LSP and to paint and make other changes to the exterior of the buildings. And it hired local people to do much of the work. This was especially important in adding to the sense of pride that residents were starting to feel about their community and adding also to their belief that the inclusive and respectful style of the work being done there was capable of producing results.

A similar shift in attitudes occurred with government officials. In 2005, Manitoba Housing treated the LSP community in a top-down fashion, making only the most limited attempts at resident engagement and seeing itself simply as a rent collector, with little if any responsibility for social development. For example, previous efforts to promote resident involvement via the creation of a residents' association entailed Manitoba Housing simply throwing a bit of money into the community and leaving locals to manage it on their own. The result was division and conflict fostered by nepotism and favouritism, which merely magnified the distrust and cynicism so prevalent in the community. For their part, Manitoba Housing officials saw this outcome as confirming their negative views of residents and their belief in the futility of community development. Perhaps not surprisingly, when we began working in LSP middle-level officials treated us almost scornfully, seeing us as naive or worse, and became a distinct hindrance to our efforts. Nevertheless, we persisted in working with the community in an inclusive and respectful way.

At the same time, we lobbied the government. We were persistent and sometimes even relentless in seeking provincial government and especially Manitoba Housing support for our various initiatives. And we had two things to strengthen our case: first, the fact that we were listening carefully to and working closely with the community, so that at least some senior government people knew that our requests came directly from the community itself; and second, the fact that we had research to back us up, because we were regularly conducting community-based studies and were writing up and widely distributing the results.

Writing and Publishing as Part of CBPR

Throughout this process, from 2005 to 2013, Jim wrote about what we were doing. He authored many internal documents, including reports, letters to governments, and strategic plans for our own purposes, always attempting to reflect accurately what Janice, Cheyenne, Carolyn, and others involved in the project were saying and doing. And he wrote for public consumption, to describe and document what we were doing and to help secure public and government support for it. Jim published chapters in three State of the Inner City Reports (CCPA–MB 2005, 2007, 2009); an essay that described "hidden" forms of resistance by Indigenous women in LSP (Silver 2009); a book on poverty and public housing in Canada that included a chapter on LSP (Silver 2011); and a chapter on adult education as community development in LSP, in a book on transformative Indigenous adult education in Winnipeg's inner city (Silver 2013a). He also published various shorter articles on LSP. These publications arose from our CBPR methodology and were intended, among other purposes, to document the process that we were engaged in at LSP and to show that there was a way forward for low-income public-housing projects other than bulldozing. It is almost certainly the case that because our efforts in LSP were being written about and published, governments were more prepared to respond positively to what we were doing. The publications were also intended to show that even the most troubled neighbourhoods can experience positive change if the hard work of community development, guided by good CD principles and a belief in people's capacities and capabilities, is joined by reasonable public investment in initiatives that the community itself identifies as being necessary.

Our research started right from the beginning, in 2005, when we interviewed residents and community workers to gather their views on life in LSP. To conduct the interviews, we hired Claudette Michell, a Cree woman who was then one of Jim's students. As two-thirds of LSP residents were of Indigenous descent, we believed that they would speak most openly and fully to an Indigenous woman who was familiar with North End life. This hypothesis was borne out. The interviews – conducted in an open-ended fashion to let people tell us what *they* perceived as important – produced rich data; residents had much to say to Claudette about their lives and about the changes they wanted to see.

The other side of this coin was that Claudette benefitted enormously as well. In addition to earning some money to support her family while studying at university, she began to develop a keen understanding of how research is done, including the importance of working according to established and appropriate ethical guidelines. In the process, her confidence in her abilities grew significantly. An important methodological point arising from this is that engaging students and community residents – particularly those from low-income, racialized, and colonized communities – in a CBPR project can have an important capacity-building character. Claudette went on to play an important role in the North End as program coordinator of the University of Winnipeg's Department of Urban and Inner-City Studies, and author of a particularly insightful essay on the transformative character of Indigenous adult education (Michell 2013).

CBPR, Public Policy, and Social Change

One could think of our work in LSP as being two sides of a coin. We cooperated closely with the LSP community in the ways described above, especially through the resource centre and the many one-on-one community engagement activities we undertook and the research that we did. This was the foundation of our work. But we also spent what often seemed an inordinate amount of time doing "political" work – lobbying the provincial government to secure the necessary funding to build and operate the institutions that the community told us it needed and planning and strategizing for those lobbying efforts. Although this entailed what sometimes seemed endless meetings and much frustration, it was the necessary complement to our grassroots work in the community. We recognized that our good work alone would not have gained government support – especially funding for the ALC and the childcare centre – had it not been for the fact that Gord McIntosh and Kerri Irvin-Ross were the ministers of housing, and Diane McGifford was the minister responsible for adult education. Each was committed to our inclusive and participatory approach to community development. Indeed, Manitoba Housing became Manitoba Housing and Community Development when Kerri Irvin-Ross became minister, symbolizing its newfound commitment to the social side of housing. The ministers and their senior officials heard us – over and over again – and they responded by insisting that their staff adopt our more community-based approach. Our lobbying alone could not have achieved this shift in Manitoba Housing's thinking; we had to have support at the top. As we said when we met to discuss this chapter, these ministers "opened the door for us; without them it wouldn't have been possible."

In our lobbying efforts, our community-based research proved valuable – it added legitimacy and credibility to what we were saying. But research alone is not enough. We learned that simply producing research findings to show that something should and can be done does not automatically mean it will be done (see Gaskell and Levin 2012, 183). Governments face many competing demands for limited dollars, most from segments of the broader community with much more economic and political clout than we had. Yet, achieving what residents needed to improve their lives required *public* dollars. We needed government support and investment. Consider the ALC, whose Michif name, Kaakiyow li Moond Likol (All People's School), was bestowed by Metis Elders at a naming ceremony. With its three-person staff, Kaakiyow costs about $230,000 per year to run, and though this is a small amount by government standards, raising such a sum is far beyond the ability of LSP residents. If CBPR is "to combine knowledge with action to achieve sustainable, social change" (Andrews et al. 2010, 1), public investment in the social-change-related goals identified by CBPR – such as adult education, literacy programs, and childcare – is essential. Thus, lobbying governments to secure public investment became a central part of our work, and our effectiveness in this task was enhanced by our research.

The same is true for the Lord Selkirk Park Childcare Centre. There is a wealth of research evidence showing the benefits of early childhood education (Friendly and Prentice 2009; Mustard and McCain 1999), but this by itself does not prompt governments to act. A major part of effective CBPR in low-income neighbourhoods is how the research is then used to advocate for a government response that serves the interests of such communities. In the case of the childcare centre, a great deal of political effort was necessary. In the end, it was funded as part of the Manitoba government's fiscal stimulus package in the wake of the 2008–09 global economic crisis. To its credit, the provincial NDP government used a large part of the stimulus package to renovate every unit in LSP and in other Manitoba Housing complexes, and to build the Lord Selkirk Park Childcare Centre. We believe that its decision to invest stimulus dollars in these projects, at a time when public housing across North America was being bulldozed, was in large part attributable to the improvements that were emerging in LSP as the result of our efforts.

In addition, the resource centre was relocated from the two units it had previously occupied to share space with the new childcare centre, thereby creating a community hub. Furthermore, the provincial government's Healthy Child Manitoba program chose to pilot the Abecedarian model of childcare at the childcare centre – we had lobbied it to do so. As a result, an outreach worker was hired to work with parents of the children at the centre, and the cost of running the resource centre – a major fundraising problem in the early years when it was reliant upon insecure project funding (Silver 2011, 129–30) – was funded on a permanent basis, consistent with CBPR's commitment to *sustainable* change.

An Asset-Based Approach

Underlying all of these principles – and an important component of CBPR in low-income communities – is a belief in people's abilities, no matter how difficult their circumstances may be. This is sometimes called asset-based community development, an approach that identifies the strengths in a community and works to build on them (Kretzmann and McKnight 1993). Building on strengths is an essential element of CBPR as well (Israel et al. 2012). We identified the good-quality low-rent housing in LSP as an enormous asset, given its rarity in the neighbourhood, which contributed to our taking a "rebuilding from within" approach to this public-housing project, as opposed to the more commonly applied bulldozing response. And we identified the significant number of strong and healthy residents, especially women, as an asset (Silver 2009). When they spoke about what would improve their lives, we listened carefully, and we acted on the assumption that many in the community had the ability and the motivation to respond positively to opportunities that were created. This assumption, so different from the poor bashing that is predominant today (Katz 2013; Swanson 2001), has been borne out by the evidence – many LSP residents have responded to the opportunities that the CBPR process has helped to create (Silver 2013b) – and is an essential aspect of the effective use of CBPR in low-income communities.

Our asset-based lens enabled us to see beyond the long-term poverty and dysfunction of the community to identify and build upon the strengths and capacities of the people of Lord Selkirk Park. Today, approximately eighty people have graduated from Kaakiyow, with their mature Grade 12. It is likely that few if any of them would have done so had we not listened to the community and worked with it and with the government to create the adult learning centre. Similarly, the literacy program is consistently full to capacity, and the childcare centre is making a significant difference in the lives of children and parents in LSP.

Limitations of CBPR in Lord Selkirk Park

There have also been weaknesses in our approach to CBPR in the Developments. Perhaps the most important of these is the fact that significant numbers of residents did not become actively involved. We worked very hard, in the wide variety of ways described above, to engage them, and we succeeded in changing attitudes, especially as it became apparent that we were respectful and that our efforts were bearing fruit. But the residents who worked with us were few in number, and their involvement was sporadic, especially in our lobbying efforts. This is typical of CBPR and of community development more generally. Flicker et al. (2007), for example, have found that in Canadian cases involving the use of CBPR researchers and CBOs have been very involved, whereas residents have been much less so. This was our experience as well.

How are we to explain this? Life is extremely difficult for very low-income people who are experiencing complex poverty (Silver 2014; CCPA–MB 2009). Many LSP residents expend all their energy simply in getting through another day. This complexity is intensified in an Indigenous community, such as the Developments, because of the destructive effects of colonization. For centuries, Indigenous people have been led to believe that they and their cultures are inferior, and this belief, widely held in the dominant society, has eroded many Indigenous people's sense of self-esteem and self-confidence. This was described in the first State of the Inner City Report (CCPA–MB 2005, 24) by the use of two metaphors:

> One is the notion of a complex web – a web of poverty, racism, drugs, gangs and violence. The other is the notion of a cycle – people caught in a cycle of inter-related problems. Both suggest the idea of people who are caught, trapped, immobilized, unable to escape, destined to struggle with forces against which they cannot win, from which they cannot extricate themselves. The result is despair, resignation, anger, hopelessness, which then reinforce the cycle, and wrap them tighter in the web.

These conditions make it extremely difficult to gain the full involvement of people such as those in the Developments in a CBPR process aimed at rebuilding from within. As Flicker et al. (2007) observe, "many models of CBR romanticize the notion that moving toward maximum community participation in all aspects of the research is optimal. However, community members are often overworked and have little time for, or interest in, involvement with the minutia of research." Nevertheless, we were consistent in soliciting and listening to the views of residents, treating them respectfully, and remaining true to their expectations about what should be happening in Lord Selkirk Park. CBPR – and community development more generally – is not an all-or-nothing method, which requires that *all* residents be involved.

CBPR as an Agent of Social Change

Whatever the limitations of resident involvement in rebuilding Lord Selkirk Park from within, it is a different place today than it was in 2005, when this process began. CBPR, as part of a broader community development process, has contributed to the progress that has been made. Unlike in the 1990s, when half the LSP units were boarded up, every unit is occupied today, turnover has diminished – so the community is more stable – and there is a wait list to get in. More than forty African families that recently arrived in Winnipeg now live in LSP, something that would never have occurred in the past due to conflicts between young Indigenous and African men. Many more residents are either involved directly in education at Kaakiyow, the literacy program, or the childcare centre or are in the paid labour force at the resource centre, the childcare centre, or beyond the Developments as the result of their educational attainment. Kaakiyow, the resource centre, and the childcare centre are all on permanent funding streams, not project funding, and thus are sustainable. As mentioned above, about eighty adult students have graduated from Kaakiyow with their Grade 12 diploma since the first graduation in June 2009. Crime, violence, and street gang activity appear to have dropped. The resource centre is a roaring success – a recent evaluation (Keyser 2012, 2) reported that it is "highly successful" and is having a "profound impact in the lives of neighbourhood residents." The childcare centre – piloting the Abecedarian model

– is producing real change in the lives of children in the Developments. As Carolyn noted, "the change in the children already is amazing." There can be no doubt that LSP is a better place to live today than has been the case for decades.

CBPR played a significant role in making these changes possible, so it seems accurate to say that this is a successful use of CBPR in a low-income community. The project was first and foremost about promoting change, from the bottom up and in ways of residents' choosing, and the research component was always in support of those objectives. It was valuable because those who work with CBOs in low-income communities are typically stretched to the limit in terms of time and resources, and thus cannot undertake the research tasks that are an essential element of the CBPR process. Jim's involvement with the SSHRC-funded Manitoba Research Alliance (MRA) gave our group access to the financial resources needed to run small qualitative research projects, and the MRA's commitment to CBPR led to our paying local people to do the research, with all the benefits that local hiring produces.

There is a long history of research in Indigenous communities that produces benefits for the researchers but that leaves nothing behind for the community (Wilson 2008, 16) – what is sometimes called "drive-by" or "fly-in" research (Andrews et al. 2010). The researchers get the academic benefits from publishing their results, including tenure, promotions, and higher salaries, but they exit the community, never to return and with nothing left in their wake. Indigenous people are rightly resentful of such exploitative practices. This has not been the case in Lord Selkirk Park. There, CBPR has contributed to producing much that has benefitted the community. In a great many respects, the Developments today are a better place to live, and CBPR has made a positive contribution to that outcome.

At the end of our meeting on April 4, 2014, the four of us agreed upon two things. First, a lot has been achieved in LSP since 2005, as described above. At some points, the process seemed to be taking forever. In large part, this was because what we were doing necessarily required time. Establishing trusting relationships in a low-income community, where such relationships have not existed before, does not occur immediately. It takes time to convince governments to act, especially to act in the interests of such a community, since almost all governments are strongly biased in favour of those with more money and power than the residents of Lord Selkirk Park. Yet in hindsight, a great deal was achieved in what now seems like a very short period – less than a decade. Perhaps the lesson here is that taking the time to build relationships and trust is essential, while simultaneously pushing governments to act swiftly in the interests of low-income communities. Research can furnish advocates with tools to make their case.

Second, we are somewhat surprised and disappointed that Lord Selkirk Park has not become more of a model for change in Winnipeg's inner city. On many occasions, one of us has said something like, "If positive change can be made in LSP, it can be made *anywhere* in the inner city." In undertaking our work in 2005, we were tackling what was probably the most difficult neighbourhood in town. It seems to us that success in such a neighbourhood, in what was actually a relatively short time, ought to have led to the replication of the approach in other inner-city neighbourhoods.

Two other comments are worth making by way of conclusion. First, CBPR can play a positive role in support of, and in cooperation with, a community-driven neighbourhood revitalization effort. Although research was not the primary purpose of our work in LSP, a good deal has been learned, much research and publication has arisen from the community-driven efforts (see Chapter 1 of this volume), and throughout the process, published and unpublished research findings lent credibility to our efforts. Second, any success that we have had in LSP has been the result of two processes occurring simultaneously: the patient, face-to-face, relationship- and trust-building form of grassroots organizing that was initiated in LSP; and the persistent and informed pressure placed on a government, at least some of whose ministers were prepared to see the merits of our demands and to act on them. When these two conditions prevail in combination, good things can be achieved, even in a very difficult low-income neighbourhood.

These conclusions fly in the face of arguments that complex urban poverty cannot be solved. It *can* be solved. This is not to suggest that poverty in Lord Selkirk Park has been solved. It has not. But the significant improvements that were made in a very short time and in a particularly challenging neighbourhood reveal what is possible. A central finding of our community-based and change-oriented project is that meaningful reductions in the severity of poverty are possible, even in difficult urban spaces such as Lord Selkirk Park and in a short period, when two conditions are met: the community identifies the actions to be taken and governments invest in those solutions. If such an approach were to be continued for a generation and more, we contend that poverty would be reduced to a bare minimum. The case of Lord Selkirk Park suggests that CBPR can play a useful role in such anti-poverty efforts.

REFERENCES

Andrews, Jeannette, Susan Newman, Otha Meadows, Melissa Cox, and Sheila Bunting. 2010. "Partnership Readiness for Community-Based Participatory Research." *Health Education Research.* https://doi.org/10.1093/her/cyq050.

CCPA–MB (Canadian Centre for Policy Alternatives–Manitoba). 2005. *The Promise of Investment in Community-Led Renewal: The State of the Inner City Report, 2005.* Winnipeg: CCPA–MB.

–. 2007. *Step by Step: Stories of Change in Winnipeg's Inner City: The State of the Inner City Report, 2007.* Winnipeg: CCPA–MB.

–. 2009. *It Takes All Day to Be Poor: The State of the Inner City Report, 2009.* Winnipeg: CCPA–MB.

Comack, Elizabeth, Lawrence Deane, Larry Morrissette, and Jim Silver. 2013. *Indians Wear Red: Colonization, Resistance and Aboriginal Street Gangs.* Halifax: Fernwood.

Flicker, Sarah, Beth Savan, Brian Kolenda, and Matto Mildenberger. 2007. "A Snapshot of Community-Based Research in Canada: Who? What? Why? How?" *Health Education Research.* https://doi.org/10.1093/her/cym007.

Friendly, Martha, and Susan Prentice. 2009. *About Canada: Childcare.* Halifax: Fernwood.

Gaskell, Jane, and Ben Levin. 2012. *Making a Difference in Urban Schools: Ideas, Politics and Pedagogy.* Toronto: University of Toronto Press.

Israel, Barbara, Eugenia Eng, Amy Schulz, and Edith Parker, eds. 2012. *Methods for Community-Based Participatory Research for Health.* 2nd ed. San Francisco: Jossey-Bass.

Katz, Michael B. 2013. *The Undeserving Poor: America's Enduring Confrontation with Poverty.* 2nd ed. New York: Oxford University Press.

Keyser, Caitlin. 2012. "2012 Evaluation of Lord Selkirk Park Resource Centre." Report prepared for Manidoo Gi Miini Gonaan, Winnipeg.

Kretzmann, John P., and John L. McKnight. 1993. *Building Communities from the Inside Out: A Path toward Finding and Mobilizing a Community's Assets.* Evanston, IL: Asset Based Community Development Institute, Institute for Policy Research.

Loxley, John. 2010. *Aboriginal Northern and Community Economic Development: Papers and Retrospectives.* Winnipeg: Arbeiter Ring.

Michell, Claudette. 2013. "Circles of Healing and Transformation: Aboriginal Women and Adult Education." In *Moving Forward, Giving Back: Transformative Aboriginal Adult Education,* ed. Jim Silver, 17–28. Halifax/Winnipeg: Fernwood/Canadian Centre for Policy Alternatives–Manitoba.

Mustard, J. Fraser, and Margaret Norrie McCain. 1999. *Reversing the Real Brain Drain: Early Years Study, Final Report.* Toronto: Canadian Institute for Advanced Research.

Sahota, Puneet Chawla. 2010. *Community-Based Participatory Research in American Indian and Alaska Native Communities.* Washington, DC: NCAI Policy Research Center.

Silver, Jim. 2009. "Unearthing Resistance: Aboriginal Women in the Lord Selkirk Park Housing Developments." In *Aboriginal Governance and Globalization: Proceedings of the International Symposium Held at the University of Winnipeg, January 31–February 2, 2008,* ed. Liliane Rodriquez. Winnipeg: University of Winnipeg Press.

–. 2011. *Good Places to Live: Poverty and Public Housing in Canada.* Halifax: Fernwood.

–. 2013a. "Adult Education as Community Development: The Case of Lord Selkirk Park." In *Moving Forward, Giving Back: Transformative Aboriginal Adult Education,* ed. Jim Silver, 129–42. Halifax/Winnipeg: Fernwood/Canadian Centre for Policy Alternatives–Manitoba.

–, ed. 2013b. *Moving Forward, Giving Back: Transformative Aboriginal Adult Education.* Halifax/Winnipeg: Fernwood/Canadian Centre for Policy Alternatives–Manitoba.

–. 2014. *About Canada: Poverty.* Halifax: Fernwood.

Swanson, Jean. 2001. *Poor Bashing: The Politics of Exclusion.* Toronto: Between the Lines.

Thomas, Clive. 1974. *Dependence and Transformation.* New York: Monthly Review Press.

Wilson, Shawn. 2008. *Research Is Ceremony: Indigenous Research Methods.* Halifax: Fernwood.

5

The Right to Housing Story
Research and Advocacy to Increase Housing Options for Low-Income Manitobans

CLARK BROWNLEE and SHAUNA MacKINNON

When the Government of Manitoba tabled its budget for 2014, opposition parties and the media immediately drew attention to a 1 percent increase in the provincial sales tax. By contrast, despite its significance, the public discourse largely ignored the announcement that the Province would scale up its investment in social housing. However, the Right to Housing Coalition (R2H) celebrated the news. Since the inception of R2H in 2006, its members had been diligent in trying to put social housing on the public policy agenda. This development demonstrated that their hard work was paying off.

The announcement was especially gratifying, given the fiscal context. In the months preceding the budget release, the minister of finance prepared Manitobans for a budget aimed at reducing the deficit. This indicated that little would be forthcoming in the way of new spending. So the announcement that the government would support the creation of five hundred new affordable rental units and five hundred new rent-geared-to-income units over the next three years was particularly satisfying. This was not the first time that R2H advocacy had achieved success. In 2009, after years of sidestepping the need for new and refurbished social housing, the Manitoba government responded to R2H lobbying with a commitment to build 1,500 new social housing units. In 2014, it announced that it had met this goal.

The 2014 budget also promised a new residential rental housing investment tax credit, providing an 8 percent credit on construction costs for private developers to build new rental housing, at least 10 percent of which was to consist of affordable units. This would complement the Province's previous commitment to invest $100 million annually over the next ten years to renovate and upgrade existing government-owned social housing.

R2H has much cause for celebration as we reflect on the progress made in Manitoba with regard to affordable and social housing and the role that it has played. Concrete progress represents years of hard work and lobbying to rectify a serious housing shortage for lower-income households in Manitoba. In this chapter, we describe how activists and researchers came together to advocate for policy change in the province and how their strategic approach to improve housing for low-income Manitobans brought measurable improvements.

The R2H Story

R2H is a Winnipeg-based advocacy coalition made up of 58 organizations and roughly 250 individual supporters. It is a case example of how policy analysts, researchers, and activists can join forces to have an impact on public policy. What eventually evolved into the R2H coalition had its genesis in 2004, when a small group of citizens became concerned about a particular housing issue in their neighbourhood. A series of events quickly steered the group to focus more broadly on the state of housing in Manitoba and to call for an increase in the supply of rental housing for low-income individuals and families. And the rest, as the saying goes, is history.

Affordable Housing as a Foundation of Inclusion

The R2H focus on housing for the most vulnerable is rooted in the belief that access to safe, affordable housing is a basic human right. Good-quality, affordable housing is one of the most important determinants of health and social well-being. The World Health Organization's Ottawa Charter for Health Promotion (1986) lists shelter as a fundamental indicator of health, and the World Health Organization (2007) identifies housing as a basic human right and as essential to good health. The United Nations International Covenant on Economic, Social and Cultural Rights also includes housing as a basic human right (United Nations 1976).

Nonetheless, governments in Canada have not enacted the necessary comprehensive policy interventions to fulfill this right. In 2007, the

UN special rapporteur on adequate housing characterized the state of homelessness and inadequate housing in Canada as a "national emergency" (UNHR 2007). The state of housing in Canada prompted the call for a national housing strategy and the mobilization of activists and policy researchers to advocate for improved responses from all levels of government.

The Role of Policy Research and Advocacy in the Right to Housing Movement

Social and economic injustice can be caused or exacerbated by policies that limit access to the resources that individuals and families require to engage in society. Housing policy in Canada is a clear example of this. Affordable and social housing in Canada has long been in decline. From the late 1940s to 1993, the federal government was fully engaged in funding the development and maintenance of social housing in Canada. Espousing the neoliberal ideology that emerged during the 1980s, the federal, provincial, and territorial governments began to move away from state intervention in housing to rely on the market as the primary source of housing development, including that for low-income households (Shapcott 2009).

In the early 1990s, Ottawa proceeded with its plans to transfer full responsibility for its housing programs to the provincial and territorial governments. By late in the decade, it had all but abandoned its role in the provision of affordable housing (ibid.). In the early twenty-first century, it re-entered the housing arena, signing affordable housing agreements with the provinces and territories. However, these focused on providing capital incentives for the private sector to develop what was termed affordable housing. Social housing – with long-term subsidies attached – was not included in the new arrangements. The deinvestment in social housing meant not only that new units were not being built, but that existing units were not being adequately maintained.

By about 2005, it became increasingly apparent that the private sector would not resolve the housing needs of low-income families (Shapcott 2009; MacKinnon and Silver 2009). However, governments, particularly the federal government, continue to avoid investing in the development, subsidization, and maintenance of low-cost housing. The resultant housing crisis became increasingly evident, with no real solution in sight. Calls for a national housing strategy were ignored by the Harper Conservatives, who deflected the issue to provincial and territorial governments. Although too recent to know for certain, the Liberal government's recently announced ten-year, $40 million national housing strategy is welcome news. Housing activists have long known that gains to be made at the local level will be limited in the absence of a strong federal commitment.

The complexity of housing policy and the jurisdictional challenges make it increasingly important for advocates to work with policy analysts and researchers to develop strategic approaches that, though not letting Ottawa off the hook, focus attention on provincial and local governments.

In the case of R2H, policy analysts, researchers, and community activists joined forces through a participatory policy research and advocacy approach that has shown some success (Bernas and MacKinnon 2015). This approach differs from traditional methods of resolving social "problems" in that it is not driven by research but rather by activists with support from policy experts and researchers. It is based on the historical lesson that complex social problems cannot be solved through research alone. Although social policy research is valuable, it is most effective when used as a tool by communities that are committed to social justice and policy change. Indeed, Canada's social safety net, as it emerged through the early to mid-twentieth century, was in response to the activism of Canadians who were concerned with social justice.

Researchers who collaborate with community activists know that the most effective social policy research responds to the needs identified by those who are directly affected by inadequate housing policy and can be used by activists in their political advocacy work.

The R2H Participatory Policy Research Approach

Participatory policy research seeks the involvement of all relevant stakeholders, especially those who are traditionally excluded from the policy process, and it engages community in identifying problems and solutions (Freudenberg et al. 2005). It integrates an analysis of the broader historical, social, cultural, and political dimensions of problems that is critical to understanding complex social issues as societal rather than personal. Bringing researchers, policy analysts, and activists together also ensures a move toward action. Participatory policy research brings researchers and activists together to understand the issues from differing perspectives but moves beyond research to advocate for policy change.

R2H has been effective for at least three important reasons: it has drawn upon policy analysis and existing and original research to put housing on the political radar in Manitoba; it has adopted a strategic approach, remaining focused and disciplined; and it has seized on political opportunities to move its ideas forward. In effect, it has exposed a critical social problem, suggested measures to address it, and become the driving force behind improved housing outcomes for low-income individuals and families in Manitoba.

Expose, Propose, Politicize

Like that of many grassroots social justice efforts, the work of R2H evolved through trial and error, and in response to an ever-changing political environment. Some individuals consistently appear at the R2H table, whereas others come and go. New housing challenges and policy concerns inevitably arise, but R2H has been disciplined in focusing on its core purpose – improving access to safe and affordable accommodation for the most vulnerable Manitobans.

Like many concerned citizens who experienced a sense of injustice and felt compelled to take action, R2H members didn't rely on textbooks and theories to guide them. Nonetheless, theory does inform their work. Here, the scholarship of Peter Marcuse comes to mind as a theoretical framework that explains the synthesis of research and action that characterizes the R2H model. Marcuse, a critical urban theorist, was a proponent of the idea of the "right to the city" as proposed and popularized by Henri Lefebvre (1968). Lefebvre defined the right to the city as both a "cry and a demand," inferring the role of citizen participation in re-claiming and re-shaping the spaces in which they live (Lefebvre 1967, 158). Marcuse builds on Lefebvre's concept of the right to the city by proposing a "Critical Planning" approach (Marcuse 2012, 37), where planners collaborate with community groups, researchers, and others to participate in socially just policy change. His framework is grounded in three essential ways that theory can aid the reclamation of rights – expose, propose, and politicize.

Expose

As Marcuse explains, the first step toward social justice is exposing, or analyzing, the root causes of injustice and finding ways to communicate this analysis to build public support. This was an early focus of R2H, when members reached out to researchers to join them in their efforts.

The R2H story began in the summer of 2004, when Ottawa decided to move the Second Division, Princess Patricia's Light Infantry, from its station at Kapyong Barracks on Kenaston Boulevard in Winnipeg to Camp Shilo, forty miles west of Brandon. As Winnipeggers adjusted to the social and economic loss of the military members and their families, they also noticed that the once busy housing portion of the Kapyong base had become a ghost town. As winter arrived, this became increasingly noticeable. Sidewalks continued to be shovelled, the smoke rising from chimneys revealed that the homes were still heated, and automated timers turned lights on and off to give the illusion of a human presence. But locals knew that the houses were vacant. It didn't take long before residents in the nearby affluent River Heights neighbourhood began to make some connections. Many asked themselves why more than 150 homes had been left untenanted, given that vacancy rates were low and dropping, and so many Winnipeg families desperately needed a place to live. They began to contemplate the possibility of making these government-owned units available to precariously housed families.

On January 5, 2005, ten people, representing seven churches and four denominations in River Heights, met to explore possibilities. Calling themselves the River Heights Ministerial Housing Action Group, they began to correspond with the Department of National Defence and learned of a federal program that encouraged the use of surplus military property for low-cost housing. The civilian who was responsible for managing the Kapyong housing stock was amenable to renting it out while decisions were being made about its future. However, that person was soon replaced, and word came from Ottawa that a lengthy process was under way to determine the eventual need for military housing in Winnipeg. Until the Kapyong units were officially declared redundant, their status would not change.

Nevertheless, the action group continued to meet and to plan ways in which the houses could be used. It was spurred on by stories of refugees and Indigenous people who were forced to live in substandard conditions. Some also experienced racism and discrimination from landlords, who exploited the highly competitive rental market to pick and choose their tenants on the basis of subjective and questionable criteria.

By the fall of 2005, the action group had met with the local MP, sent a petition to the minister of defence, and prepared a position paper that outlined the need for housing. The paper included a plan in which the Kapyong homes could be used while the long-term review was taking place. It cited the interest and support of the Winnipeg community.

The revelation that more than 150 heated and entirely livable homes were standing empty while families remained in desperate need eventually struck a responsive chord. Media began to contact the action group for information and personal stories. A local MP, who was then the president of the Treasury Board, promised that a deal could be reached once the upcoming federal election was over.

The action group decided to strengthen its efforts by broadening its appeal, membership, and objectives. In pursuit of this, it held a public meeting on January 6, 2006, in a boardroom at Crossways in Common, an inner-city church-owned facility. The group had recently learned that the Peguis First Nation was interested in the Kapyong land and housing as a potential piece of property for a land settlement claim, so it invited Peguis leaders to the meeting. Having also read some research produced by Shauna MacKinnon, it invited her as well, asking her to speak about the growing affordable-housing crisis in Canada.

The organizers reserved a room at Crossways in Common to accommodate what they anticipated would be a small gathering. When crews from the four main television stations, various reporters, and a stream of interested citizens arrived, they scrambled to arrange for a larger space.

The meeting turned out to be a pivotal moment that would shape the work of the coalition. First, the action group explained the Kapyong issue. This was followed by a presentation about the broader housing problems of Manitoba, including a brief overview of public policy related to housing in the province and Canada generally. The group discussed the housing shortage for low-income Canadians and the policy negligence that created and sustained it. It examined the market failure to provide affordable rental units and the federal and provincial government policies that were not meeting the need for social housing. It talked about the shifting role of the Canada Mortgage and Housing Corporation (CMHC), which was no longer involved in affordable and social housing. It dealt with Ottawa's policy of redirecting CMHC resources to general revenue, effectively making the provinces responsible for the creation of social housing. It called attention to the expiring social housing operating grants that provided the needed rent subsidies for social housing, a problem that was becoming increasingly critical as mortgages on social housing expired. For attendees who were primarily interested in Kapyong, the revelation that a far bigger crisis was percolating throughout the country came as a bit of a jolt. And the complexity of the issues was reinforced when the Peguis First Nation representatives reminded the group of their treaty entitlement to surplus land on Kapyong. The lively discussion ended with a plan to meet again to determine how to proceed with what was now clearly evident – that Manitoba's housing problem was far bigger than the Kapyong issue.

Any hope for action on Kapyong soon dissipated, with the election of a Conservative minority government. The president of the Treasury Board lost his seat, and the action group's political allies no longer had the power to move the agenda forward. Nonetheless, the newly formed R2H would continue with its efforts. Its first meeting, on February 21, 2006, was attended by fifteen people, representing Indigenous interests, resettlement agencies, seniors' organizations, and churches. A draft letter to Prime Minister Stephen Harper had been circulated, calling on his government to make the empty Kapyong units available for social housing on an interim basis while the Department of National Defence decided on its long-term needs. More importantly, the letter asked Harper to recognize that Ottawa should resume the active role it had once played by investing profits made by CMHC into the creation of new social housing and sustaining the existing stock, which was now in decline. Discussed, revised, and later signed by fourteen groups, the letter was copied widely.

Propose: Years of Growth, Learning, and Seeking Solutions

Since that first meeting in 2006, R2H has continued to expose housing issues through research and activism. It also proposes solutions. Its model is consistent with what Marcuse (2009, 194) describes as "working with those affected to come up with actual proposals, programs, targets, strategies, to achieve the desired results." Although R2H initially concentrated on Kapyong, research revealed that there was a larger issue to contend with, so it began to work on this while also continuing with Kapyong. By now, the public and the media were anxious to see the Kapyong houses put to practical use. R2H began a series of meetings with MPs, MLAs, Cabinet ministers, housing experts, and a local senator. Hopes of reaching an interim solution persisted. In an early victory, the Manitoba minister of family services and housing agreed to subsidize the rent of any Kapyong units that R2H managed to secure from National Defence. R2H continued to draw attention to Kapyong as a way of highlighting broader housing issues. Its members organized information pickets along on the busy street beside the vacant homes. Over the next several years, the corner of Kenaston Boulevard and Corydon Avenue became the scene of several actions, complete with signs, handouts, and press conferences. But the emphasis on Kapyong eventually faded, and R2H set its sights on other issues. This occurred for a few reasons.

First, though several units remained untenanted at Kapyong, Ottawa eventually assigned the more desirable ones to its own employees. Second, there was no indication from the federal government generally or from National Defence itself that their policy regarding the homes was about to change. Seeing no new developments on the horizon, the media soon tired of the issue. Finally, the ongoing work of policy analysts and researchers who had joined R2H demonstrated how serious the housing situation had become. It was now painfully obvious that even if all the empty units at Kapyong were made available for civilian occupancy, the overall need for affordable accommodation would remain virtually undiminished. The need to focus on the broader social housing issue was becoming increasingly clear to R2H.

R2H was disappointed in the outcome at Kapyong, but it had learned an important lesson – though the strategic use of demonstrations could help raise public awareness, effecting a shift in policy required much more than this. When the coalition started seriously to assess the bigger housing picture in Manitoba, it concluded that public awareness of the problem was minimal, with the concomitant result that the political attention it received was also minimal. Raising awareness as a means to elevate housing issues in the public policy discourse became an early objective for R2H. During the first few years, municipal, provincial, and federal elections came and went, with housing rarely mentioned. Prior to an election, R2H would typically ask for and receive a policy statement from each party, but little changed once the election was over. The task became how to put pressure on three levels of government while simultaneously providing accurate information to the public via the media so that the politicians would feel pushed to make housing a higher priority. R2H began to see itself as a place where organizations and individuals could bring information and ideas, and develop strategies for moving forward. Throughout this time, its members continued to analyze housing policy and conduct research. Much of this work was published through the Canadian Centre for Policy Alternatives–Manitoba (CCPA–MB), which remains an important ally, as it publishes and circulates policy updates, analysis, and primary research on housing issues.

One lesson that R2H learned over the years was to use research strategically and to suggest policy solutions that were practical and realistic. In October 2007, it decided to propose to the provincial government a target for new rent-geared-to-income units. Researchers and analysts recommended that it aim for 1,500 units to be established in Manitoba over a five-year period. In fact, the true need was three times this number, but R2H chose the smaller target of 1,500 for two reasons. It knew that the Province would dismiss its calls for 4,500 new units by citing its inability to proceed if the other two levels of government were not at the table. By dropping the number to 1,500, R2H cut off this line of retreat, countering the Province's claims that its hands were tied by concentrating on what it *could* do. Furthermore, R2H estimated that the price of creating the 1,500 units over five years would represent less than 1 percent of the provincial budget. This amount was so tiny that it could not possibly be framed as prohibitive, and R2H argued that it would be palatable to the public.

The strategy of proposing a realistic and costed measure proved effective. It has helped R2H to remain disciplined, focused, and relentless. It has also helped the coalition to respond to the Province's attempts at deflection by producing reports of what it has done rather than dealing with what is most needed. For activists who are not policy experts, circumventing the smokescreen of bureaucratic bafflegab is perhaps the best course. Simply saying, "Thank you very much for that, but how many new rent-geared-to-income units have you built?" keeps the discussion on track.

Although R2H has directed its main efforts at the provincial government, it has not abandoned its focus on the other levels of government. It also continues to recognize the role of the private and not-for-profit sectors, and has established task groups to deal with these areas. Advocacy efforts directed at the federal government are the least active because they have been the least fruitful. Municipal advocacy efforts have also been difficult, but R2H continues to push for a more substantial municipal commitment.

Since researchers, analysts, and activists first joined forces in 2006, they have produced several research papers, articles, op-eds, and other information to raise the profile of housing issues in Manitoba. In addition to their policy-focused work, researchers have conducted qualitative research to ensure, as Marcuse describes, that those directly affected by policy are included in exposing, proposing, and politicizing for policy change. Examples of such work include "The Real Housing Shortage in Winnipeg" (MacKinnon 2005a), the first article that drew attention to the looming crisis. This was followed by "What's Happening to Low Income Rental Housing in Winnipeg's Inner City?" (MacKinnon 2005b). In 2006, the proposal for 1,500 new units in five years was first outlined in the CCPA–MB's alternative provincial budget, *Investing in Tomorrow, Today* (CCPA–MB 2006). That year also saw the release of an essay titled "Social Housing, Neighbourhood Revitalization and Community Economic Development" (Skelton, Selig, and Deane 2006). In the next year, "Housing: It's Time to Set Targets" (MacKinnon 2007) again emphasized the need for new units.

A lengthy report, *Putting Our Housing in Order* (CCPA–MB 2008), included four individual studies that illustrated the complexity of both the need and the potential solutions. In 2009, a brief report titled "The Trouble with Housing for Low-Income People" (MacKinnon and Silver 2009) assessed the failure of the private sector in meeting the needs of low-income renters. *The View from Here: Manitobans Call for a Poverty Reduction Plan* (CCPA–MB 2009) again advocated for 1,500 new units over five years as the minimum needed to address the crisis in Manitoba.

Skelton and Mahé (2009) looked at the housing challenges of people living with mental illness. Shauna MacKinnon (2008a, 2008b) discussed the privatization of public housing and the attack on rent regulations. MacKinnon and Lafreniere (2009) also drew attention to northern Manitoba's very dire shortage in "The Housing Crisis in Thompson."

Smirl (2012) wrote about the problems caused by the increasing conversion of rental units to condominiums. In *Home-Ownership for Low-Income Households* Jesse Hajer (2009) researched home ownership as an option for low-income households, noting both the benefits and the limitations. MacKinnon (2010) and Brandon (2015) discussed housing in the broader context of the social determinants of health.

Cooper (2011) scrutinized the relationship between neoliberal economic policy and the shortage of housing, as well as the increasing gap between social assistance allowances and rental rates. *Rooming Houses to Rooming Homes* (Lottis et al. 2014) explored the challenges created by the shrinking number of rooming houses, which are increasingly needed for the most difficult to house. And Silver (2011) debunked myths about public housing in *Good Places to Live: Poverty and Public Housing in Canada*.

As noted, R2H has made of point of including the precariously housed through its qualitative research. An important component of its model is to ensure that the lived experience of those affected by inadequate housing policies is at the forefront of what it does. R2H-aligned researchers have conducted various qualitative studies to illustrate the essential nature of accommodation for individuals and have gathered powerful stories in the process. These have inspired the coalition to persist in advocating for policy change, even when its efforts seemed futile. And they have helped R2H reach a broader public – increasing the understanding of the pressing need for housing. For example, in "I Just Want to Have a Decent Home" (MacKinnon 2009), an individual struggling with mental health issues recounted his efforts to find reasonable housing. A shortage of social housing had forced him to live in private sector housing, where the rent was far beyond his means. As he explained,

My yearly income is $9,667. After expenses are paid I am left with $2,703. That's $225 a month to cover everything including food, bus fare, clothing, toiletries, and laundry. Everything. I have lived in my apartment for three years. I feel safe and comfortable there. But the rent increase is forcing me to find somewhere else to live. There is nothing available ... I just want to have a decent home. (MacKinnon 2009, 1)

Some studies revealed that poor housing hindered the ability to function in other areas of life. One individual interviewed for the 2008 State of the Inner City Report told researchers: "I couldn't even do high school because I wasn't in a safe place. At the end of the day, you've got to have somewhere to do your stuff, you know?" (Brody, Arthurson, and Kliewer 2008, 41).

The research also uncovered stories of what good housing can achieve. For example, in *You Know You're Not Alone* (Cooper 2012), residents of six Winnipeg public-housing developments explained how public housing with strong on-site programming had added to their quality of life and to feeling safe and secure in their homes (see also Chapter 9 of this volume).

Politicize: From Educate to Activate

Politicization is the third critical step in reclaiming the right to the city. According to Marcuse (2009, 194), it is the "sense of clarifying the political action implications of what was exposed and proposed, and supporting organizing around the proposals by informing action."

By all accounts, R2H has successfully exposed housing issues in Manitoba, but it has also proposed solutions and brought about change. Activists, researchers, and policy analysts work side by side, recognizing the strengths that each individual brings to the table. Qualitative and quantitative research further exposes the depth and breadth of the issue and the implications for those affected. Through this work, researchers are able to identify concrete and costed policy solutions, which has led to a strategic and disciplined policy advocacy campaign focused on clear and measurable "asks."

Its collaborative model and discipline have helped R2H move forward, and have enabled it to seize political opportunities when they arise. This became apparent in 2009, when Premier Gary Doer announced his resignation, triggering a leadership race within the governing New Democratic Party (NDP). Knowing that the victor would be the next premier of Manitoba, R2H moved swiftly, lobbying the three candidates to endorse its request that 1,500 units of social housing be built over five years. This was a crucial moment for R2H. The Doer government had not made a clear commitment to increase the supply of much-needed social housing. R2H knew that getting the leadership hopefuls to commit to concrete targets during their campaigns meant that, for the first time in recent memory, advocates would have both a target and a timeline to hold policy makers to account.

The remaining two candidates endorsed the request, and soon after Greg Selinger became the province's new premier, he confirmed his commitment in the Speech from the Throne that preceded the 2010 budget. Social housing advocates, for whom victories had been few and far between since the 1980s, were re-energized. As described above, further gains at the provincial level have been realized since that time, and R2H continues its advocacy efforts with the other levels of government.

Although Manitoba's housing problem remains unresolved, R2H has become a force to be reckoned with. Certainly, the provincial political environment has been an important factor in this, but the preparedness of R2H to seize an opportunity when it presents itself has been critical to its success. Its ability to capitalize on the moment is grounded in the persistent, collaborative, strategic, disciplined, and patient approach of researchers, analysts, and activists.

Research and policy advocacy are commonly perceived as separate realms, but R2H has come to see them as symbiotic. Both are equally important. All too often, researchers are sequestered in ivory towers, hoping that policy advocates and activists will use their good work to effect change. Although advocates *do* often seek out research to aid their efforts, activists and researchers rarely work together over the long term to make change happen. R2H has learned that instigating policy change requires a long-term commitment by multiple stakeholders with varying skills and expertise, working together as equals in the fight for social justice.

R2H began as a small group of concerned citizens, whose interest in a local issue drew them into the policy world of affordable housing. Since that time, they have created a sophisticated activist group that has earned the respect of policy makers in Manitoba. It has developed a depth of understanding not only of housing issues, but also of how to expose social justice issues, how to propose viable solutions, how to politicize the issues using research and public policy analysis, and how to seize the opportunities to move its policies forward.

At the time of writing, Manitoba had recently entered a new political era, with the election of a Conservative government after sixteen years of an NDP government. Although austerity measures taken by the current government have many worried about the future of social housing in Manitoba, the implications are yet to be seen. What we do know is that R2H is strong and determined to keep safe, affordable, and social housing on the public policy agenda in Manitoba.

REFERENCES

Bernas, Kirsten, and Shauna MacKinnon. 2015. "Public Policy Advocacy and the Social Determinants of Health." In *The Social Determinants of Health in Manitoba,* ed. Lynne Fernandez, Shauna MacKinnon, and Jim Silver, 295–308. Winnipeg: Canadian Centre for Policy Alternatives–Manitoba.

Brandon, Josh. 2015. "Housing and Health in Manitoba." In *The Social Determinants of Health in Manitoba,* ed. Lynne Fernandez, Shauna MacKinnon, and Jim Silver. Winnipeg: Canadian Centre for Policy Alternatives–Manitoba.

Brody, Jill, Devon Arthurson, and Benita Kliewer. 2008. "Voicing Housing Experiences in Inner City Winnipeg." In *Putting Our Housing in Order: State of the Inner City Report, 2008,* 20–61. Winnipeg: Canadian Centre for Policy Alternatives–Manitoba.

CCPA-MB (Canadian Centre for Policy Alternatives–Manitoba). 2006. *Investing in Tomorrow, Today: The 2006 Manitoba Alternative Provincial Budget.* Winnipeg: Canadian Centre for Policy Alternatives–Manitoba. https://www.policyalternatives. ca/sites/default/files/uploads/publications/Manitoba_Pubs/2006/2006_Manitoba_ Alternative_Budget.pdf.

–. 2008. *Putting Our Housing in Order: State of the Inner City Report, 2008.* Winnipeg: Canadian Centre for Policy Alternatives–Manitoba.

–. 2009. *The View from Here: Manitobans Call for a Poverty Reduction Plan.* Winnipeg: Canadian Centre for Policy Alternatives–Manitoba. https://www.policyalternatives. ca/sites/default/files/uploads/publications/reports/docs/poverty_reduction_plan_ fullreport_052809.pdf.

Cooper, Sarah. 2011. "Housing for People, Not Markets: Neoliberalism and Housing in Winnipeg's Inner City." In *Neoliberalism: What a Difference a Theory Makes – State of the Inner City Report, 2011,* 20–36. Winnipeg: Canadian Centre for Policy Alternatives–Manitoba.

–. 2012. *You Know You're Not Alone: Community Development in Public Housing.*
Winnipeg: Canadian Centre for Policy Alternatives–Manitoba. http://www.policy
alternatives.ca/sites/default/files/uploads/publications/Manitoba%20Office/
2012/04/You%20Know%20You%27re%20Not%20Alone%202012.pdf.

Freudenberg, Nicholas, Marc Rogers, Cassandra Ritas, and Mary Nerney. 2005.
"Policy Analysis and Advocacy: An Approach to Community-Based Participatory
Research." In *Methods in Community-Based Participatory Research for Health,* ed.
Barbara Israel, Eugenia Eng, Amy Schulz, and Edith Parker, 349–70. San Francisco:
Jossey-Bass.

Hajer, Jesse. 2009. *Home-Ownership for Low-Income Households: Outcomes for
Families and Communities.* Winnipeg: Canadian Centre for Policy Alternatives–
Manitoba. https://www.policyalternatives.ca/sites/default/files/uploads/
publications/Manitoba_Pubs/2009/Home_ownership_for_Low_Income_
Households_April2009.pdf.

Lefebvre, Henri. 1967. "The Right to the City." In *Writings on Cities,* ed. E. Kofman
and E. Lebas, 63–184. London: Blackwell.

–. 1968. *Le droit à la ville.* Paris: Anthropos.

Lottis, Jovan, and Molly McCracken, with Mary Burton, Isabel Jerez, and Art Ladd.
2014. *Rooming Houses to Rooming Homes.* Report. Winnipeg: Canadian Centre
for Policy Alternatives–Manitoba. https://www.policyalternatives.ca/sites/default/
files/uploads/publications/Manitoba%20Office/2014/05/Rooming%20Houses
%20to%20Homes%20final%20report.pdf.

MacKinnon, Shauna. 2005a. "The Real Housing Shortage in Winnipeg." *Fast Facts*
(CCPA–MB), March 3. https://www.policyalternatives.ca/sites/default/files/
uploads/publications/Manitoba_Pubs/2005/FastFacts_March3_05.pdf.

–. 2005b. "What's Happening to Low Income Rental Housing in Winnipeg's Inner
City?" *Fast Facts* (CCPA–MB), March 2. https://www.policyalternatives.ca/sites/
default/files/uploads/publications/Manitoba_Pubs/2005/FastFacts_March2_
05.pdf.

–. 2007. "Housing: It's Time to Set Targets." *Fast Facts* (CCPA–MB), March 17. http://
www.policyalternatives.ca/sites/default/files/uploads/publications/Manitoba
_Pubs/2007/FastFacts_May17_07_Housing.pdf.

–. 2008a. "Privatization of Public Housing: Who Really Benefits?" *Fast Facts* (CCPA–
MB), December 22. https://www.policyalternatives.ca/publications/reports/
fast-facts-privatization-public-housing.

–. 2008b. "Rent Control in Manitoba: Challenging the Myths." *Fast Facts* (CCPA–MB),
December 23. https://www.policyalternatives.ca/publications/reports/fast-facts
-rent-control-manitoba-2.

–. 2009. "I Just Want to Have a Decent Home: 'Joe's' Story." *Fast Facts* (CCPA–MB), July 8. http://www.policyalternatives.ca/sites/default/files/uploads/publications/ Manitoba_Pubs/2009/FF_A_decent_home_070809.pdf.

–. 2010. "Housing: A Major Problem in Manitoba." In *The Social Determinants of Health in Manitoba,* ed. Lynne Fernandez, Shauna MacKinnon, and Jim Silver. Winnipeg: Canadian Centre for Policy Alternatives–Manitoba.

MacKinnon, Shauna, and Charlene Lafreniere. 2009. "The Housing Crisis in Thompson." *Fast Facts* (CCPA–MB), April 29. https://www.policyalternatives.ca/ publications/reports/fast-facts-housing-crisis-thompson.

MacKinnon, Shauna, and Jim Silver. 2009. "The Trouble with Housing for Low-Income People." March 5. Winnipeg: Canadian Centre for Policy Alternatives–Manitoba. https://www.policyalternatives.ca/publications/reports/trouble-housing -low-income-people.

Marcuse, Peter. 2009. "From Critical Urban Theory to the Right to the City." *City* 13 (2–3). http://dx.doi.org/10.1080/13604810902982177.

–. 2012. "Whose Right(s) to What City?" In *Cities for People, Not For Profit: Critical Urban Theory and the Right to the City,* ed. Neil Brenner, Peter Marcuse, and Margit Mayer. London: Routledge.

Shapcott, Michael. 2009. "Housing." In *Social Determinants of Health: Canadian Perspectives,* 2nd ed., ed. Dennis Raphael, 221–34. Toronto: Canadian Scholars Press.

Silver, Jim. 2011. *Good Places to Live: Poverty and Public Housing in Canada.* Halifax: Fernwood.

Skelton, Ian, and Richard Mahé. 2009. *'We Got Evicted ... Did I Leave That Out?' Stories of Housing and Mental Health.* Report. Winnipeg: Canadian Centre for Policy Alternatives–Manitoba. http://www.policyalternatives.ca/sites/default/files/ uploads/publications/Manitoba_Pubs/2009/stories_of_housing_and_mental_ health.pdf.

Skelton, Ian, Cheryl Selig, and Lawrence Deane. 2006. "Social Housing, Neighbourhood Revitalization and Community Economic Development." June 28. Winnipeg: Canadian Centre for Policy Alternatives–Manitoba. https://www. policyalternatives.ca/publications/reports/social-housing-neighbourhood -revitalization-and-community-economic-development.

Smirl, Ellen. 2012. "Rising Rents, Condo Conversions and Winnipeg's Inner City." August 3. Winnipeg: Canadian Centre for Policy Alternatives–Manitoba. https:// www.policyalternatives.ca/publications/reports/rising-rents-condo-conversions -and-winnipegs-inner-city.

UNHR. 2007. "United Nations Expert on Adequate Housing Calls for Immediate Attention to Tackle National Housing Crisis in Canada." Text available at http://www.povnet.org/node/2227.

United Nations. 1976. *International Covenant on Economic, Social and Cultural Rights.* http://www.ohchr.org/EN/ProfessionalInterest/Pages/CESCR.aspx.

World Health Organization. 1986. "The Ottawa Charter for Health Promotion." http://www.who.int/healthpromotion/conferences/previous/ottawa/en/.

–. 2007. *Global Age-friendly Cities: A Guide.* Geneva: WHO.

PART 2

WALKING BESIDE

———

6

Doing Research in Hollow Water First Nation
Methodological Memories

ROSA EVELIA SANCHEZ GARCIA

In 2008, the Province of Manitoba passed Bill 6, the East Side Traditional Lands Planning and Special Protected Areas Act. The act enables First Nations on the east side of Lake Winnipeg to request special protection for Crown lands they have traditionally used. The research project discussed in this chapter resulted from a request of the Kukooms (which means grandmothers in Ojibwa), a community group of Hollow Water First Nation, which lies on the southeast shore of Lake Winnipeg. The Kukooms were looking for someone to conduct research that would support their request for special protection in accordance with the act.

This chapter describes my experience as a non-Indigenous researcher who worked with the Kukooms and other members of Hollow Water First Nation to document the stories of Elders regarding traditional borders and the use of Crown land as a food source.

Background

The Kukooms of Hollow Water consist of about forty women, who are interested in finding solutions to the challenges facing their community. In pursuit of this, they have led several advocacy activities. In 2010, for example, the financial problems of Hollow Water motivated them to stage a peaceful protest to demand accountability from band leaders (Welch and Martin 2010). Due to growing concerns about the negative impact of external political and economic factors on the environment of their traditional territories, they were encouraged to explore the potential benefits of Bill 6. They decided to request the designation of a traditional use planning area.

The ecological deterioration of Hollow Water's territories threatens the community's food-harvesting practices, putting its cultural and physiological health in jeopardy. Bill 6 provides hope for undoing some of the damage or at least for preventing future harm. It enables Indigenous groups to "request that an area of Crown land in the east side management area that they have traditionally used be designated as a traditional use planning area."[1] The community must submit a written request to the provincial minister that sets out the boundaries of the planning area and that demonstrates the level of support for the proposed designation from other Indigenous groups that have traditionally used the land.

The Kukooms needed to conduct research to define the boundaries of the traditional territories. In 2011, acting on the recommendation of a Kukoom who had been a student of Dr. Peter Kulchyski's at the University of Manitoba, they asked him for help. He suggested that Emily Grafton and I conduct the project, the purpose of which was to establish the boundaries of the proposed planning area and to identify other Indigenous communities that shared the land with Hollow Water.

Emily and I travelled to Hollow Water during the summer of 2011. Our fieldwork was based on semi-structured interviews with Elders who shared their stories. We held feasts and gatherings to obtain feedback on the research process. During our time in the community, the Kukooms invited us and other research participants to share in traditional ceremonies and prayers. In October 2011, we went back to Hollow Water to present the first draft of our findings to the Kukooms and other residents. The Kukooms circulated the preliminary findings among community members to obtain their feedback, which was incorporated into the final report. In the fall of 2012, we delivered the final report to the Kukooms, with the hope that it would help them attain a traditional use designation through Bill 6, if Hollow Water decided to pursue that course. We also hoped that the research results would further the process of collecting the valuable stories and memories of the Elders.

Theoretical Framework:
Decolonization Theory and the Tribal Paradigm

Throughout the project, we observed the guidelines for decolonizing research (Smith 1999). When one conducts Indigenous research, it is essential that the theoretical positioning does not discard historical analysis. Critical theorists object to post-positivism, post-modernism, and post-colonialism because these terms universalize marginalization and ignore historical analysis. "Post-colonial" means that colonialism is a thing of the past. Thus, those who employ the post perspective when they undertake Indigenous research are at liberty to jettison historical analysis. By contrast, we ensured that it was always present in our project. Decolonization theory recognizes that although the appearance of colonialism changes over time, the relationship between the colonizer and the colonized persists (Kovach 2009).

Our project also followed the requirements of the tribal paradigm regarding research ethics, data sharing, and tribal sovereignty (Harding et al., 2012). Tribal methodology documents the historical experience of colonial relationships to integrate some aspects of decolonization theory into the methodology. According to the tribal paradigm, the research methodology should be in line with Indigenous values, include some form of community accountability, benefit the community, and ensure that the researcher is an ally for the social and economic progress of the community and will not hurt it (Kovach 2009).

Our methodology aligned with Indigenous values, as the community participated in the research design and in organizing the social, spiritual, and academic events that accompanied the research process. The values of the Kukooms and their community were clearly spelled out in a letter of intent that the group had written to the provincial government in 2010.[2] The Kukooms' philosophy is based on the sharing circle, which symbolizes equality regardless of the economic or social status of group members. The Kukooms are guided by Anishinaabe law, which is founded on the circle, the clan system, and the seven sacred laws. These laws are wisdom, courage, honesty, humility, kindness, love, and sharing (Angel 2002).

Community members demonstrated their accountability by engaging in the project and by providing feedback when we met in October 2011 to disseminate our first draft. Seven months later, a Kukooms member gave us a copy of the draft with an organized and detailed set of suggestions and recommendations from research participants and other residents who had important knowledge to contribute. The community also showed its accountability by providing us with a letter of support to include in our request for ethics approval and by giving verbal or written consent to participate in the project.

The research methodology was of obvious benefit to Hollow Water, as it would support its effort to capitalize on Bill 6. Our results also formed the basis for a second project that documented the potential for community economic development in Hollow Water. Financed by the Manitoba Research Alliance, it explored the possibilities for the creation of social, cooperative, community-owned, and/or private enterprises that could generate employment and increase food security in Hollow Water. Our methodology also benefitted the community by building capacity in two young women, who voluntarily assisted the research team and thus learned the fieldwork basics of conducting semi-structured interviews.

The Ethics Research Board of the University of Manitoba granted approval of our project, and we followed its recommendations to avoid inflicting any possible harm on the community.

Community Motivation and Initial Involvement in the Research

In their 2010 letter to the Province of Manitoba, the Kukooms had expressed their desire to designate Hollow Water's land as a traditional use planning area but had not identified its boundaries. Nor did the letter demonstrate support for this designation from Indigenous groups that shared the land. Under the terms of Bill 6, both are mandatory. The Kukooms knew that research would be needed to acquire this information. When they learned that Emily Grafton and I would be conducting it, they immediately set a date for our first meeting in Hollow Water. We were introduced to various community members, including political leaders, Kukooms representatives, and two young women who were students in the Native Studies Department at the University of Manitoba. They were supporters of the Kukooms, and they volunteered to assist in the research. The people we met during this visit expressed their interest in supporting the project.

Data Collection Method

Our first official meeting with the Kukooms and other concerned community members occurred during our second visit to Hollow Water, which lasted two days. On the evening of the first day, we participated in a prayer and a sweat lodge ceremony, both of which are traditional preparations for an endeavour that draws on the wisdom and success of the ancestors. With the help of the Kukooms, we held a feast, which allowed us to build rapport with residents.

Next day, we had scheduled focus group meetings, with an opening traditional prayer and food breaks. Emily and I had prepared topics and questions for the focus groups and for storytelling, via which we planned to collect the information we needed. An evident weakness of our approach revealed itself when most of the participants arrived too late to hear our instructions regarding the focus groups, despite having received an email in advance and having been reminded personally the evening before. Further, we needed the participants to discuss the questions only with the members of their specific groups, but this did not occur, as people from various groups talked to each other. We quickly realized that focus groups were not the best option for our project. Although focus groups are more flexible and can collect more insights than statistical surveys and other quantitative methods (Morgan 1997), they constrained participation in Hollow Water by imposing time limits on discussions and by excluding aspects of the Indigenous talking circle model (Bartlett 2005; Running Wolf and Rickard 2003), with which community members were more familiar.

Indeed, the participants spontaneously used a talking circle methodology to tell us what our research should document. As this was happening, the Kukooms prepared a list of key Elders, whose wisdom and traditional knowledge suggested that they would be good interview subjects. Emily and I simply observed and documented what was unfolding. Without using a moderator or resorting to time limits, the participants ensured that everyone had a chance to speak. Nor did they take food breaks: instead, the food was put on a table so that people could help themselves without interrupting the process. Although our original plan for the meeting had not succeeded, the Kukooms and other community members helped us to refine the focus group questions and identify additional research variables. Their input helped us to design the interviewing method that we later used. After two days in Hollow Water, Emily and I took this information back to Winnipeg, aware that we needed to use an alternative data collection method.

Ultimately, we decided to conduct semi-structured interviews that would allow for storytelling. This would provide for more flexible discussion time in locations selected by the participants themselves. This decision was also informed by several sources in the literature that emphasize the importance of oral tradition for Indigenous people such as the Ojibwa and the Cree (Hallowell 1992; McLeod 2007; Benton-Banai 1979; Blaeser 1996). As Minh-ha (1989) points out, the oldest archives in the world originated from women who used storytelling to communicate their memories from speaker to listener and from body to body. Storytelling is a process in which realities are conveyed by speakers and retold by listeners. We believed it was important to honour this non-structured methodology to align with Indigenous epistemology and the realities of Hollow Water. We interviewed people either in their homes or in the place we were staying, depending on their preference. The interviews took between one and a half and three hours, depending on how much time and information participants were able to provide. This gave enough time for them to engage in storytelling.

In addition to semi-structured interviews, we conducted talking circles to get feedback from the community on the research process and results. This decision was prompted by our first meeting, in which the participants spontaneously used a talking circle to provide feedback on our questions and prepare a list of potential interviewees. Talking circles facilitate group cohesion while encouraging dialogue and respect for individual differences (Bartlett 2005; Running Wolf and Rickard 2003). They assist interaction between interviewer and interviewee while decolonizing the interview method by applying Indigenous methodologies (Chilisa 2012). We used talking circles at three points during the project: at the first meeting; when conducting fieldwork to exchange thoughts with the Kukooms on the research process; and when disseminating the preliminary findings to participants and the community.

Community Involvement

As described above, the first meeting generated important contributions that were critical to the selection of an appropriate methodology. The list of potential interviewees initiated the non-probabilistic recruitment strategies, such as snow ball and group support (Bryman 2008), that were used to select participants. These strategies, which are based on providing referrals, succeeded because the Kukooms had both credibility and a good relationship with the community.

To ensure strong results, we needed to interview a group of individuals who could solidly represent Ojibwa values and culture, and who also had experience with traditional and/or non-traditional land and food-gathering activities. Interviewees included Elders whom the Kukooms had recommended, non-Elders whom the Elders suggested, and others who wanted to participate because they were sympathetic to the work of the Kukooms. Most interviewees were Elders, as their testimony is recognized as the primary source of Indigenous history and perspective. This history is fundamental to proving and exercising the unique land rights of Indigenous people in Canada, which are protected by the Constitution (Federal Court–Aboriginal Law Bar Liaison Committee 2012).

In selecting interviewees, I did not differentiate between Elders and non-Elders, but it seemed very natural for community members to do so. The Kukooms told me that they identified Elders "by their knowledge." This is consistent with Stiegelbauer (1996, 41), who identifies Elders as people who have "enough life experience to have something to offer those behind them. In a sense, Elders are 'experts on life.' Their exact expertise may depend on the nature of their experience, but in one way or another it involves some aspects of traditional knowledge and culture, or an interpretation of their experience in traditional terms." Simpson (2001), a scholar of Ojibwa descent who has worked in Hollow Water, remarks that some Indigenous processes can take fifty or sixty years to master. Many Indigenous scholars perceive Elders as the experts and themselves as the students. To think otherwise would be lacking in respect for the Elders and for Indigenous people. Simpson emphasizes that although her academic skills can be useful to Indigenous people, Elders and other community experts always direct and control her research projects.

Without the support of Hollow Water Elders and other community members, we would have had great difficulty in choosing and approaching the appropriate interviewees for the project. Local residents were most effective at selecting Elders, given their knowledge of their culture. They also helped us to identify the areas of knowledge that each Elder had mastered as well as the correct protocol to ask for his or her consent to be interviewed. We always approached Elders by offering tobacco to ensure that by accepting it, they agreed to share their knowledge with us. I learned a great deal from the Elders and other community members throughout the research process.

Residents contributed to the success of the research in other essential ways. Some key Elders did not speak English or simply preferred to speak about their cultural values and traditions in Ojibwa. Community members were fundamental in overcoming this challenge. One Kukoom spent considerable time translating questions and answers as we interviewed people in their homes. We were very fortunate to have found a local person who would undertake this task. Had we used a translator from outside, who was unfamiliar with the culture, our results might not have been as strong. Obtaining a faithful record and translation of what people mean and think is essential to understanding the institutions that guide their behaviour.[3] Without good translators, we would not have acquired a true understanding of the institutions that guide Hollow Water's traditional approaches to land, and thus the usefulness of our research report would probably have been diminished.

Hallowell (1960) provides a good example of how not knowing the language creates confusing interpretations of what native speakers actually mean. He points out that the idea that Ojibwa distinguishes between animate and inanimate nouns has been imposed by Europeans on the Algonquian languages. A close examination of Ojibwa shows that the distinction between animate and inanimate nouns appears to be arbitrary in some cases, with some nouns labelled animate when an outsider to the language would not expect them to be. When outsiders try "to understand the cognitive orientation of the Ojibwa there is an ethno-linguistic problem to be considered: What is the meaning of animate in Ojibwa thinking?" (ibid., 22, 23). Also, Minh-ha (1989, 74) stresses that anthropologists should familiarize themselves with a Native language "to render the verbal contour of native thought as precisely as possible." Knowing the language adds to the expertise of anthropologists since it helps achieve a faithful record and translation of the Native mentality.

Our interview process was also enhanced by the two young female members of the Kukooms who had volunteered to assist us. They drove to people's homes to confirm their availability for the interview and were present during interviews to listen, take notes, and clarify our questions or comments. DeWalt and DeWalt (2002) emphasize that interviewers must be active listeners, which implies observing while jotting down and making mental notes during the conversation. The presence of the two young Kukooms not only helped us conduct effective interviews, but also allowed them to learn. They have become a very important human resource in meeting the future research needs of Hollow Water.

Although Hollow Water First Nation lies about three hours from Winnipeg, it has neither a hotel nor a restaurant. When we failed to get a hotel room in nearby Manigotagan or Pine Falls, the Kukooms found us a place to stay. A resident who kindly conducted a sweat lodge and shared sacred stories with us and the Kukooms offered us his teepee and access to his home. When scheduled community feasts were held, some of the Kukooms prepared and organized them. Thanks to the community's participation and commitment to the project, we overcame the problems posed by the language barrier and the lack of accommodation.

Impact of the Project on the Community

The project allowed for a representative sample of the community to develop a well-informed opinion of the value of Bill 6. Although the Kukooms were familiar with the act, most people in the community were not. Several meetings were organized to inform them of it and of how the Elders' stories about traditional land use would assist Hollow Water in accessing its potential benefits. We provided the same information to research participants when asking for their consent to be interviewed.

A benefit of this measure was demonstrated by the large turnout at the meeting in which we presented the first draft of our results. Some of the attendees were new to us, and some were political leaders, whose support would be fundamental in completing the Bill 6 application. Feedback on the preliminary findings included comments and complementary information from key people who had not initially agreed to be interviewed. Their contribution enhanced the findings, and this broader participation helped unify the community around the use of Bill 6.

Prior to our involvement, the Kukooms were among the few community members who wanted to explore the potential value of Bill 6. Some residents declined to be interviewed because they doubted that Bill 6 would confer any benefits. However, as we carried out the research, they began to see its worth and agreed to participate in the process. Bill 6 requires Indigenous communities to supply a map in which a certain area is clearly demarcated as their traditional land. However, the people of Hollow Water did not traditionally have land borders. They shared the land with other Indigenous communities. Therefore, they saw no need for a map to define their territory. Some residents feared that the creation of such a map could be taken to mean that the community's traditional land consisted solely of what appeared there, with the tacit inference that it had legally surrendered all rights to any other areas.

In a way, the idea that Hollow Water's traditional territories lacked borders was confirmed during the meeting in which we presented our first draft. This included a map based on fieldwork data, and it indicated that the Hollow Water territories overlapped with lands used by other Indigenous groups. I suggested that the map be redrawn to delete the overlapping borders so that Hollow Water would not need to negotiate with other communities to apply for Bill 6. However, the people who attended the meeting generally suggested that the map with overlapping borders would not conflict with what they wanted, in terms of access to land. They had no wish to obtain ownership of a limited piece of property, since, in their view, "nobody can own it." In fact, they wanted to share the stewardship of the land with other communities as their ancestors did.

As of January 2016, Hollow Water had not requested a traditional use planning area designation under Bill 6. However, the research provided it with a key piece of information that it would need to supply if it did make such a request. Also, in a land use planning meeting that I had with community members and band authorities, some Elders suggested that the research report would be relevant in supporting any potential land claim that Hollow Water might make.

Another impact of the project was that it helped the Kukooms gain greater recognition among residents and political leaders as an all-female advocacy group that spoke on behalf of the community. The Kukooms had been looking for more local women to become involved in discussing and proposing solutions to pertinent issues. To facilitate this, they had hoped to establish an office, where women could meet to identify and address concerns. When we delivered our final report, the Kukooms informed us that they had obtained the necessary resources to set up the office. Their leadership role in several Hollow Water events had shown what they were capable of achieving, but their participation in the research project was fundamental in confirming their credibility and in accessing the resources to establish the office. Supporting the consolidation of an all-female Indigenous group and strengthening the ability of women to exercise their right to participate in community decisions are important accomplishments. Building the capacity of women to advocate for themselves is particularly significant, given that it is not promoted by Indigenous economic development policies, which have been criticized for lacking gender sensitivity (Whiteduck and Peebles 2009). This occurs even though Indigenous women have been identified as the most disadvantaged group in Canada (Walters et al. 2004; Bernier 1997; Fiske 2006; Fiske and Browne 2006).

Our work at Hollow Water helped build capacity in other ways. The two young women who volunteered to assist us developed knowledge and experience in conducting interviews. As a result, they are now important resources with research skills that the Kukooms and Hollow Water can rely on in the future.

Reflections

Hollow Water's concept of time taught me a new way to organize my own time and allowed me to optimize and make more enjoyable my subsequent work visits there. Learning about Indigenous ideas regarding time helped me to understand that an effective and respectful relationship with Indigenous people requires integrating parts of their culture into that relationship. Smith (1999) describes Western concepts of time as linked to production. During the Industrial Revolution, the middle class began to distinguish between work time, leisure time, education time, and religion time. By contrast, Indigenous people see time as elastic: praying, eating, socializing, and working can occur at any moment, sometimes simultaneously, and are not hived off from each other. Janca and Bullen (2003, 41) point out that whereas Western people perceive time as linear, for many Indigenous communities "time calendars consist of multiple and simultaneously existing time categories such as 'practical time,' 'social time,' 'religious time,' 'dream time,' etc."

I encountered this Indigenous concept of time while conducting fieldwork in Hollow Water. My visit there was earmarked as working time, but it also included time for praying, traditional ceremonies, eating, talking, joking, storytelling, and interviewing, among other things. These activities gave me a global sense of the social, cultural, and economic functioning of the Hollow Water people, which enriched the project and made me feel comfortable and welcome. Also, once I understood that the time I spent there was not linear and that it represented more than just working time, I realized that I was in some way decolonizing the research methodology. If, when we designed our fieldwork, Emily and I had had a better understanding of Indigenous ideas about time, we might not have selected inappropriate methodologies such as the focus group, thereby avoiding stress and wasted time.

The Kukooms and other residents at Hollow Water demonstrated their immense generosity and commitment to the project by translating interviews, finding potential interviewees, driving us to the homes of participants, taking notes, conducting traditional ceremonies, organizing feasts, and providing accommodation. We took this as a sign that they trusted us, which strengthened our own commitment to meeting their research needs. It is important to emphasize that the project would not have been realized without the Kukooms. They were present throughout. Their commitment to preserving the traditional values of their community triggered the need for the project. They introduced us to residents and ensured we had everything we needed to carry out the fieldwork. They circulated our preliminary findings to obtain feedback and approval, which allowed us to refine the findings in a final report. In summary, the Kukooms were the leaders of the project. I admire their strength and determination to contribute positively to the lives of their fellow community members.

Like the Kukooms, I initially felt confident that Bill 6 would be of benefit to Hollow Water. But some people did not agree. Throughout the research process, both defenders and critics of the value of Bill 6 were able to listen to each other's concerns and perhaps revise their initial perspectives. The outcome of this exchange could lead to a community decision not to request a traditional use planning area designation under Bill 6. In any case, it will be an informed decision, thanks to the community-based participatory research method used to carry out the project.

Conclusion

The method used in conducting this research generated several benefits that would not otherwise have arisen. First, it enabled community members to get involved and identify with the findings. This increases the likelihood that they will feel comfortable using the results if they do eventually request a planning area designation under Bill 6. Second, it enabled a reciprocal exchange of skills between the participants and the researchers. I will apply these skills in future projects, and I hope that having people with newly acquired basic fieldwork skills will similarly help Hollow Water to meet its future research needs. And third, the residents became our colleagues, which made it easier to learn and take direction from each other. This reduced the risk that, as non-Indigenous individuals, we would discard the historical analysis and assume that colonization had ended. The community's participation in the process demanded the use of tribal methodologies, which helped decolonize the project.

Anyone who undertakes community-based participatory research should be aware that some important residents may choose not to be involved in it, especially if its objectives do not match the traditional institutions of the community. This was our experience, as some people disagreed with the project's objective of facilitating a planning area designation through Bill 6. As we listened to their reasons for refusing to participate, we learned about Hollow Water's traditional institutions on land rights, which differed from those conveyed in Bill 6. Had we not conducted community-based participatory research, this useful exchange would not have occurred, as many other methodologies do not involve direct interaction between the community and the researcher. Many researchers would see the refusal to participate simply as an unfortunate limitation. However, depending on the reasons for refusal, it could become an asset. For us, understanding why skepticism regarding Bill 6 had prompted certain people to distance themselves from our project allowed for deeper insights into community institutions on land rights. Policy makers could capitalize on these insights to design policies that are more consistent with Indigenous values.

When non-Indigenous researchers work with Indigenous people, they sometimes experience culture shock. In a way, this was true for us, when we had to adjust to the community's language and concept of time. Our research method helped to address these challenges by allowing us to develop relationships with residents that enabled us to know, accept, and feel more comfortable with each other. Working shoulder-to-shoulder with them taught me some life lessons, as well as developing my academic knowledge. I was both amazed and humbled by the wisdom, generosity, strength, and perseverance of the Elders, the Kukooms, and the Hollow Water community. I will always feel honoured and grateful to have worked with them.

As mentioned above, Hollow Water has not yet used the project to continue an application under Bill 6. Our research method allows me to understand and respect its reasons for not proceeding with a request. Ultimately, it may decide never to do so. Regardless of what happens, the research process enabled community members to understand, reflect on, and take a position regarding the potential benefits and limitations of Bill 6 for Hollow Water, and this is a positive outcome. Furthermore, the research helped strengthen the capacity of a group of Indigenous women to support each other and participate in important community decisions.

ACKNOWLEDGMENTS

I would like to express my gratitude to Professor Peter Kulchyski at the University of Manitoba, director of the project that led to this chapter, and to Emily Grafton, my partner in the same project. Also, I thank the Manitoba Alternative Research Food Alliance (MAFRA) for its financial support, as well as the Kukooms and the members of Hollow Water First Nation. Without their various contributions, neither the project nor this chapter would have been possible. I alone am responsible for the content of this chapter: it expresses my own ideas and thoughts, which are independent of Peter Kulchyski, Emily Grafton, MAFRA, and Hollow Water.

NOTES

1 Manitoba, *The East Side Traditional Lands Planning and Special Protected Areas Act*, SM 2009, c. 7, pt. 2, s. 5(1), http://web2.gov.mb.ca/laws/statutes/ccsm/_pdf. php?cap=e3.
2 Letter of Intent to the Provincial Government to Access the Possibilities to Protect Aboriginal Traditional Land Raised by Bill 6.
3 The term "institutions" in this chapter refers to the theory of institutions. Broadly defined, institutions are "systems of established and prevalent social rules that

structure social interactions. Language, money, law, systems of weights and measures, table manners, and firms (and other organizations) are thus all institutions" (Hodgson 2006, 2).

REFERENCES

Angel, Michael. 2002. *Preserving the Sacred: Historical Perspectives on the Ojibwa Midewiwin*. Winnipeg: University of Manitoba Press.

Bartlett, Judith. 2005. "Health and Well-Being for Métis Women in Manitoba." *Canadian Journal of Public Health* 96 (1): S22–S27.

Benton-Banai, Edward. 1979. *The Mishomis Book: The Voice of the Ojibway*. Saint Paul, MN: Indian Country Press.

Bernier, Rachel. 1997. *The Dimensions of Wage Inequality among Aboriginal Peoples*. Analytical Studies Branch Research Paper Series, Statistics Canada Catalogue no. 11F0019MPE – No. 109. Ottawa: Statistics Canada.

Blaeser, Kimberley M. 1996. *Gerald Vizenor: Writing in Oral Tradition*. Norman: University of Oklahoma Press.

Bryman, Alan. 2008. *Social Research Methods*. Don Mills: Oxford University Press.

Chilisa, Bagele. 2012. *Indigenous Research Methodologies*. Los Angeles: Sage.

DeWalt, Kathleen M., and Billie R. DeWalt. 2002. *Participant Observation: A Guide for Fieldworkers*. Walnut Creek: AltaMira Press.

Federal Court–Aboriginal Law Bar Liaison Committee. 2012. "Aboriginal Litigation Practices Guidelines." http://cas-cdc-www02.cas-satj.gc.ca/fct-cf/pdf/Practice Guidelines%20Phase%20I%20and%20II%2016-10-2012%20ENG%20final. pdf.

Fiske, Jo-Anne. 2006. "Boundary Crossing: Power and Marginalization in the Formation of Canadian Aboriginal Women's Identity." *Gender and Development* 14 (2): 247–58.

Fiske, Jo-Anne, and Annette Browne. 2006. "Aboriginal Citizen, Discredited Medical Subject: Paradoxical Constructions of Aboriginal Women's Subjectivity in Canadian Health Care Policies." *Policy Sciences* 39 (1): 91–111. http://www.jstor. org/stable/25474293.

Hallowell, A. Irving. 1960. *Ojibwa Ontology, Behavior, and World View*. New York: Columbia University Press.

–. 1992. *The Ojibwa of the Berens River, Manitoba: Ethnography into History*. Fort Worth: Harcourt Brace.

Harding, Anna, Barbara Harper, Dave Stone, Catherine O'Neill, Patricia Berger, Stuart Harris, and Jamie Donatuto. 2012. "Conducting Research with Tribal Communities: Sovereignty, Ethics, and Data-Sharing Issues." *Environmental Health Perspectives* 120 (1): 6–10.

Hodgson, Geoffrey M. 2006. "What Are Institutions?" *Journal of Economic Issues* 40 (1): 1–25. http://www.geoffrey-hodgson.info/user/image/whatareinstitutions. pdf.

Janca, Aleksandar, and Clothilde Bullen. 2003. "The Aboriginal Concept of Time and Its Mental Health Implications." *Australasian Psychiatry* 11 (1): 40–44. doi:10.1046/j.1038-5282.2003.02009.x.

Kovach, Margaret. 2009. *Indigenous Methodologies: Characteristics, Conversations, and Contexts.* Toronto: University of Toronto Press.

McLeod, Neal. 2007. *Cree Narrative Memory.* Saskatoon: Purich.

Minh-ha, Trinh T. 1989. *Women, Native, Other.* Bloomington: Indiana University Press.

Morgan, David. 1997. *Focus Groups as Qualitative Research.* Los Angeles: Sage.

Running Wolf, Paulette, and Julie A. Rickard. 2003. "Talking Circles: A Native American Approach to Experiential Learning." *Journal of Multicultural Counseling and Development* 31 (1): 39–43. doi:10.1002/j.2161-1912.2003.tb00529.x.

Simpson, Leanne. 2001. "Aboriginal Peoples and Knowledge: Decolonizing Our Processes." *Canadian Journal of Native Studies* 21 (1): 137–48. http://www3. brandonu.ca/cjns/21.1/cjnsv21no1_pg137-148.pdf.

Smith, Linda Tuhiwai. 1999. *Decolonizing Methodologies: Research and Indigenous Peoples.* New York: Zed Books.

Stiegelbauer, Suzanne M. 1996. "What Is an Elder? What Do Elders Do? First Nation Elders as Teachers in Culture-Based Urban Organizations." *Canadian Journal of Native Studies* 16 (1): 37–66. http://www3.brandonu.ca/cjns/16.1/Stiegelbauer.pdf.

Walters, David, Jerry White, and Paul Maxim. 2004. "Does Postsecondary Education Benefit Aboriginal Canadians? An Examination of Earnings and Employment Outcomes for Recent Aboriginal Graduates." *Canadian Public Policy* 30 (3): 283–301. http://www.jstor.org/stable/3552303.

Welch, Mary Agnes, and Nick Martin. 2010. "Grandmothers Occupy Hollow Water Band Office." *Winnipeg Free Press,* March 12. http://www.winnipegfreepress.com/local/grandmothers-occupy-hollow-water-band-office-87459232.html.

Whiteduck, Francine, and Dana Peebles. 2009. "Gender Analysis of the New Federal Framework for Aboriginal Development: Discussion Guide and Annexes." *Journal of Aboriginal Economic Development* 6 (2): 46–63. http://iportal.usask.ca/docs/Journal%20of%20Aboriginal%20Economic%20Development/JAED_v6no2/pp46-63.pdf.

7

Engaging *Dibaajimowinan*
"Stories" in Community-Based Research
at Asatiwisipe Aki, Manitoba

AGNIESZKA PAWLOWSKA-MAINVILLE

One of the Elders I have become friends with in Poplar River, Jean, loves to bead and sew. She makes mukluks, moccasins, gloves, belts, wrist warmers, shirts, and many other things. Her beautiful beadwork is based on a technique that was passed on to her from her mother and grandmother. It was "a long process to learn," she tells me. When I tried it for myself and discovered how difficult it was, I gained much respect for the women who have the skill, patience, and dexterity to do it. When I first began, Jean explained how to proceed. The thread must be strong, and the loops needed to pass around and then tuck in underneath each bead. Her words were lost on me until she suggested that I watch while she finished beading a pair of moccasins. I started to learn how to sew the beads in a straight line, but I could not get them to stay close to the hide. Jean showed me which needles and technique would lock the beads tightly to the hide. But it wasn't until I brought my own work and followed Jean step by step that I finally started placing the tiny beads right.

I have many memories of the time I spent with Jean. I recall the smell of hide filling the room as I opened my sewing kit. I recall the taste of the tea I drank as Jean and I talked and listened to the occasional stories her husband, Walter, would chime in with. I remember feeling comfortable in the quiet and warm home that I have visited so many times in the last few years. I remember laughing, eating supper together, watching Jean and Walter's sons fiddle around on their guitars, and teaching their young granddaughter how to read the multiplication table.

Jean's family lives in Poplar River First Nation, a small and remote Aboriginal community on the east side of Lake Winnipeg in Manitoba. In 2007, Poplar River, along with four neighbouring communities, announced its determination to permanently protect its trapline territory through a UNESCO World Heritage site proposal. The nomination, Pimachiowin Aki, is an example of First Nations communities taking charge of their future to ensure long-term protection of their traditional lands. This is a story of how one non-Aboriginal researcher followed this community's unique position within the World Heritage site proposal to protect its territory and local values. The community-based research process that was used relied on academic methodologies such as participant observation, longitudinal research, and interviews with Elders and resource harvesters, as well as on my prior knowledge as an individual, as a researcher, and as a guest in the territory.

I also depended on a number of socio-cultural contexts arising out of Anishinaabe traditions in Poplar River, specifically, on *mawadishiwe,* "visiting" in Anishinaabemowin (Ojibwe), on *odaniibiishimidaa,* "let's have tea," and on *dibaajimowinan,* "stories." Although these words are taken from Anishinaabemowin, the constructs that inform them were useful in my work elsewhere, with the Makeso Sakahican Inninuwak as well as during my time spent with the Shutagotine Dene in the Western Arctic and Naskapi of Kawawachikamach, Quebec. These tools have enabled me to be part of a research project that created the potential for policy change affecting Aboriginal rights and for a space for mutual learning, where the line between the researched and the researcher often became blurred.

Dibaajimowin, "the Story"

We just want to protect the land, so that people don't come and spoil our land. It's a nice land, nice hunting place for the moose and the other animals ... we want to protect, so that we can survive on wild meat like moose. That's why we want to protect our land.

– Ken Douglas, local Elder, 2008

According to residents of Poplar River, numerous companies have tried to log the trees, dam the rivers, and mine the area for several years. For example, in 2007 Manitoba Hydro announced its long-planned project to build a high-voltage direct-current transmission line known as BiPole III across the east side of Lake Winnipeg, where the *asatiwisipe aki,* Poplar River land, is located. The community responded, arguing that this area – the "lungs of North America" – needed to be protected because it signified *mino-bimaadiziwin,* "the good life" of the people. And so, it decided to put a First Nations face back on the boreal forest of the east side of Lake Winnipeg by first ensuring interim protection under the Manitoba Parks Act, and then by nominating its traditional territory as part of a UNESCO World Heritage site known as Pimachiowin Aki, "the land that gives life."

The Pimachiowin Aki nomination was officially submitted to UNESCO in 2012 by the First Nations, two provincial parks, and two provincial governments. The three-hundred-page nomination is the first in Canada to be submitted based on both natural and cultural heritage values. All four communities involved believed it was important to submit the nomination to protect their ways of life and traditional lands, and to sustain the intact ecosystem for the well-being of all. Being part of the universally recognized World Heritage site program would be a precedent-setting achievement for First Nations in the boreal forest. Each First Nation involved would be responsible for the stewardship of its respective territory as per its own land management plan. Responsibility for the stewardship of natural and cultural resources reflects the self-determination of First Nations and the "ways of the Old People," as the elders and harvesters of Poplar River would put it. Many local Elders have stated that the harvesters were the stewards of the lands and resources. For Poplar River, the First Nations–led designation represents an ecologically sustainable vision of community-controlled economic and political development.

After a tumultuous few years, during which the role of resource development within economic growth was presented, debated, and re-presented, Manitoba Hydro's BiPole III transmission line project was relocated to the west side of Lake Winnipeg, and the decision about the status of the Pimachiowin Aki World Heritage site is still pending.

The Story of Me, the History

Many stories have a protagonist – this story too – and so, I must introduce myself. When they introduce themselves, Anishinaabe and Inninu people make a point of mentioning family, place of origin, and sometimes a clan, and providing background about oneself. This is likewise imperative for anyone who conducts Indigenous research. It is especially important when a non-Indigenous person comes into the community to "do" research because contexts such as colonialism, power, race, gender, and rights come into play. Acknowledging the existence of power relations and the fact that they play a significant role in the outcome of research and research data is fundamental. Said (1978, 20) argues that "strategic location" is "a way of describing the author's position in relation to the material he writes about." Therefore, if one is to "engage" in an Indigenous community, a point of reference must be made in relation to the research project.

The first thing that people in Poplar River noticed about me was my skin colour and gender. In this Anishinaabe community, I was identified as *mooniya-ikwe*, white woman. This forced me to recognize that my "whiteness" – and the privilege that comes with this – is embodied through me in my position as outsider. As a non-Indigenous woman and researcher from outside the community, I was aware that my position of privilege meant that I would require time to establish trust in the community. I discovered that during my early visits, *I* was in some ways being researched. People often came up to me and asked who I was, what I was doing in Poplar River, and what I thought about the community. Since I could not change the fact that I was an outsider, I recognized that I had my work cut out for me. Many of my preconceived ideas about *how* research was conducted needed to be transformed. So, after exploring many different approaches, after numerous visits and countless stories exchanged with residents over tea, I learned a great deal about what community-based participatory research means. So please, grab a cup of tea and let me tell you some stories.

Poplar River's primary objective was to gain permanent protection for its traditional territory through provincial government mechanisms and the UNESCO bid. If these failed, it would go to court, and I was brought in as the community's "Plan B" in 2007. The chief and council wanted someone to collect oral histories and stories from local Elders and residents in the event that they needed to take legal action to protect their lands. My work was to help with that endeavour. The protection of the land in Poplar River was spearheaded by the community, and later the broader World Heritage site initiative was led by the partnership of the Pimachio-win Aki First Nations. My role was to support these efforts by collecting narratives from local Elders and harvesters, and to provide research and policy recommendations.

Initially, I examined Poplar River's resistance to BiPole III, but my later research emphasized resource stewardship through intangible cultural heritage. I also explored Indigenous forms of resource stewardship as an Aboriginal and treaty right (Pawlowska-Mainville n.d.). This work was intended to support the UNESCO nomination with stories of land use that could be placed at the community's planned cultural interpretive centre. I undertook community-based fieldwork, participatory observation, and key-informant interviews chronicling the use of global mechanisms to meet local needs. The more time I spent listening to local voices, the more people were interested in being interviewed and in having their stories heard. The relationships that developed became the foundation of my long-term research in Poplar River.

I spent much time participating in activities and in the daily life of the community. This allowed me to engage with key residents, with whom I worked most closely throughout the research. Many people told me that the research needed to be useful to Poplar River, which provided me with an encouraging sense of direction. I attempted to guide my research so that the results could help achieve significant and positive change that promotes social equity. I was happy to know that the chief and council were involved in the process by outlining ways that the research could benefit the community and that they foresaw using it in the interpretive centre.

Frequent visits to Poplar River allowed me to obtain feedback on how I was doing and gave residents many chances to ask questions. I put up posters that outlined the project and described a little about myself in an effort to make this information more accessible. I relied heavily on Anishinaabemowin to connect with more Elders and harvesters. The community provided me with official letters of support for my work and with accommodation in the local school's teacherage, the mission, and members' homes. On occasion, Poplar River leaders subsidized my groceries, introduced me to some Elders, and supplied information, maps, news, and data.

Being welcomed in a home or invited for tea to exchange narratives furnished a kind of feedback that validated the research process. The friendships I developed gave opportunities to share new developments regarding the research in a way that was less formal than a PowerPoint presentation or official meeting. It was significant for me that the research had generated enough interest among the leaders and community members that they wanted to see summaries of my research report. I designed the final report to make it accessible to everyone and distributed a two-page summary of the findings to community members. In return, I received photos, personal notebooks, and sometimes even letters that residents hoped would be included in the final text (Pawlowska-Mainville n.d.). This was an important development. Although the chief and council were involved from the start, residents became increasingly interested as I became more engaged in their community. I was still an outsider but no longer a stranger.

Mawadishiwe, "Visiting"

It's nice to see you again.
– *Ken Douglas, 2009*

Ken, a local Elder, was my first "interview subject" when I began my work with Poplar River in 2007. Our one-hour talk was a typical research interview: I asked questions, Ken responded, and I jotted down his answers. As is customary in Western research, and with Ken's permission, I placed an audio recorder on the table to capture his replies. When we met again eight years later, the process looked much different. We sat at the table, drinking coffee and talking about my marriage, the land, recent hunters, and local buzz. The "research interview" had transformed into a conversation between two long-time friends who were learning from each other and exchanging opinions and worries, thoughts and stories. A casual conversation with a familiar person can result in a more significant exchange than might otherwise occur, and I continued to learn from Ken, but in a more meaningful way.

By definition, community-based participatory research (CBPR) requires that researchers spend a great deal of time in the community under study. Throughout this project, I travelled frequently to Poplar River, visiting and developing relationships with residents. I believe that the project would not have been as successful if I hadn't engaged in longitudinal research that allowed me time to develop trusting connections. For example, I recall the day I first met Walter at his house in Poplar River. I was introduced to him by a councillor who told me that Walter had a wealth of knowledge and was someone I could learn from. Two days later, I was invited to the family's home for a dinner of boiled moose meat. That day was the beginning of a long and warm-hearted friendship between the family and me. I also learned a great deal through my many formal and informal conversations with Noah, a fiery harvester from Makeso Sakahican. Developing trusting relationships with Ken, Noah, and others allowed me to learn far more than I would have done if I'd relied solely on the academic research methods I studied at university.

Working with Indigenous Elders requires an understanding of cultural norms, practices and protocols, and social constructs. One important practice in Poplar River is that of mawadishiwe (visiting). This enabled me to establish relationships of trust prior to formally gathering research data. Spending time getting to know people is, I believe, the key to conducting good research with members of a community.

My visits to Poplar River included participation in local activities and events, including games and sport competitions. I also spoke with many individuals about subjects other than my research. This allowed me not only to connect at a human level but also to gather stories that defined how Poplar River community members as a collective related to the issues driving the research topic. What began as Western-influenced research relationships, where data were gathered through key-informant interviews, evolved into dialogues in which stories were exchanged between two people rather than extracted from the interviewee by the researcher. On many occasions, seemingly unrelated activities presented me with stories that complemented the research and sometimes even provided me with a new perspective on how best to tackle a particular subject. I found that working with people was better than conducting research on a people. Surprisingly, some of the best "testimonies" I received took place while I walked up and down the aisles of the local grocery store!

These regular visits reduced the power relations that are often present in the research process, creating space for a respect-based dialogue. As community members became less inclined merely to say what they thought I wanted to hear, our exchange became more honest and meaningful. This taught me the importance of developing trusting relationships. For example, I initially planned that my interaction with Ken would entail a single formal interview. However, the two of us also had at least twenty informal discussions over the course of one year and have probably spoken about two hundred times during the past decade. Instead of obtaining data in the formal sense, I established trust through numerous *mawadishi-wewinan* (visits), leading to a deeper and more open sharing of information. Frequent mawadishiwewinan in CBPR, in which informal discussions allow the researcher to introduce, explain, elaborate, or provide more information without using overly scholarly language, also empower First Nation members in this collaborative process.

Indigenous research methods view storytelling as an integral form of knowledge (Smith 1999). Stories are often shared through informal discussions with one or two key informants, occurring over a long period. Had I subscribed to traditional Western methods, visiting Poplar River sporadically, I may have learned that many community members support the World Heritage site. However, I would not have learned why Elders, harvesters, councillors, and others do so.

Odaniibiishimidaa, "Let's Have Tea!"

Sometimes if you don't have anything to eat, you can offer some tea. This is a good thing to offer something like that. I am used to that. My mom used to teach me a lot about that. Even if you don't have any tea. Even if you don't have tea or coffee at home or whatever. Water, give them some water; that's the best way you could do, and from there, they know you're respectful, they know that you will be a respectful guy. Then people will come to you ...

And that's what my mom and dad would tell me a lot about that.
This is the way I am using it now; and this is the way I feel for
you, using it this way, offering me this and all that. This is the
way I like it. That's like when you go somewhere else and visit.

— *Abel Bruce, Elder, 2013*

Although the idea of mawadishiwe comes first in longitudinal research
because it demonstrates a commitment to establishing relationships,
odaniibiishimi (have tea) quickly follows. These "methods" have been
employed by some of the best scholars working with Indigenous communities, most notably Hugh Brody (1975, 2004) in his work with the
Inuit, Peter Kulchyski (2005) with the Dene, and Julie Cruikshank (1990)
with the Athapaskan and Tlingit women. Others, such as Brown and Peers
(2005), Brownlie (2003), Feit (1995), Nadasdy (2003), Richardson (1991),
and Tanner (1979), are also examples of individuals connecting with community members through visiting, having tea (and sharing meals), and
exchanging stories as part of the research process. Brody (1975, 163), for
example, describes his experience of sharing food: "I often visited the home
of an elderly man. The visits had become one of the most relaxed parts of
my work; the old man, his family, and I talked, drank endless cups of tea,
and often ate together." Drinking endless cups of tea gave Brody the space
and time to talk with the Elder and learn more about him and from him.
Cruikshank (1990, 372) also writes that women would share their stories
during tea time: "We all had lunch together; afterward, while we were
drinking tea, Mrs. Ned began speaking."

These shared experiences also reconfigure the relationship between
the researcher and the Aboriginal community. During them, two individuals who were once linked solely through a research project can become
connected as friends. When food or tea are shared, sincerity comes naturally. This kind of engagement allows the researcher to become truly
interested in the individual, rather than simply in obtaining data. Informal
discussions over *aniibishaabo* (tea) allow questions to be tailored to a
community member's specific role. For example, it would be unproductive
(not to mention inappropriate) for me to ask Elders to discuss Canada's
policy regarding UNESCO World Heritage sites or to request that a young
councillor talk about his life-long experience as a head trapper. Neither

individual would have much to say, and I would probably be laughed at for my ignorance in asking impertinent questions that reflect little understanding of local dynamics. The CBPR process therefore allows for knowing the community members and their roles as well as for an adaptive design that can lead to lasting friendships. This was not something I had expected to experience.

As the project evolved, my relationship with the interview participants became more complex. Trust, respect, and affection grew with time, and the Elders developed a sense of empowerment. As I spoke with the Elders, harvesters, and community members it became evident that despite my university education, I knew very little and that I needed to depend on them to teach me. It was the Elders and local residents who introduced me to all the unequivocal knowledge about the worth of the World Heritage site. In one instance, I had an Elder and trapper named Abel over for aniibishaabo. As we spoke, I realized that not only did I know very little, but that I was reliant on him to teach me. I was not the expert – Abel was. With time, the quest for knowledge becomes a humbling experience. The more a researcher speaks with an Elder, the more she discovers that in reality, the Elder determines which "data" are important.

The Elders, especially the few with whom I have a close relationship, guided my work and research in Poplar River, and I thought of them as my collaborators. They shared stories and personal experiences that they thought I needed to know. This helped shift the power of the research relationship to them because they held all the knowledge, and I, the researcher, was learning from that knowledge to disseminate it further on behalf of the knowledge holders. In academia, this dependence can be viewed as putting the researcher in an inferior or subjective position. In my research, it seemed to empower the "Native informant" (Spivak 1999), who was increasingly willing to share the wealth of knowledge with the trusted person and eager learner. One Elder, Abel, said, "It is good what you are doing. You can go and take what you have learned here and take it out" (Abel Bruce, pers. comm. 2013). I sometimes felt that my role was to provide a mechanism for disseminating some of those voices that tend to be obliterated in the larger scope of political meta-narratives. Findings are indeed presented in written format by the researcher, but they are ultimately a reflection of recommendations made to the researcher by the

Elders or community members. Therefore, long-term involvement becomes not only a method used to conduct effective and relationship-building research, but also signifies a form of unique collaboration where research is guided by community members and will have practical relevance. Throughout the research process, I would casually describe what I wanted to learn so that participants could think about my questions and respond when they were ready. Some preferred to take their time and ponder my questions. Likewise, I sometimes needed to think about the stories I was told – sometimes for years – before understanding the relevance.

The Inside Story

The research relationship changes when you work with community members over a long period, and they welcome you into their lives by sharing personal information and introducing you to family members. My affection for some Poplar River residents grew as a result of the relationships I formed over several years. I initially went to Poplar River simply to conduct research through fieldwork. I had not anticipated developing such strong feelings for some of my colleagues there or becoming so deeply affected by things that happened to them. For example, I did not expect to cry when Stanley, the person who made me feel so welcome the first time I visited alone, died tragically. I was surprised at the heartfelt happiness I felt when a friend finally got married. I was also surprised at the trepidation I felt upon being placed in an uncomfortable situation with a local man. And, when I discovered that a thirteen-year-old female had been cutting her arms, I did not anticipate feeling torn in deciding whether to tell someone and thus risk having her removed from her home or to say nothing and let her continue hurting herself. The shock and sincere pain that is felt each time stories like this are heard surpass all academic boundaries.

Ethical questions also arose in the research process. During a wonderful discussion with an Elder, I had to decide when I could appropriately bring out my recorder and ask him to sign a consent form to obtain the data he had just shared. I sometimes struggled with how best to articulate the context in which I acquired information from a child or a non-interviewed participant and how to acknowledge these voices as part of the research. I often found myself wondering if my role as researcher might be interpreted as an intrusion in the life of the community. I was also unexpectedly faced with the dilemma of deciding whether to intervene when serious issues arose.

Orienting my moral compass when instincts and academic responsibilities conflicted was sometimes difficult. For example, it can be devastating to learn about sexual abuse and other severe crimes committed by trusted community members or to see other effects of colonialism manifested by close friends. These issues persist in numerous Aboriginal communities throughout Canada, and becoming engaged without being affected at a personal level is difficult. The challenges that I encountered in Poplar River were a direct consequence of my long-term involvement there. After one establishes close relationships with certain people over tea and shared personal stories, it is difficult not to feel affected by their struggles and successes. These complicating factors are delicate issues for many researchers, and I am still navigating formal ethics and my own values for solutions.

Additionally, the fact that I was a woman shaped how I conducted my research – and myself as an individual. More so than my race, my gender determined how the research process was carried out and what data could be obtained. For example, because I was female I could not just hitch a ride with any man, because sitting with him in a car could be seen as inappropriate, especially if he had a partner. If a male friend stayed too long at my place, and others saw his car parked outside late into the night, assumptions could be made. Going on a hunting trip that involved overnight camping with men would have been unacceptable for me if there were no women present. In one instance, my unfamiliarity with social protocols regarding gender relations led to an unpleasant and dangerous situation. A brief conversation I had with a man in a public place created conflict between him and his girlfriend, which escalated to violence and police involvement. In another community, I joined a hunting trip that involved boat travel, unaware that women who participated in such trips were not viewed positively. Both cases were resolved in the end, but they taught me that CBPR can be a different experience for women and that observation of social and cultural norms must be carefully made to avoid unsafe circumstances. Therefore, the stories and data I could gather through my CBPR were to some extent limited by my role as a woman.

Challenging the Meta-Narrative

Often, Western methods of conducting research, such as formal interviews with strangers, completing surveys, and filling out forms, may not be welcome in First Nations, where experience with outside researchers and Western methods has been destructive for generations. I learned very quickly that impersonal data collection methods, used to obtain the largest possible amount of information, are resisted in First Nation communities. I've also learned that well-intentioned university practices of requiring research participants to provide written consent for interviews is problematic. Many First Nation members are very reluctant to sign these forms, for good reason.

When done well, CBPR that better aligns with Indigenous ways of knowing can generate tools that Indigenous communities can use to advocate for their inherent rights. I believe this form of research can create a space where "two societies with disparate worldviews are poised to engage each other" (Ermine 2007, 193) to develop a framework for dialogue regarding Indigenous-Canadian relations. CBPR can be an attempt to represent narratives and experiences of Indigenous people.

In my research, informal interactions were an open space where I could hear Indigenous perceptions and stories, and re-present them to support community endeavours. This research was useful in challenging the meta-narratives around economic development in First Nations. Listening to various dibaajimowinan (stories) about community land use and aspirations for economic development enabled me to disseminate those stories as information to support the case for self-determination over natural and cultural resources.

The plurality of information and experiences that I obtained from members of Poplar River First Nation also enabled me to join with scholars who argue that a broader interpretation of Aboriginal and treaty rights is needed in Canada. In that sense, rather than continually validating the larger meta-narrative around this issue, CBPR ultimately trusts the experience of First Nations as valid knowledge. The CBPR process enabled me to support the often under-represented grassroots voices and help legitimize their unique knowledge. This is what makes CBPR projects beneficial and worthwhile.

Conducting CBPR with an Aboriginal community requires a commitment to eradicate the faults associated with the dominance of Western
forms of knowledge aligned with Eurocentrism. Because Eurocentrism is so
pervasive, special attention must be paid to the framing of re-presentations
so that research findings will not be used to inaccurately depict Aboriginal
people and society. Amidst the various portrayals of Poplar River and the
World Heritage site initiative, my biggest challenge was to truthfully represent the community without romanticizing or perpetuating negative
perceptions in a way that could damage the community and its aspirations. Close relationships with individuals enabled me to examine the World
Heritage site nomination in Poplar River, listen to both local and grand
narratives, and then re-present those discourses in a way that contributed
to the mino-bimaadiziwin, the good life, of the community. CBPR is indeed
about listening to dominant narratives and retelling them from an action-
based perspective, where meaningful changes can be experienced by the
community.

Moreover, my experience with CBPR has also taught me that relationship building can be time consuming and expensive. Regular travel
to remote communities to catch up with First Nation members can be
costly, and researchers often have limited time and funds to conduct their
work. As a student, I depended on research grants and a flexible work
schedule to visit and work in the fly-in Anishinaabe community. Further,
relationship-building activities are not always recognized as part of the
work. For example, I conducted research for an organization that required
me to spend approximately twelve hours per day travelling to communities, purchasing snacks for meetings, and sharing tea with residents so
they could share their stories with me comfortably. However, I was paid
only for the regular eight hours of work because developing relationships with the community was not counted as part of the job. Likewise,
some organizations, governments, and ethics boards might view informal
methods of conducting research as inappropriate because they do not observe formalities and produce very few official documents, and because
data collection via informal means is seen as potentially inaccurate. The
fact that organizations and researchers who have little time and funds to
establish relationships continue to work with small communities, and
that informal methods that better align with Indigenous values and beliefs

are yet to be acknowledged, suggests the continued dominance of Western methods.

From the beginning, my objective was to work alongside Poplar River and to support its aspirations to ensure mino-bimaadiziwin. The CBPR process allowed me to engage so completely with the community that the line between research and life often blurred. The fieldwork component of the project has been more about friendships, adventures, feasts, tea times, travel, and stories than about data, statistics, and the number of interviews conducted. In this way, CBPR moves away from a study of the informant and toward a communal process of working for shared goals.

The Rest Is History: Some Conclusions

I believe that CBPR is an intellectually vibrant process that can help researchers become better investigators and activists. Fieldwork represents one of the best methods to identify the needs and uniqueness of Indigenous communities. CBPR can shift our understanding of indigeneity and how we talk about the relationship between the colonizer and the colonized. It is about being connected to the community versus looking at it from the outside. For me, it is also about learning how to navigate my role as non-Aboriginal, as a female, *and* as a researcher in a First Nation. CBPR gave me access to intricate knowledge and profound friendships that would not have been available through other research methodologies or positionalities.

Exploring the complexity, richness, and depth of the community at the local level enabled me – as a scholar, researcher, and individual – to critically reflect on my own work and the World Heritage site nomination. Rather than confining research to one theory, method, or discipline, CBPR allows for the integration of a variety of philosophical ideas and ways of knowing. It requires the researcher to be physically present in the community to better understand grassroots voices. CBPR requires scholars and local Indigenous critical thinkers to work together and exchange their knowledge, experiences, narratives, and even tea so that changes can be made at the local level and in society as a whole.

As a non-Aboriginal researcher driven by action that influences social change, I was determined from the outset that my work would contribute to Poplar River and would not extract anything from it. Knowing that the relationship between Aboriginal communities and researchers is often strained, I attempted.to redefine that relationship in my own way. One of my goals was not to do research for its own sake. Rather, I wanted to facilitate opportunities for Aboriginal resource stewardship, provide another perspective or case study to support Aboriginal rights, and supply results that helped address the economic needs of the local community. The unique needs of diverse Indigenous groups demand comprehensive examination to identify the distinct position, character, and aspirations of each one. This meant that I needed to hear local voices and to present and share them through the dissemination of research reports.

The research process allowed for interaction, active learning, and dialogue between two worlds that would otherwise rarely communicate: the Aboriginal community and academia. Establishing trust between these worlds created opportunities for growth, ongoing alliances, and supplementary projects that build on local capacity. CBPR was a tool to assist the community in the World Heritage site nomination and in its broader aims toward self-determination. Its perceptions about the importance of the land and resources to mino-bimaadiziwin show that Indigenous people continue to rely on the land and that this UNESCO site is as much a cultural landscape as it is a site of natural beauty.

Finally, a research process that respected the socio-cultural constructs of mawadishiwe (visiting), odaniibiishimidaa (let's have tea), and dibaaji-mowinan (stories) provided me with a deeply rewarding experience. Most importantly, however, I hope that the research we did together will be useful to Poplar River in years to come.

ACKNOWLEDGMENTS

I would like to say *gichi-miigwech* to Poplar River First Nation for enduring my presence to this day, for welcoming me, for the friendships made, and for putting up with my numerous questions and academic expectations. This publication and much of the research would not have been completed without the generous support from the Manitoba Research Alliance, the Social Sciences and Humanities Research Council, and the Northern Scientific Training Program. I take full responsibility for any errors in what is written here, which is grounded in my own reflections and experiences.

REFERENCES

Brody, Hugh. 1975. *The People's Land: Eskimos and Whites in the Eastern Arctic.* Harmondsworth: Penguin.

–. 2004. *Maps and Dreams.* Vancouver: Douglas and McIntyre.

Brown, Alison, and Laura Peers. 2005. *Pictures Bring Us Messages/Sinaakssiiksi Aohtsimaahpihkookiyaawa: Photographs and Histories from the Kainai Nation.* Toronto: University of Toronto Press.

Brownlie, Jarvis. 2003. *A Fatherly Eye: Indian Agents, Government Power and Aboriginal Resistance in Ontario, 1918–1939.* Don Mills: Oxford University Press.

Cruikshank, Julie, in collaboration with Angela Sidney, Kitty Smith, and Annie Ned. 1990. *Life Lived Like a Story: Life Stories of Three Yukon Native Elders.* Lincoln: University of Nebraska Press.

Ermine, Willie. 2007. "The Ethical Space of Engagement." *Indigenous Law Journal* 6 (1): 193–201.

Feit, Harvey. 1995. "Hunting and the Quest for Power: The James Bay Cree and Whiteman Development." In *Native Peoples: The Canadian Experience,* ed. R.B. Morrison and C.R. Wilson, 2nd ed., 101–28. Don Mills: Oxford University Press.

Kulchyski, Peter. 2005. *Like the Sound of a Drum: Aboriginal Cultural Politics in Denendeh and Nunavut.* Winnipeg: University of Manitoba Press.

Nadasdy, Paul. 2003. *Hunters and Bureaucrats: Power, Knowledge, and Aboriginal-State Relations in the Southwest Yukon.* Vancouver: UBC Press.

Pawlowska-Mainville, Agnieszka. "Using the Global to Support the Local: The Pimachiowin Aki UNESCO World Heritage Site at Asatiwisipe Aki through Intangible Cultural Heritage." PhD diss., University of Manitoba, Winnipeg.

Richardson, Boyce. 1991. *Strangers Devour the Land.* White River Junction, VT: Chelsea Green Publishing Company.

Said, Edward W. 1978. *Orientalism.* New York: Vintage Books.

Smith, Linda Tuhiwai. 1999. *Decolonizing Methodologies: Research and Indigenous Peoples.* New York: Zed Books.

Spivak, Gayatri Chakravorty. 1999. *A Critique of Postcolonial Reason: Toward a History of the Vanishing Present.* Cambridge, MA: Harvard University Press.

Tanner, Adrian. 1979. *Bringing Home Animals: Religious Ideology and Mode of Production of the Mistassini Cree Hunters.* Social and Economic Studies, No. 23. St. John's: Institute of Social and Economic Research.

8

Systemic Violence in Winnipeg's Street Sex Trade
Methodological and Ethical Issues

MAYA SESHIA

Violence is common in Winnipeg's street sex trade. Since the late 1980s, there have been at least twenty recorded unsolved murders of women and transgendered women who worked in this trade (CBC News 2007), and women continue to go missing, especially from the West End and North End, two marginalized and stigmatized inner-city areas of Winnipeg. Indigenous women are overrepresented in the city's street sex trade and are disproportionately the targets of this violence (Kingsley, Krawczyk, and Mark 2000). The circumstances that brought them to the streets, along with the dehumanization and violence they encounter, are rooted in past and present colonialism (Razack 2002). Some attacks are motivated by gendered and racist violence (Comack and Seshia 2010). In many cases, women's bodies are literally evicted from the city, dropped off or disposed of in isolated fields on its outskirts. Sherene Razack (2014, 60) observes that this spatial racial urban cleansing "inscribes settlers' claims on the ground and upholds the racial order on which colonialism depends" (see also Bourgeois 2015; Lowman 1998; Kingsley, Krawczyk, and Mark 2000). In short, anyone who wishes to comprehend Winnipeg's street sex trade and the violence experienced within it must view it through a lens of colonialism – and the gendered racial, spatial, and classed violence colonialism entails.

Some research does focus on violence directed at adult street sex workers in the United States and Canada (Fraser and Lowman 1995; Lowman 1998, 2000; Dalla 2002; Prenger 2003; Lewis et al. 2005; Jeffrey and MacDonald 2006, 89–93). However, in-depth studies specific to Winnipeg are limited (Brannigan, Knafla, and Levy 1989; Gorkoff and Runner 2003; Nixon and Tutty 2003a, 2003b; Seshia 2005; Brown et al. 2006; Canadian National Coalition of Experiential Women 2006, 19–30). Thus, in 2007, I undertook a project that examined systemic violence in Winnipeg's inner-city street sex trade. The research involved close collaboration with an inner-city health, outreach, and resource centre for women and with individuals who worked in the street sex trade or had done so in the past. It built on relationships I had already formed and work I had done with the organization and the individuals who use its services (Seshia 2005). In a 2005 project, I had conducted qualitative research with women and transgendered women who worked in the trade. Participants in this study stressed that the dehumanizing violence they encountered on the streets was a pressing issue. In addition, staff at community organizations that provided support to sex workers expressed concern about the violence, and this too provided impetus to further examine the nature of and solutions to this problem.

The 2007 project used qualitative and quantitative research methods. It was guided by the idea that experiential women – women who have been or are in the street sex trade – are the most knowledgeable about the subject and best able to articulate their experiences and provide solutions to the violence. Participants are seldom consulted respectfully, so a goal of the research was to provide a space for them to voice their opinions and advocate solutions. Twenty diverse women – artists, activists, inner-city community members, students, mothers, daughters, sisters, and aunties – were key contributors to the project. Participants were asked about their perceptions of and experiences with violence in the sex trade, and they were also asked to share their ideas about how to diminish it and to increase their safety. To uncover information about the nature of violence, I quantitatively analyzed "bad date" and "street hassle" reports. Drawing on participants' opinions and the findings from the quantitative analysis, I attempted to answer two questions: What factors explain this violence? What strategies might be taken to address it?

The views of participants, coupled with findings from the bad date and street hassle reports, led to the conclusion that violence is systemic, constituting a pattern that is gendered, racialized, class-based, and spatialized in nature (Goulding 2001; Razack 2002; Amnesty International 2004;

Comack and Seshia 2010; Seshia 2010). There was no single cause; instead, a fusion of factors motivated attacks. Street sex work takes place in the marginalized spaces of the inner city, where violence can be perpetrated with little consequence or care (Razack 2014, 2002). Canada's prostitution laws and the view, expressed by some police officers, that violence simply "comes with the streets" intensifies the spatial marginalization and brutality. In Winnipeg, street sex workers are often poor and racialized, and are further stigmatized because of their occupation and inner-city residency, and sometimes because they are transgender. In combination, these factors produce an exceptionally violent environment in which assaults are common, normalized, and tacitly accepted by dominant society, the police, and the law. In addition to law reform, long-lasting solutions involve addressing sexist, racist, and colonial attitudes that mark some people as less human, as well as root causes – such as poverty, and past and present colonialism – that lead to the overrepresentation of poor and often racialized individuals in Winnipeg's street sex trade (Seshia 2010).

Research on violence in the sex trade raises a number of ethical and methodological issues, which are magnified when the project involves interviews with the workers themselves. The politics of researching and writing about the sex trade have generated a great deal of scholarly debate, and much literature exists on the controversies associated with interviewing sex trade workers (Bowen 2005; Cwikel and Hoban 2005; Davidson 2008; Jeffrey and MacDonald 2006; Martin 2013; Razack 1998; Sanders 2006; Shaver 2005). Developing an ethical methodology was one of the most crucial yet challenging aspects of this project. I grappled with the following questions, which I still struggle to resolve: How can the power imbalances between the researcher and participants best be addressed? Is the project exploitative? Does it make a difference? Who ultimately benefits from it?

Locating the Academic Researcher in the Research

Maddy Coy (2006, 428) notes that, "in social research, the researcher is rarely subject to the same scrutiny as [the] researched." However, since the 1990s and especially after 2000, a positive shift has occurred, and those doing research are increasingly being subjected to much-needed critical inquiry. Scholars who write about the trade have been faulted for position-ing themselves as the "experts." In consequence, the knowledge and voices of the workers are silenced, and research that may not accurately reflect the realities of their occupation is publicized. To avoid this imbalance of power, Margo St. James observes that "any theory that comes out about prostitution should come from the inside out, not from the outside in" (quoted in Bell 1987, 86). In addition, the desire to rescue women from prostitution and/or a prurient interest can motivate academics to study sex work and sex workers.[1] Coy (2006, 428) asserts that there is "an element of voyeurism and fascination born of the othering of women who sell sex and the perceived transgression of codes of 'femininity.'" Razack notes that such motivations compel some academics to travel into spaces of prostitution and have fleeting investigative encounters with women whom dominant society constructs as deviant. This type of research "is a planned, temporary foray into degeneracy that in the end only confirms the traveler in her position of privilege because she is able to emerge unscathed" (Razack 1998, 353). Such voyeurism "is precisely the process involved in a man's use of a woman's body in prostitution" (ibid.). Razack (ibid., 376) insists that scholars must begin to reflect critically on their own role as privileged social investigators who conduct fieldwork and write about prostitution.

Throughout the course of my project, I was troubled by my position-ality as an academic researching sex trade workers' perceptions of and ex-periences with violence. The topic had its genesis in the concerns of the workers themselves and of staff at community organizations that provided support to them. I strove to incorporate their advice about how the project should develop. In various ways, I attempted to give back by volunteering for the organizations and by being involved in activism around the topic. Nevertheless, I constantly questioned my role. What right did I have to ask such deeply personal questions? Whose knowledge was being privileged? What power dynamics did the project involve? And why was I even under-taking such work? Contemplating these questions, confronting the possi-bility that the project might be exploitative, and frequently engaging in obsessive self-reflection was paralyzing. Paradoxically, this process of self-reflection, though essential, sometimes meant that the project became more about me than about the research topic and the participants. A balance between honest reflexivity and completing a project that best captured the views of participants was needed, but achieving it was not easy. I often found myself struggling with doubts about my role as a researcher and the power it involved, and I grappled with pessimism about what the research would ultimately accomplish.

My motive for undertaking this study was personal. As a mixed-raced woman, my reality has been shaped by my gender, class, and race. Reflecting on my own life experiences, I realized that oppressions and privileges regulated my life and the lives of those close to me. The desire to understand how my life is structured by relations of power, the yearning to better comprehend and take action against the oppressions that I and those close to me have experienced, and the longing to resist gendered, racial domination all compelled me to build solidarity with others who had somewhat similar but, importantly, also unique experiences. I also wanted to give back to organizations that had helped me become conscious about the power dynamics in Canadian society. In 2004, these partially selfish motivations led me to a women-centred organization, where I started volunteering at an inner-city drop-in that was open to individuals who were working or had worked Winnipeg's streets. Participants in the drop-in aided me in my undergraduate work. I hope that my work assisted with activism, education, and positive change, but the truth remains that I also benefitted academically from the knowledge of participants.

I continue to struggle with the question of whether this work perpetuates oppression and is itself exploitative. I anxiously wonder if I have occupied the same role as the "john." Speaking to this issue, the English Collective of Prostitutes asserts that academics who undertake research about sex work are "pimping off women as much as men have ever done" (quoted in Coy 2006, 428). Though I recognize my privileged status as a member of the academic community, I believe that this work is necessary to resist systems of domination and to combat the violence that is so prevalent in Winnipeg's street sex trade. In this regard, Razack's (1998, 365–66) reflection regarding her own work on violence against female sex workers is helpful:

> Positioning myself as a scholar ... and critic who wants to attend to the hierarchal relations and to the violence of prostitution, does not annul

the respectability that writing this article and taking this position brings. I still remain the female social investigator ... and my efforts to name the violence can be taken up as the traditional role of Lady Bountiful rescuing her unfortunate sisters ... [However], if I account for the violence and understand how it secures my own position of respectability, I can advocate for strategies that will end prostitution. In doing so, I contribute to undermining the systems of oppression that structure my own marginalization.

Guiding Principles, Research Methodologies, and Ethics

Coy (2006, 428) notes that individuals who work the streets are often the focus of research but have reaped few benefits from studies about their lives. In a similar vein, activists point out that research studies on Winnipeg's inner city in general, and Indigenous people in particular, "should be undertaken in a way that [is] participatory and respectful" and "should contribute in some way to the community" (Silver et al. 2006, 7). Following this advice, and in hopes of ameliorating power imbalances between the researcher and study participants, my project was guided by the relationship-based model of research. This model is premised on respect, reciprocity, long-term relationships, and "sincere, authentic investment in the community" (Kovach 2005, 30). It also enables participants to shape and reshape the research focus and direction.

This study was based on the idea that experiential women – women who have worked in the street sex trade – are the most knowledgeable about their experiences and are best able to provide successful solutions. This is consistent with the community development (CD) approach, which Peter Gorzen, Joan Hay, and Jim Silver (2004, 3) describe as "the process by which people in a neighbourhood participate collectively in working to solve problems that they themselves identify." From the outset, reciprocity, respect, and establishing ongoing communication between myself and the participants were critical to this project. Feminist participatory action models fit with these goals, and it therefore seemed fitting to use this methodology. Participatory action research "synthesizes the knowledge of communities and academics" (Coy 2006, 422). This methodology aims to produce holistic and practical knowledge by situating communities involved in studies as the most knowledgeable (ibid.). Jan Barnsley and Diana

Ellis (1992, 9) observe that the participatory model of research is "an on-going process for change" and is not viewed as "an end in itself." This methodology, combined with the ethics associated with the relationship model of research, requires the principal investigator to become involved in communities. This compels her to listen to and learn from the individuals who participate in the process. Developing genuine connections encourages the researcher to give back to those involved. This framework is conducive to self-reflection and reflexivity. As a result, the social investigator must scrutinize her own privileged role and power, as well as the impact of her presence and work on communities; reciprocity and critical self-reflection help "lessen the likelihood of exploitative forms of research that mostly benefit the careers of academic researchers" (Frisby et al. 2005, 368).

In accordance with these principles, I closely collaborated with the organization and the individuals who participated in the project. Two months before its scheduled start date, I submitted a proposed project outline to the organization's program director. She subsequently offered suggestions and expressed her support. Throughout the project, I provided regular updates at biweekly staff meetings, where the research process was discussed. I circulated research questions to individuals affiliated with the organization and adjusted the questions accordingly. I spent much of my time at the organization, where I worked in an office space, did volunteer administrative tasks for a Winnipeg grassroots coalition, and volunteered as a casual outreach worker at the drop-in. In short, I tried to give back as best I could.

In keeping with CD and the feminist participatory action methodology, I consulted women who had supported themselves by working in the street sex trade. To recruit participants, I displayed two posters at the organization, outlining the study's purpose. Information about the project also spread by word of mouth. As a result, a number of individuals who rarely utilized the organization's services took part in the study. In total, I completed twenty qualitative interviews between February and April 2008.

The interviews were loosely structured, and questions were open-ended (Barnsley and Ellis 1992, 14). We used a questionnaire guide, but it did not dictate our discussions. Interviews were not subject to time constraints, and though all participants said they felt comfortable being recorded, I always honoured any request to omit certain material. I asked them to reflect on the research dynamics and discussions, and to provide their thoughts and critiques. Due to their input, the wording of some questions was adjusted, and additional advice was integrated into the research process. As I wrote up the project, I spoke with a number of participants about its progress, and we discussed the paper's development. Whenever possible, I sought guidance from some participants about a variety of challenges I confronted.

Ethics Process

Respecting the emotional, psychological, and cultural dignity of participants, undertaking research that was just and fair, minimizing possible harms, and maximizing benefits were crucial to this project. The ethics application was reviewed by the community organization with which I worked, the University of Alberta Research and Ethics Board, and the University of Manitoba Research Ethics Board. The most important criterion for taking part in this study was the willingness to be involved. I ensured that interested individuals knew of its purpose and what would be done with the information they shared. For instance, before an interview began, participants were told that they had the right to withdraw their consent during and after it, and that they could decline to answer questions without penalty. They independently evaluated the project, discussed concerns, and asked questions, and they were required to read a detailed consent form. In addition, before they formally agreed to take part, I spoke in detail about the project, and we reviewed the consent form. Ensuring their anonymity was also crucial, so I always omitted participants' names and all identifying information. Consent forms, the recording device, and the transcribed data were stored in a locked file cabinet to which only I had access. Because so many people took part, and in order to maintain anonymity and to differentiate between participants' responses, pseudonyms were used.

At the end of participants' interview, participants and I reflected on the interview process and discussed concerns, questions, and emotions that might have arisen during it. Some expressed interest in talking further, outside the interview context. Thus, a number of conversations continued afterward, and participants were told that they could contact me if they wanted to chat on another day.[2] Everyone was given a card with the community organization's number and hours of operation. The card also listed the names and phone numbers of emergency counselling and shelter services.

In appreciation of participants' involvement, and to compensate for the income they lost during it, an honorarium was provided. This brought up a host of ethical dilemmas. Coy (2006, 425) notes that "payment can signify commodification of participants' knowledge and allow the researcher to exercise ownership of the knowledge." Prostitution Alternatives Counseling and Education, a Vancouver-based organization that undertakes programs and research led by sex workers, acknowledges the issues associated with compensation but makes a telling point: "When payment is offered to populations that are impoverished, the idea of free and informed consent appears compromised. Money or compensation will affect one's decision to participate. Does this then mean that only the rich can participate in research?" (Bowen 2005, 14). In recognition of this dilemma, I made clear to participants that receiving an honorarium did not tie them to the project. That is, they could withdraw from the study after the interview process. The interview would be erased, content from the discussion would not be used, and I would not ask participants to return the honorarium.

Reflections and Revisions

Before I began interviewing, I was versed in the literature about violence directed at sex workers. Much of it discusses the relationship between prostitution laws and the high levels of violence in the sex trade; however, I was not fully convinced that the law on communicating for the purposes of prostitution was responsible for the violence.[3] Thus, I did not initially intend to incorporate it into my analysis. Clearly, I had my own biased assumptions at that point.

Participants challenged my academic knowledge and biases. The issues they discussed were directly related to the communicating law. Thus, to do justice to these concerns, I altered the project's framework. I also sought guidance and advice from a number of participants, who provided invaluable feedback.

Quantitative Data Analysis

In addition to conducting qualitative interviews, I collected quantitative data to uncover details about perpetrators of violence. To do so, I analyzed bad date and street hassle reports from 2002 to 2007 published by the community organization. A bad date is any form of violence (physical, sexual, verbal, emotional, mental, economic, or spiritual) committed by a client or a predator posing as a client. A street hassle is violence inflicted by someone who is not a client or is not posing as a client (Comack and Seshia 2010, 204). These can include members of the public, resident groups, and police. Information about the offenders (such as their sex, age, race, and type of vehicle) as well as details about the incident (such as general location and type of abuse) were coded and then input into SPSS software for analysis. Identifying information was omitted (such as licence plate numbers, specific details about the car, and distinct characteristics of the person). To ensure the anonymity of the victim, identifying information was not recorded.

Focusing on street-level customers has important limitations. Leslie Ann Jeffrey and Gayle MacDonald (2006, 128) note that affluent men tend not to purchase sex from women who work the streets because they can afford escort and massage services. Similarly, Chris Atchison and John Lowman (2006, 283) state that numerous studies "suggest that communicating law enforcement [which predominantly focuses on the street-level sex trade] captures men mostly from the lower socio-economic segment of the prostitution trade." Because class is interconnected with race, and because men who are poor and racialized in Canada are over-policed, generalizations about street-level customers derived from police data and men surveyed in john schools are seriously limited. But Lauri Gilchrist reports a disturbing finding about the men who sexually exploit children in the Lord Selkirk Park neighbourhood of Winnipeg's North End. As she explains, its sexually exploited youth "are mostly Aboriginal children, some as young as eleven," and "the majority of men who come to this area are white and middle class" (quoted in Fontaine 2006, 118). I hoped that the bad date analysis would shed light on the perpetrators of violence and provide insight into possible systemic factors related to it. The analysis clarified the nature of the violence as well as its spatialized and gendered aspects: offenders were typically male, their targets were women and individuals who identified as women, and most incidents occurred in Winnipeg's inner city, though a significant portion took place outside city limits.

Policy Implications

My interviews with the twenty participants confirm the systemic gendered, racialized, classed, and spatialized character of the stigma attached to street sex work in the inner city (Comack and Seshia 2010; Seshia 2010). Combined, these factors dehumanize those who work the streets. The study relied on solutions recommended by participants whose lives were regulated by oppressive conditions, such as intense poverty; their most pressing concern was daily survival for themselves and their families. As a result, their suggestions were often practical and immediate (Seshia 2010). Most focused on enhancing everyday safety.[4] One woman recommended that outreach kits include a notebook and pen so that sex workers could record important information about bad dates and street hassles (such as licence plate numbers and descriptions of offenders). A handful of participants suggested longer outreach hours and a twenty-four-hour safe house. A two-spirited woman said, "More outreach or a safe house that is open twenty-four hours is what I would like to see. But, unfortunately, it lands on government funding so governments sure wouldn't value funding that because, again, we're sex trade workers."

A number of participants commented that assaults they had reported to police were not always taken seriously and that some officers felt that violence simply came with the streets. This blame-the-victim mentality, coupled with the fear of being arrested for prostitution, dissuaded the women from reporting assaults. To resolve this problem, a few participants suggested that a confidential sexual assault telephone line could be set up for sex trade workers. All thought that having access to a cell phone would increase their sense of security.

In terms of public policy changes, a number of women expressed the desire to have a safe space where they would not be criminalized. One recommendation was "having a safe place to go do dates ... even a safe house to go do dates." A second participant said, "In my opinion, any city, town, whatever, needs a safe prostitution place," and another woman commented, "I don't see the point of keeping it [prostitution] illegal." One woman felt that prostitution would "probably be somewhat safer, not a lot, but somewhat," if it were decriminalized. The Standing Committee on Justice and Human Rights and the Subcommittee on Soliciting Laws (Canada 2006, 86) agreed, reporting that "the social and legal framework pertaining to adult prostitution does not effectively prevent and address prostitution or the exploitation and abuse occurring in prostitution, nor does it prevent or address harms to communities." Notably, in December 2013, the Supreme Court of Canada struck down a number of prostitution laws, including those that affect the street-level trade, because they harmed and endangered the lives of sex workers. Laws relating to communicating for the purposes of prostitution, living off the avails of prostitution, and bans on brothels were deemed to violate Canada's Charter of Rights and Freedoms. They were subsequently reformed.[5] Further reforms could occur under the Liberal government, which came to power in 2015.

These solutions are critical, but as one participant noted, more is required to eradicate systems of domination that create gendered, racialized, classed, and spatialized systemic violence (Razack 1998, 375). These systems include white power and privilege, patriarchy, capitalism, and colonialism, all of which order, regulate, and sustain the Canadian nation-state. Long-lasting solutions to violence involve addressing sexist, racist, and colonial attitudes that dismiss some people as less human than others. Root causes – such as poverty and ongoing colonization – that lead to the over-representation of economically marginalized and often racialized individuals in Winnipeg's inner-city street sex trade need to be addressed. In the words of one two-spirited participant,

> Until you change the very fabric of what this country is built up and made out of, then we're not going to get anywhere. It's still going to be the same in fifty to a hundred years. More Aboriginals are going to be dying in vast numbers. More Aboriginal children are going to be dying ... It has to start with the very fabric of society ... Until the actual governing body or the main members of society actually wake up and smell the coffee, only then will we get somewhere.

Success and Limitations

This project was both ethically and methodologically challenging, yet it generated a number of positive outcomes. Foremost, it provided a crucial space for participants to voice their concerns and advocate solutions to violence. Participants frequently mentioned that simply talking about the problem was itself a healing process. Although some felt that the situation could not be improved, a number indicated that sharing their stories, brainstorming solutions, and advising me on how the project could better achieve its goals were powerful acts. Indeed, a number of the immediate recommendations pertaining to drop-in hours and outreach were shared with staff at the community organization. As a result, they conducted a survey to determine whether their hours and days of operation were meeting participants' needs. Beyond these small but significant outcomes, the stories that women shared, coupled with the quantitative findings, shed important light on the systemic nature of violence in the sex trade. Drawing attention to the gendered racial and spatialized nature of violent encounters is important because this information can be used to advocate for systemic change and comprehensive policies that get to the root of the problem. To address violence in the sex trade, we must first understand it and then name it (Jiwani 2006); the stories women shared and the solutions they offered assist with the monumental task of getting to the heart of systemic oppression in Canada.

Finding common themes in the narratives of twenty diverse women was extremely difficult. Each interview supplied a great deal of detailed and varied information, and every woman had her own concerns, solutions, and conceptions about safety and the sex trade. My academic position sometimes posed a challenge. For example, the original guiding questions were lengthy and wordy. Thankfully, participants made many suggestions on how to reframe them.

If I were to do this research over again, I would make certain changes. For example, though conducting a large number of interviews did confer benefits, I would decrease the number of participants interviewed. Taking this step would improve my ability to report back to interviewees by sharing transcriptions and drafts of the paper, which I couldn't always do with twenty people. I was able to report back to those who regularly came by the community organization, but a number of participants did not, and following up with them was difficult. Thus, I would reduce the participant number to ten. Moreover, I would divide the interview process into three stages and, if funding allowed, provide honoraria for each part. The first part would involve discussions about violence in the sex trade and solutions to address it. During the second part, we would go over the interview transcripts. Here, I would ask participants if the transcriptions were accurate, and I would delete, alter, or add any information they felt was necessary. In the third stage, I would present a draft of the paper to the participants and would integrate their comments, critiques, and suggestions into the final version. Finally, I would add a concluding phase to the research process – generating an action plan. Based on participant feedback, this would concentrate on drawing attention to the concerns articulated and developing strategies to implement both the non-policy and public policy solutions recommended. Creating a thorough action plan to raise awareness about violence and to organize around the solutions might result in comprehensive changes that could address the root cause of the violence.

Conclusion

This project revealed that violence in Winnipeg's inner-city street sex trade is gendered, spatialized, and racialized. Although it raised a number of ethical dilemmas, grappling with them was a necessary part of the project. In future studies, reducing the number of interviewees, altering the interview process, and developing an action plan would be useful. Successes of the project are difficult to quantify, but it provided a forum in which sex workers could voice their concerns and put forth solutions. Moreover, the act of naming the systemic nature of violence – violence that is all too often misconstrued or dismissed by dominant society in Canada – is in itself significant. In 2014, Prime Minister Stephen Harper characterized Canada's systemic gendered, racialized, colonial violence as a "crime" rather than "a sociological phenomenon" (quoted in Renzetti 2014, A2). In this context, naming systemic violence is a powerful act, one that is crucial if real change is to occur.

NOTES

1 Rescue strategies can result in colonial responses and can perpetuate colonial stereotypes (for instance, that black women, women of colour, and Indigenous women lack agency and are in need of assistance or saving).
2 Because these conversations occurred while I was volunteering as an outreach worker at the drop-in, not during an interview, ethical considerations prohibited their use, so they were not included in the project.
3 The "communicating law" was enacted in December of 1985. This law "prohibit[ed] communicating in a public place for the purposes of buying or selling sex" (Lowman

1998, 1). According to this law, adult sex trade work was technically legal; however, communicating for the purposes of prostitution was not. The aim of the law was to reduce the visibility of street sex work and respond to perceived nuisances (such as increased traffic and litter) and their impact on businesses (Prenger 2003, 5). This provision was intensely scrutinized. Academic and government funded reports repeatedly demonstrated that this law had not achieved its objectives (Canada 2006). More concerning, however, was the discriminatory nature of the law, as well as the violent atmosphere it fostered. The communicating law negatively implicated economically marginalized, often racialized, women who already experienced systemic violence (Canada 2006, 52–53). A number of studies also demonstrated that this provision decreased safety in the street sex trade and further contributed to violence within the sex trade. Among other things, this law forced sex workers to work in isolated areas; decreased the time they had to assess potential clients and negotiate services; and magnified distrust of police, making it less likely that sex workers would seek assistance and/or report incidents of violence (Lowman and Fraser 1995; Jeffrey and MacDonald 2006; Lowman 1998, 2000; Prenger 2003). In December 2013, the Supreme Court of Canada struck down a number of prostitution laws, including the communicating law.

4   For a fuller discussion of the gendered, racialized, and spatialized violence that participants encountered, see Comack and Seshia (2010) and Seshia (2010). In addition, solutions recommended by participants are given in more detail in Seshia (2010).

5   For an insightful discussion about the federal Conservative government's response to the Supreme Court decision – Bill C-36, the Protection of Communities and Exploited Persons Act – see Davies (2015). For background information and analyses of proposed law reforms in Canada, see Ka Hon Chu and Glass (2013) and Powell (2013). For an analysis of various opinions around law reform in Canada, see Lowman and Louie (2012).

REFERENCES

Amnesty International. 2004. "Stolen Sisters: A Human Rights Response to Discrimination and Violence against Indigenous Women in Canada." http://www.amnesty.ca/sites/default/files/amr200032004enstolensisters.pdf.

Atchison, Chris, and John Lowman. 2006. "Men Who Buy Sex: A Survey in the Greater Vancouver Regional District." *Canadian Review of Sociology and Anthropology* 43 (3): 281–96.

Barnsley, Jan, and Diana Ellis. 1992. *Research for Change: Participatory Action Research for Community Groups.* Vancouver: Women's Research Centre.

Bell, Laurie, ed. 1987. *Good Girls Bad Girls: Sex Trade Workers and Feminists Face to Face.* Toronto: Women's Press.

Bourgeois, Robyn. 2015. "Colonial Exploitation: The Canadian State and the Trafficking of Indigenous Women and Girls in Canada." *UCLA Law Review* 62 (6): 1426–63.

Bowen, Raven. 2005. "Research Ethics: A Guide for Community Organizations." Draft report produced for Prostitution Alternative Counseling and Education Society. http://www.pace-society.org/wp-content/uploads/2014/04/Community _Research_Guidelines.pdf.

Brannigan, Augustine, Louis Knafla, and Christopher Levy. 1989. *Street Prostitution: Assessing the Impact of the Law, Calgary, Regina, and Winnipeg.* Ottawa: Department of Justice Canada, Research, Statistics, and Evaluation Directorate.

Brown, Jason, Nancy Higgitt, Christine Miller, Susan Wingert, Mary Williams, and Larry Morrissette. 2006. "Challenges Faced by Women Working in the Inner City Sex Trade." *Canadian Journal of Urban Research* 15 (1): 36–53.

Canada. Standing Committee on Justice and Human Rights and Subcommittee on Soliciting Laws. 2006. *The Challenge of Change: A Study of Canada's Prostitution Laws: Report of the Standing Committee on Justice and Human Rights.* Ottawa: Standing Committee on Justice and Human Rights. http://www.ourcommons.ca/ Content/Committee/391/JUST/Reports/RP2599932/justrp06/sslrrp06-e.pdf.

Canadian National Coalition of Experiential Women. 2006. *Nation Wide Focus Groups on Social Service Barriers, Violence, and Addictions: Final Report.*

CBC News. 2007. "Winnipeg's Murdered Women Deserve Task Force, Say Aboriginal Groups." CBC. September 6. http://www.cbc.ca/news/canada/manitoba/winnipeg -s-murdered-women-deserve-task-force-say-Aboriginal-groups-1.690739.

Comack, Elizabeth, and Maya Seshia. 2010. "Bad Dates and Street Hassles: Violence in the Winnipeg Street Sex Trade." *Canadian Journal of Criminology and Criminal Justice* 52 (2): 203–14.

Coy, Maddy. 2006. "This Morning I'm a Researcher, This Afternoon I'm an Outreach Worker: Ethical Dilemmas in Practitioner Research." *International Journal of Social Research Methodology* 9 (5): 419–31.

Cwikel, Julie, and Elizabeth Hoban. 2005. "Contentious Issues in Research on Trafficked Women Working in the Sex Industry: Study Design, Ethics, and Methodology." *Journal of Sex Research* 42 (4): 306–16.

Dalla, Rochelle, L. 2002. "Night Moves: A Qualitative Investigation of Street-Level Sex Work." *Psychology of Women Quarterly* 26 (1): 63–73.

Davidson, Julia O'Connell. 2008. "If No Means No Does Yes Mean Yes? Consenting to Research Intimacies." *History of the Human Sciences* 21 (4): 49-67.

Davies, Jacqueline M. 2015. "The Criminalization of Sexual Commerce in Canada: Context and Concepts for Critical Analysis." *Canadian Journal of Human Sexuality* 24 (2): 78–91.

Fontaine, Nahanni. 2006. "Surviving Colonization: Anishinaabe Ikwe Gang Participation." In *Criminalizing Women: Gender and (In)justices in Neo-Liberal Times,* ed. Gillian Balfour and Elizabeth Comack, 113–30. Halifax: Fernwood.

Frisby, Wendy, Colleen Reid, Sydney Millar, and Larena Hoeber. 2005. "Putting 'Participatory' into Participatory Forms of Action Research." *Journal of Sport Management* 19 (4): 367–86.

Gorkoff, Kelly, and Jane Runner. 2003. "Introduction: Children and Youth Exploited through Prostitution." In *Being Heard: The Experiences of Young Women in Prostitution,* ed. Kelly Gorkoff and Jane Runner, 12–28. Black Point, NS/Winnipeg: Fernwood/Research and Education for Solutions to Violence and Abuse.

Gorzen, Peter, Joan Hay, and Jim Silver. 2004. *Aboriginal Involvement in Community Development: The Case of Winnipeg's Spence Neighbourhood.* Winnipeg: Canadian Centre for Policy Alternatives–Manitoba.

Goulding, Warren. 2001. *Just Another Indian: A Serial Killer and Canada's Indifference.* Calgary: Fifth House.

Jeffrey, Leslie Ann, and Gayle MacDonald. 2006. *Sex Workers in the Maritimes Talk Back.* Vancouver: UBC Press.

Jiwani, Yasmin. 2006. *Discourses of Denial: Mediations of Race, Gender, and Violence.* Vancouver: UBC Press.

Ka Hon Chu, Sandra, and Rebecca Glass. 2013. "Sex Work Law Reform in Canada: Considering Problems with the Nordic Model." *Alberta Law Review* 51 (1): 101–24.

Kingsley, Cherry, Marian Krawczyk, and Melanie Mark. 2000. *Sacred Lives: Canadian Aboriginal Children and Youth Speak Out about Sexual Exploitation.* Toronto: Save the Children Canada.

Kovach, Margaret. 2005. "Emerging from the Margins: Indigenous Methodologies." In *Research as Resistance: Critical, Indigenous, and Anti-oppressive Approaches,* ed. Leslie Brown and Susan Strega, 19–36. Toronto: Canadian Scholars Press/Women's Press.

Lewis, Jacqueline, Eleanor Maticka-Tyndale, Frances Shaver, and Heather Schramm. 2005. "Managing Risk and Safety on the Job: The Experience of Canadian Sex Workers." *Journal of Psychology and Human Sexuality* 17 (1/2): 147–67.

Lowman, John. 1998. "Prostitution Law Reform in Canada." Draft paper. http://184.70.147.70/lowman_prostitution/HTML/ProLaw/propol.pdf.

–. 2000. "Violence and the Outlaw Status of (Street) Prostitution in Canada." *Violence against Women* 6 (9): 987–1011.

Lowman, John, and Laura Fraser. 1995. *Violence against Persons Who Prostitute: The Experience in British Columbia.* Technical Report. Ottawa: Department of Justice Canada, Research, Statistics and Evaluation Directorate.

Lowman, John, and Christine Louie. 2012. "Public Opinion on Prostitution Law Reform in Canada." *Canadian Journal of Criminology and Criminal Justice* 54 (2): 245–60.

Martin, Lauren. 2013. "Sampling and Sex Trading: Lessons on Research Design from the Street." *Action Research* 11 (3): 220–35.

Nixon, Kendra, and Leslie M. Tutty. 2003a. "'Selling Sex? It's Really like Selling Your Soul': Vulnerability to the Experience of Exploitation through Child Prostitution." In *Being Heard: The Experiences of Young Women in Prostitution,* ed. Kelly Gorkoff and Jane Runner, 29–43. Black Point, NS/Winnipeg: Fernwood/Research and Education for Solutions to Violence and Abuse.

–. 2003b. "That Was My Prayer Every Night—Just to Get Home Safe." In *Being Heard: The Experiences of Young Women in Prostitution,* ed. Kelly Gorkoff and Jane Runner, 69–85. Black Point, NS/Winnipeg: Fernwood/Research and Education for Solutions to Violence and Abuse.

Powell, Marie. 2013. "Moving beyond the Prostitution Reference: *Bedford v. Canada.*" *University of New Brunswick Law Journal* 64: 187–207.

Prenger, Jill. 2003. "Treat Prostitutes as Equal Canadians: A Case for Decriminalization and Federal Regulations." *Criminal Reports Articles,* 6th series, 1–17.

Razack, Sherene. 1998. "Race, Space, and Prostitution: The Making of the Bourgeois Subject." *Canadian Journal of Women and the Law* 10 (2): 338–76.

–. 2002. "When Place Becomes Race." In *Race, Space, and the Law: Unmapping a White Settler Society,* ed. Sherene Razack, 1–20. Toronto: Between the Lines.

–. 2014. "'It Happened More Than Once': Freezing Deaths in Saskatchewan." *Canadian Journal of Women and the Law* 26 (1): 51–80.

Renzetti, Elizabeth. 2014. "What Unites These Slain Native Women? An Inquiry Might Tell Us." *Globe and Mail,* August 22. https://www.theglobeandmail.com/opinion/what-unites-these-slain-native-women-an-inquiry-might-tell-us/article20180291/?arc404=true.

Sanders, Teela. 2006. "Sexing Up the Subject: Methodological Nuances in Researching the Female Sex Industry." *Sexualities* 9 (4): 449–68.

Seshia, Maya. 2005. *The Unheard Speak Out: Street Sexual Exploitation in Winnipeg.* Report. Winnipeg: Canadian Centre for Policy Alternatives–Manitoba.

–. 2010. "Naming Systemic Violence in Winnipeg's Street Sex Trade." *Canadian Journal of Urban Research* 19 (1): 1–17.

Shaver, Frances M. 2005. "Sex Work Research." *Journal of Interpersonal Violence* 20 (3): 296–319.

Silver, Jim, Parvin Ghorayshi, Joan Hay, and Darlene Klyne. 2006. *In a Voice of Their Own: Urban Aboriginal Community Development.* Winnipeg: Canadian Centre for Policy Alternatives–Manitoba.

9

Not Alone
Research as a Relational Process

SARAH COOPER with MAUREEN BARCHYN

A non-profit organization that provides services to Winnipeg families, Family Dynamics began working in public-housing complexes in 2002, establishing six family resource centres that offer programs to local tenants. Staff were curious to know how the people who used the programs felt about the centres and what kind of impact the programs were having on their lives. So, in 2010, Family Dynamics approached the Canadian Centre for Policy Alternatives–Manitoba (CCPA–MB) with a request to partner on a research study.[1] The CCPA–MB recognized the potential connections with its ongoing work in Winnipeg's inner city and the opportunity to build a relationship with an organization it had not worked with previously. It also hoped to learn more about the situation of low-income households outside the inner city and to consider what policies and practices might benefit them.

Established in 1936, Family Dynamics has evolved over time to meet the changing needs of families across the city. Its mandate is to "bring programs, partnerships and resources together to empower and strengthen families and communities."[2] Currently, one of its focuses is on low-income families living in public housing.

This research project arose from the realization that low-income communities face social and economic structural injustices, including access to information about their lives. Both the CCPA–MB and Family Dynamics felt strongly that the project should not contribute to the marginalization of the participating communities and that attention to process was important in recognizing and addressing issues of power. For this reason, the project's approach was modelled on participatory forms of research that were intended to give the communities a voice in research design and implementation.

The CCPA–MB hired me (Sarah Cooper) as a principal researcher. For about sixteen months, I worked with staff at Family Dynamics and at the resource centres, and with community interviewers to design and carry out the research plan. Drawing on conversations with staff at Family Dynamics and the CCPA–MB, this chapter offers my perspective on the benefits and challenges that emerged through the research process.

The Family Resource Centres

Family Dynamics operates six family resource centres in Winnipeg. All are situated in public-housing complexes outside the inner city, and range in size from 42 units to 147 units. Westgrove Family Resource Centre is at the western edge of the city, in Charleswood; Tuxedo Family Resource Centre is southwest of downtown; Mayfair Family Resource Centre lies just outside of downtown, in Osborne Village;[3] St. Anne's Family Resource Centre and Woodydell Family Resource Centre are in St. Vital, toward the south end of the city; and Community Resource Centre is in Transcona, toward the eastern edge of Winnipeg. Each centre has two staff coordinators who administer and run the programs, and manage the many volunteers and part-time staff.

Participation rates at the centres are high. People come to access the food bank or use the washing machine, phone, fax, and computers. They also take part in cooking, literacy, arts and crafts, and children's programs (among others), as well as annual community celebrations for special days. Many stop by for a cup of coffee or a snack, for a chat with a neighbour, or just to get out of the house for a while. The centres play an important role as neutral spaces where everyone is welcome, and they enable people to access resources and meet basic needs without having to travel downtown, where many social services are located.

The approach of the resource centres is guided by the Woodydell Model. Developed at the Woodydell Family Resource Centre (the first Family Dynamics centre), this is an educational model that puts family relationships, particularly parent-child relationships, at the core of the community. The model builds on the strengths of each person in creating a responsive, respectful, and nurturing space at the centre. It relies on grassroots leadership and engagement to provide programs and activities.

This model reflects Family Dynamics' long-term commitment to the communities with which it works. By hiring local residents as much as possible and encouraging volunteerism in its centres, Family Dynamics builds capacity and skills, and contributes to a sense of dedication and accomplishment in the community. The model also shifts much of the decision making about the centres to the tenants of the complexes. Each centre has an advisory committee, where all interested tenants can have a say in what happens there. Through the networks and connections of Family Dynamics, tenants can access resources and programs, and can, through the advisory committees, decide which resources and programs will best serve their needs. Staff coordinate the meetings, and decisions are made by consensus among those who participate. Staff provide support and act as liaisons with Family Dynamics, funders, and other partners to carry out the decisions made by the advisory committee.

The focus of these committees – and that of Family Dynamics – is to identify and address local priorities, and to support the community in meeting its own needs. Past experience has shown that resource centre programs will not succeed if tenants are uninterested or opposed; they simply do not participate. Having tenants take the lead in deciding on programming ensures a greater chance of success and also means that they are more likely to get programs that are useful to them. As a result, each centre has a different character and provides different programs and resources, depending on local priorities. Ensuring that the research project had the support of the advisory committees was a key element in developing the research plan.

Framing the Research

Our intent was to create a process that would benefit the community. The CCPA–MB had already used participatory research (see, for example, MacKinnon et al. 2008), and it fit well with Family Dynamics' grassroots approach to community development. The project was largely led by staff – by the primary researcher in partnership with staff at Family Dynamics – but the advisory committees and community interviewers were important in determining how it would be carried out. This approach begins with the idea that the people who live in poverty – in this case, the tenants who visit the resource centres – have important experience and knowledge, and that they have a right to participate in discussions and decisions that will affect their lives (Bennett and Roberts 2004). It is intended to include both research and action, focused not just on gathering information but also on applying it to change policies or practices that marginalize or oppress (Brown and Strega 2005). Participatory research is also a co-learning process, in which researchers and community members learn together (Israel et al. 2008).

To this end, the project relied on input from tenants who lived in the public-housing complexes. Through meetings with the advisory committees, they contributed to the research design and methods, and to gathering and analyzing the data for the final report. The project also enabled them to provide anonymous feedback regarding possible improvements at the resource centres. A key aspect was the hiring of interviewers from the complexes. In part, this was intended to build capacity, as it enabled the tenants to gain skills by working as members of the research team. However, it also benefitted the project itself, because the interviewers had significant expertise through their lived experience of public housing. They were familiar with the challenges that interviewees faced and had a common frame of reference for discussing the centres and the complexes. This lessened the distance between interviewer and participant, and may have helped the latter to feel more comfortable in sharing their thoughts (MacKinnon et al. 2008).

Shawn Wilson (2008) notes that Indigenous research is grounded in a practice of relationality. He describes many types of relationships that a researcher or research participants might bring to a project, including with other people, with the environment and the land, and with ideas and knowledge. Relationships with historical processes and power dynamics that oppress or privilege could also be included here, as they frame how we connect with others and with the environment around us. These links inform how people understand and engage with the world, and in a sense, we know the world through our relationships. Developing a relational approach to research requires recognition of the relationships around us and understanding that everyone is shaped by his or her life experiences and associations with others. It also requires accountability to the relationships and consideration of them over the long term.

As our project unfolded, a relational research model emerged. Throughout, it depended on discussion, negotiation, and compromise. It became a web of relationships that included the researcher, other members of the team, the participants, and beyond them the people who lived in the six public-housing complexes. The research was affected by relationships with structural factors such as poverty, discrimination, and colonialism. It was also affected by each person's relationship to the environment in which the research was conducted – the family resource centres – and by his or her life experiences. The project relied on relationships of trust and necessitated consideration of the long-term sustainability of the link between researcher and community (Cargo and Mercer 2008). It depended on the participants' relationships with the resource centres and with staff. It also depended on the ongoing connection between Family Dynamics and the communities, in some cases predating the establishment of the centres, and on the commitment of Family Dynamics to continue working there.

Each of these relationships interacted with, and pulled on, the research process differently. The project was not a top-down process of data collection and analysis that culminated in a final report. Instead, it was a process of engagement and interaction – a ceremony, as Wilson (2008) puts it. Although projects commonly focus on their end product, the process itself was the core of this research. It is here that ideas and relationships develop; it is here that effects beyond the initial goal of the research itself emerge.

Relationships along the Way

The goal of our project was to better understand the impact of the family resource centres on the public-housing tenants who used them. Through interviews with tenants, focus groups with centre staff and volunteers, and surveys distributed to every household in the six complexes, the project painted a picture of how the centres helped tenants meet every day needs and how they affected individuals, families, and communities. The final report, *You Know You're Not Alone: Community Development in Public Housing* (Cooper 2012), describes these findings, using the words of the participants themselves. It also presents a number of recommendations for policies and programs that would strengthen the centres and, through them, the communities they serve.

The research process consisted of three main stages: preparation, data collection, and analysis and conclusions.

Preparation

The preparation phase laid the groundwork for everything else. It consisted of gathering the contextual data that would inform the data collection and analysis, and outlining the research process. More importantly, it was about beginning to develop the relationships that would sustain the project.

Several existing relationships made it possible to begin the process. The Manitoba Research Alliance, which is housed within the CCPA–MB, researches strategies to address poverty in Manitoba; the groundwork it has developed for participatory research and the relationships it has nurtured over several years helped to frame the approach of this project. The project's methodology was reviewed and approved by the University of Winnipeg's Human Ethics Research Board to ensure that participants would be treated fairly and ethically. The Province of Manitoba, which funds the Family Dynamics resource centres, agreed to provide funding through Manitoba Housing and Community Development to hire a principal researcher, as the project would examine issues relating to community development in the six public-housing complexes. In addition, the United Way of Winnipeg contributed funding for honoraria for the community interviewers and interviewees, and for interpreters and childminders to reduce barriers to participation in interviews.

Perhaps the most obvious relationship is between Family Dynamics and the CCPA–MB. We began with meetings between the staff of these two organizations and between myself as the principal investigator and the staff and community members at the resource centres. These meetings set the tone for the project. The staff met in the Family Dynamics office and talked about what the project might look like. They provided background on the centres and on what they hoped to get from the project. The CCPA–MB staff talked about their approach to research. We agreed that the research process and outcomes needed to benefit the communities and that the more they could be involved, the better. Both Family Dynamics and the CCPA–MB were interested in taking a participatory approach.

Thus, we decided that the next step should be to introduce the idea to the advisory committees. At each centre, I presented the project to staff and the committees to hear what they had to say about it. These meetings established the connections that would underpin the project. They drew on the existing relationships between the centres and the housing complexes, relationships that came out of the deep commitment to the community demonstrated by Family Dynamics and by the staff at each centre. Through these relationships I was able to connect with the tenants and staff.

Attending advisory committee meetings enabled me to see each centre and to meet the staff and some of the tenants. By visiting each centre at least three times during the course of the research, I got to know the communities, and they got to know me as well. I was able to better understand the differing approaches of the centres and to learn about the programs they offered.

The initial visits also enabled the advisory committees to ask questions and provide input about the research: how it would be carried out, who would participate, how they would be selected. These discussions also raised issues of how the information would be used and whether the final report would be available to the community. The research outline that was developed through conversations between researchers and Family Dynamics staff included interviews with tenants as well as focus groups with staff and volunteers. The advisory committees wanted to know how interviewees would be selected, how to ensure that the selection process was fair, and who should participate.

At one centre, the committee wanted to include as many interviewees as possible. However, the funding covered only eight interviews per centre, a limit that could preclude other people from participating in the study. Given that even the smallest of the six complexes had 42 households and the largest almost 150, eight interviews per centre did not seem like many. How could we include as many voices as possible in the research? Also, staff were interested in learning why some people chose not to come to the centres. To address these concerns, we decided to distribute a survey to every household in each complex. The surveys would be anonymous and would enable everyone to give feedback on the centres.

Once the initial groundwork had been laid, the next step was to hire interviewers. Through discussions with Family Dynamics staff, we decided to hire one person from each centre to conduct the interviews. The centre staff did the hiring, as they had a process in place for employing community

members for short-term casual work. They understood the complex relationships in the centres and housing complexes, and had a sense of
who would best handle the sensitive dynamics of interviewing their neighbours. Interviewers needed to be good listeners, reliable, and willing
to attend job training. Through this process, six excellent interviewers
were hired.

To ensure that the interviewers had the necessary skills, we held a
training session with them and Family Dynamics staff. Over the course
of a morning, we talked about the purpose of the research, what the interviewers would be doing, and how they would do it. We discussed some
technicalities of interviewing and the importance of maintaining confidentiality. We then reviewed the interview guide and the use of the digital
recorders, and ended with some practice interviews. We also shared lunch
to get to know each other and build a sense of the team.

Data Collection

In the data-gathering process, tenants, staff, and volunteers shared significant ideas and experiences through interviews, surveys, and focus groups.
The staff at the centres were very accommodating and welcoming, and
they played a key role in facilitating the research. They distributed the
surveys, worked with the interviewers, and included the research project
in advisory committee agendas.

The interviewers worked with the staff to select the participants and
set up the interviews. Notices were posted in the centres, and flyers were
distributed to each home to let people know about the project. Care was
taken to ensure that all tenants had an equal opportunity to participate.
Child minding and language interpretation were offered, and interviews
were held at the centres, which were familiar and neutral spaces. Potential
interviewees signed up at the centres, and if more than eight people did
so, their names were put in a hat and selected at random. Interviewees
received an honorarium to acknowledge their time and contribution.

As the interviews took place, surveys were distributed to each household and were also available at the centres for people to fill out. Several
people in each complex filled out the surveys, and a few even took the time
to mail them directly to the research office. Although the responses to the
surveys differed little from the comments made in interviews and focus

groups, they provided an additional avenue for participation and reinforced the opportunity to contribute to the project.

When the interviewers had completed their work, they too were interviewed. Although their responses may have been influenced by those of other participants, the scheduling of their own interviews gave them additional time to think about the questions and to consider their replies in a holistic context.

Once the interviews were under way, I began to work on the other major component of the project, focus groups with staff. The intent of these was to hear from staff and core volunteers about how the centres operated. Differing groups participated at each centre: in some, it was the staff, including the coordinators and family support workers; in others, both the staff and volunteers attended. The staff and volunteers were more involved than the tenants with the daily life of the centre and had a different view of its role. A focus group was also held with the management staff in the main office, who were responsible for longer-term strategic planning and decision making about the centres. They had a big-picture perspective on the purpose of the centres.

This variety meant that the conversation differed in each focus group, but all the discussions revolved around how to apply each community's strengths to address the challenges faced by the centre and the tenants. Conversations ranged from what staff and volunteers had learned through their experiences in the centres to how tenants – both as individuals and as families – and the community had changed and grown as they participated in resource centre programs. They also shared some of the challenges and turmoil that had arisen over the years as the centres established themselves, as well as some of their plans for the future. Many staff said that the focus groups were helpful in providing time away from the demands of the centre. The opportunities for conversation outside the confines and pressures of the regular program helped staff, volunteers, and tenants to reflect on the life of the centres and to consider strengths and opportunities for future directions.

Changes in the day-to-day life of the community affected people's level of engagement and how they were able to contribute. For example, when I attended a meeting at one centre, I noticed that staff seemed unusually quiet, and the atmosphere was strained. I learned later that a local child had been hit by a car the day before. It was not only the immediate family that was affected, but staff, volunteers, and other residents as well. This was a reminder that the daily experiences and relationships of all community members affected their participation in the project in both obvious and hidden ways.

Sometimes, these experiences related to interpersonal tensions, whether current or in the past. Throughout the course of the project, tension sometimes arose among staff, between staff and research team members, and among community members. Although most did not affect the research directly, they did require careful handling. In one instance, confidentiality was breached at a centre. The two tenants who were involved had a history of friction, with the result that tensions flared up between them and in the community. As the principal researcher, I felt responsible for the breach, so I consulted with staff at Family Dynamics and my research supervisor about how to proceed. I wrote letters of apology to the two tenants and hand delivered them, along with Maureen Barchyn from Family Dynamics. I also apologized to the staff at the centre, who had spent considerable time talking with the two tenants and mediating the conflict, which in the end seemed to be resolved satisfactorily.

Analysis and Conclusions

The last stage of the project consisted of analyzing the data, writing the final report, and relaying the findings to the communities. I visited the resource centres, sharing the preliminary analysis with the advisory committees to determine whether it made sense and if it reflected what community members had intended to convey. I also met with staff at Family Dynamics to share the findings. As the research process drew to a close, we decided to hold a celebration to acknowledge the work and contributions of the many participants in the project.

The community interviewers had spent a lot of time thinking and talking to their neighbours and fellow tenants about the questions in the interviews. This, plus their experience of the centres and public-housing complexes, meant that they were particularly well suited to identify the key issues and ideas that emerged through the research. We gathered again at the Family Dynamics office to talk about the data they had collected and about the preliminary findings. Each interviewer spoke about the themes that had arisen during their interviews, and as a group we identified the positive elements of the resource centres and the areas that could be improved. The interviews had also asked about what programs or elements could be added at the centres, and we spent some time prioritizing the many changes that had been suggested. This step was very helpful in defining the major themes of the interviews and in revealing the direction the analysis would take.

Once the initial analysis was completed, I returned to the centres to talk to tenants and staff, bringing a newsletter that summarized the purpose of the research and the initial results. I gave a short presentation on the findings, which was followed by a discussion period. This meeting was beneficial in two ways. First, it provided a forum for tenants who had not been interviewed, allowing them to share their ideas, to hear about the experiences of others, and to discuss the strengths and challenges in the resource centres. Second, the meeting supplied us with feedback from tenants and staff, revealing whether the information gathered – and more importantly, how it was interpreted and framed – accurately represented the views and experiences of the tenants. I had not expected them to be very interested in the findings, but in fact most were highly engaged, as they saw their lives reflected in the research. It validated their experiences and told them that many other people in the complexes shared those experiences. As I gave my presentation, many tenants nodded in acknowledgment or jumped in with comments. At each centre, they deepened the initial analysis by emphasizing and clarifying various points and adding new ideas. This helped to confirm that the tenants' perspectives were accurately represented and that the analysis was on the right track. It also furthered the analysis, moving the discussion to a deeper level.

Through the analysis, a tension emerged between the ideals of the Woodydell Model and the priorities identified by some tenants. I felt it necessary to include their voices, but I also wanted to ensure that I understood the Family Dynamics interpretation of the model, so I met with staff. We clarified that though the implementation of the model sometimes caused problems, it was constantly evolving to meet the needs of the centres. Although navigating this issue was a challenge, the research helped staff to better understand the tenants' concerns about the Woodydell Model.

Once the final report was completed, we held a celebration to recognize the efforts of the many people who worked in the study. From the research participants, to the resource centre staff, to the community interviewers, to staff who managed the project, each person contributed to the final product. This last milestone in the project brought together about sixty people from all the centres, the research team, and the participating and funding organizations, who gathered at the Woodydell Resource Centre, the first centre operated by Family Dynamics. There were snacks and drinks, and it was a beautiful spring day. Copies of the final report were available for all, and additional copies were sent to each resource centre for those who could not attend. We decided at the last moment to hold the event outside, as the indoor space was very crowded. Shauna MacKinnon, the CCPA–MB director, emceed the event, Maureen Barchyn spoke on behalf of Family Dynamics, I talked about the research findings, and Tammy Wilson, one of the community interviewers, spoke about her experience with the project. We also held a contest to find a cover image for the report; all the submissions were framed and displayed at the celebration, and the artist of the winning image was recognized. People ate snacks, visited, and enjoyed the spring sunshine.

Final Thoughts

Although the project finished in 2012, the relationships that it developed continue to have an impact. The resource centres still provide a common space in the public-housing complexes for people to gather and meet their neighbours. The interviewers' participation in the project provided them with practical work experience; indeed, one interviewer went on to work for Family Dynamics as a family support worker. The close relationship between CCPA–MB and Family Dynamics remains strong. In the last few years, the two organizations have partnered on a few more research projects, notably focusing on the refugee support programs offered by Family Dynamics.

The findings from this project were shared with Province of Manitoba policy makers, as well as the United Way and other funders. The current emphasis on evidence-based practice requires social service agencies to demonstrate that their programs are of value to their clients. Although it is relatively easy to collect quantitative data (such as how many people attend a given program), gathering data that measure changes in behaviour or self-esteem is more difficult. Reports such as this one provide qualitative evidence that the family resource centres are having a significant impact on individuals, families, and communities in the complexes. Family Dynamics uses the report as a fundraising tool and to illustrate how the centres benefit the families and individuals who use them. Its position has been strengthened by a report from a neutral observer that shows how the work being undertaken at the centres benefits the tenants and community.

By building on existing relationships and cultivating new ones, this project created a space to talk about the resource centres, with all their benefits and challenges, and became a process of hope and an opportunity for change. Involving relationship building, community interviewers, and a flexible approach that adapted to meet the needs of each community, it strove to tell the stories of the centres in the words of tenants, staff, and volunteers. Thus, it aligned philosophically with the capacity-building work already under way in each centre. In this case, the whole was greater than the sum of its parts.

Although the relationship building and research described here required more time and energy than a typical project, the validity of the process, the quality of the data, and the depth of the analysis were all stronger because the project design, methods, data collection, and analysis were not concentrated solely in the hands of the principal researcher. Instead, the resource centre advisory committees contributed to the design and methods, community interviewers used their lived experience in drawing out stories from participants, and both they and the advisory committees informed the analysis of the collected data. The end result was a stronger, more powerful report that built upon the skills and contributions of every person, and every relationship, that was part of the research process.

ACKNOWLEDGMENTS

The original project, "You Know You're Not Alone," would not have happened without the collaboration of many people. I acknowledge the contributions of the community interviewers, Rebecca McIvor, Shelley Nepinak, Hero Palani, Candice Reske, Jennifer West, and Tammy Wilson; the staff at the resource centres; and Maureen Barchyn,

Carol Billett, Sukhy Mann, and Holly Puckall at Family Dynamics. I would like to thank Lynne Fernandez, Jillian Glover, Shauna MacKinnon, Tim Scarth, and Karen Schlichting at the CCPA–MB for their support. I acknowledge the financial support of the Province of Manitoba and the United Way of Winnipeg's Organizational Development Fund. Thanks also to the anonymous reviewer for comments on this chapter.

NOTES

1 Until 2012, and during the time when the research project was under way, Family Dynamics was known as The Family Centre of Winnipeg.

2 Family Dynamics, n.d., http://www.familydynamics.ca/about/.

3 This centre is now closed, as is the public-housing complex. Family Dynamics has opened a new centre in Elmwood.

REFERENCES

Bennett, Fran, and Moraene Roberts. 2004. *From Input to Influence: Participatory Approaches to Research and Inquiry into Poverty.* York, UK: Joseph Rowntree.

Brown, Leslie, and Susan Strega. 2005. "Introduction: Transgressive Possibilities." In *Research as Resistance: Critical, Indigenous and Anti-oppressive Approaches,* ed. Leslie Brown and Susan Strega, 1–18. Toronto: Canadian Scholars Press.

Cargo, Margaret, and Shawna L. Mercer. 2008. "The Value and Challenges of Participatory Research: Strengthening Its Practice." *Annual Review of Public Health* 29: 325–50.

Cooper, Sarah. 2012. *You Know You're Not Alone: Community Development in Public Housing.* Winnipeg: Canadian Centre for Policy Alternatives–Manitoba. http://www.policyalternatives.ca/sites/default/files/uploads/publications/Manitoba%20Office/2012/04/You%20Know%20You%27re%20Not%20Alone%202012.pdf.

Israel, Barbara A., Amy J. Schultz, Edith A. Parker, Adam B. Becker, A.J. Allen III, and J.R. Guzman. 2008. "Critical Issues in Developing and Following CBPR Principles." In *Community-Based Participatory Research for Health: From Process to Outcomes,* ed. M. Minkler and N. Wallerstein, 47–66. San Francisco: John Wiley and Sons.

MacKinnon, Shauna, et al. 2008. *Is Participation Having an Impact? Measuring Progress in Winnipeg's Inner City through the Voices of Community-Based Program Participants.* Winnipeg: CCPA–MB.

Wilson, Shawn. 2008. *Research Is Ceremony: Indigenous Research Methods.* Halifax: Fernwood.

PART 3

DETOURS

———

10

Together We Have CLOUT
The Story of Making a Film Together

CAROLE O'BRIEN

This chapter chronicles the making of *Together We Have CLOUT,* a film that owes its existence to the quality of trust built during a number of collaborative community-based participatory research (CBPR) projects between non-Indigenous researchers associated with the Canadian Centre for Policy Alternatives–Manitoba (CCPA–MB) and the members of Community Led Organizations United Together (CLOUT), a coalition of community-based organizations. CBPR was used not only to explore the challenges faced by Indigenous residents of Winnipeg's inner city but also to disseminate positive stories about this neighbourhood, which is often perceived as a blight on the city. Chapter 2 describes the relationship between CCPA–MB researchers (referred to as "we" and "us" herein) and CLOUT, which enabled this film to be made.

Making a film is always a risky endeavour, requiring the juggling of several human, technical, and environmental factors that often cannot be controlled. Despite these innate challenges, film is a powerful tool for telling stories. As such, it can facilitate dialogue, a complex and messy practice in a decolonizing context since it can elicit strong emotions from our deeply rooted roles as oppressor and oppressed (Bishop 2002). Storytelling is also at the heart of CLOUT's approach to community development, where the stories and the voices of community members are regularly used in the design of programs and services – an approach that aligns well with Indigenous research models (Smith 2008). Film's strength as a tool for storytelling is the reason we considered using it as a community research tool. And ultimately, this prizing of stories as a means to transmit community knowledge was key to CLOUT members' ability to envision themselves engaging with us to make a film.

That this conversation occurred at all was due to the high level of trust that already existed between us and CLOUT members, in large part because the CBPR model we used resembled CLOUT's own Indigenous approach to community development. This trust was key to CLOUT's openness to using film to bring inner-city stories to a wider audience. It also contributed to CLOUT's ability to fully engage in the filmmaking process and accept our suggestion of filmmaker (the author of this chapter), in the belief that we would accurately and sensitively portray both the coalition and the story they wanted to communicate.

Making *Together We Have CLOUT* (O'Brien 2011) had a positive impact on CLOUT members, who were the primary participants in this collective project. However, the story of making the film actually begins in controversy, in a political decision that clearly demonstrated how little CLOUT's efforts at community development were understood by politicians and how much the stories of inner-city residents needed to be brought to a wider audience.

The Film Began with a Media Story

In the spring of 2010, the City of Winnipeg decided to donate more than $200,000 per year, for fifteen years, to support a plan by Youth for Christ (YFC) to construct and operate a recreation and drop-in facility in an inner-city neighbourhood. That the youth in this North End area were already being well served with culturally relevant drop-in programs by a network of community-based organizations (CBOs), some of which belonged to CLOUT, did not factor in the political decision to fund a faith-based group.[1] However, what surprised CLOUT members even more was the fact that YFC planned to proselytize youth as part of its programming. The City's failure to consult with the community or allow public assessment of the YFC project prior to making the decision was also frustrating to CLOUT. Like most Winnipeggers, CLOUT members heard about the decision from the local media (Roussin and Christensen 2010).

This failure to consult suggested two things: (1) the community-building work of CLOUT was little known outside the inner city, despite years of delivering services to residents, and (2) municipal politicians understood neither the need for culturally relevant programs in the inner city nor the nature of CLOUT's community development practices, despite years of collaborative research projects with CCP–MB that showed the effectiveness of its unique service model.

As CLOUT's research partners, we too were baffled by this political decision. It not only defied the positive results of CLOUT's work but also suggested that we had been less effective at disseminating CLOUT's story than we had hoped. Seeing the negative repercussions for CLOUT, we realized that we needed to heighten its visibility beyond the inner city. So, we were delighted when CLOUT members agreed to explore film as an alternative model as part of our ongoing participatory research projects. That I (Carole O'Brien) also happened to be a filmmaker also meant that I was naturally drawn to using the strong storytelling capabilities of film as a knowledge mobilization tool.

Systemic Barriers to Aboriginal Storytelling

Before shooting began, we met with CLOUT members to discuss what the film would include. We all felt it needed to be situated in the context of a city deeply divided and shaped by colonialism, systemic racism, and neoliberal capitalism – the backdrop to CLOUT's community development work in the North End and the everyday realities of Winnipeg's inner-city Aboriginal population (see Chapter 12 in this volume; MacKinnon et al. 2008). This division is also exacerbated by a large rail yard that separates the North End from the more affluent neighbourhoods to the south. CLOUT's story, which we tried to tell on film, is one of resistance to these dynamics and to mainstream social service delivery models.

The film enabled CLOUT members to break some of these systemic barriers and expose the complex colonial realities that underpin them. It also gave them a forum to describe their unique decolonizing and collaborative community development approach, which is based on listening to people's stories and foregrounding them in decisions about programming. In the film, one CLOUT member contrasted this approach with its mainstream counterpart: "We've done it the mainstream way and it doesn't work. We've been told by the community that it doesn't work. The model of CLOUT works and I think it's effective because ... it's about what we bring to the table and that's the voices of the people we work with." Another remarked, "It's a model that's respect. Believe that people have something to offer. If you try to help someone, then you need to know from that person what it is they need. And what they have already, you know?"

These comments also reveal the identity and role dissonance that fuels CLOUT members' resistance to the mainstream as they try to apply an Indigenous worldview to their community development practices. They work within (and despite) complex relationships with mainstream or colonial institutional structures, as well as between and across culturally diverse contexts (Baikie 2009; Hart 2009). This dissonance was key to the creation of CLOUT in 2003, during the Aboriginal Child Welfare Initiative devolution process in Manitoba, which saw a new governance structure developed to address Manitoba's poor track record of serving Aboriginal children and families (in response to recommendations of the Aboriginal Justice Inquiry). Many inner-city CBOs that worked to keep Indigenous children out of the child welfare system feared that the new model would focus on the mainstream approach, which was grounded in separation and intervention rather than integration. Although these CBOs supported the devolution of responsibility for Indigenous children to First Nation and Metis organizations, they were also concerned about being excluded from the process. Since CLOUT's inception, its collectivist nature has enabled member organizations to resist the mainstream approach to social services – a story that is clearly told by CLOUT members in the film.

CLOUT's Own Story of Resistance

Together We Have CLOUT alternates between scenes of CLOUT members enjoying themselves at various North End community gatherings and scenes in which these women, all directors of CLOUT member organizations, talk to the camera about their work. They describe their resistance to colonialism with decolonizing community development practices based on Indigenous values and teachings as well as their resistance to neoliberal expectations that social services be delivered homogeneously. Over the years, the women became critical of the increasingly restrictive, ineffective, and heavily bureaucratic funding structures imposed on them, and of the mainstream tendency to focus on single issues and/or on intervention rather than prevention. This approach did not work in the inner city, largely because it provided narrowly defined social services while systemically dismissing local knowledge and solutions. The CLOUT members who appear in the film were also frustrated by the multitude of short-term programs imposed by these funding structures as "a horrendous waste of talent and energy" (O'Brien 2013, 92) and by the resulting instability in their programming.

The women talk about how they resist these systems, mostly through conscientious communication. For example, to avoid competing for scarce program funding, they collectively determine which CLOUT organization is best suited to deliver a particular program, and the coalition as a whole then supports its proposal for funding. They also try to provide a continuum of services through the various CLOUT organizations as a tactic to decrease duplication while supplying comprehensive services and making the most of funding sources. As one women points out, "I think inner-city organizations really make a buck stretch. And there are a lot of resources out there that could be used in a much more effective way."

In the film, CLOUT members decry the time they waste in repeatedly explaining to funders how colonial complexities affect Aboriginal lives in the inner city. They speak of their frustration with the mainstream tendency to simplify complex and interrelated social problems such as poverty into separate parts. To them, homogeneous solutions are not appropriate for the inner city. As one CLOUT member explains, the use of "simple" language is part of the problem, since it obscures the complexity of everyday realities in the North End: "Trying to describe the solution, for CLOUT, it takes longer, because ... CLOUT is much more holistic and integrated. It isn't compartmentalized. You can't just deal with housing, without dealing with all the rest of it" (quoted in O'Brien 2013, 106).

CLOUT's criticisms of the increasingly restrictive neoliberal funding policy model are echoed by many progressive social researchers and analysts. They condemn the emphasis on efficiency, homogenization, and individualism in the marketplace (Keil 2002), which diminishes efficiency while widening the economic gap and creating more separation, more poverty, and more social instability (LaRocque 2010; Keil 2002; Bishop 2002). They point out that neoliberalism has severely weakened CBOs over the years: as governments pursue the neoliberal agenda, community-based organizations at the front lines are forced into becoming the public face of government cuts to social programs (Gough 2002), while the inherent inefficiencies of neoliberal funding models effectively turn CBOs into "unwitting allies" of the system (Storper 1998). Neoliberalism has also encouraged a shift away from public policy and accountability (Harvey 1992), favouring a charity model and band-aid solutions, a change that CLOUT members also disparage and try to resist.

In the film, they describe this resistance as a decolonizing practice that embraces complexity, difference, and interconnection. This collectivist and holistic practice is also effective from a programming perspective (MacKinnon et al. 2008), since it gives them a stronger voice and greater political influence. CLOUT members see this model – of building on people's strengths and cultivating local, grassroots relationships through listening and dialogue – as the source of their power to resist mainstream systems and to take political risks through a unified voice. One woman notes, "My power is that the community is behind me ... I have the power to bring people together, because they believe in what we do. And they see the results in what we do, and they are a part of it. So there's ownership. And they would fight for it also" (quoted in O'Brien 2013, 112). The power of this practice is evident in the contrapuntal quality of the women's voices in the film, as in this excerpt denouncing racism in Winnipeg: "Live their lives! Go through what they went through! And see how many tools you have to work with! And see how your life goes! Like, really *see* that!"

The Story behind the Camera

Our ability to support CLOUT along this new research journey in film depended on a few factors, the most crucial of which was our openness to decolonization as a practice that "questions institutional power and privilege and the rationale for dominance, and acknowledges the intertwining role state, societal and institutional structures play in producing and re-producing inequalities" (Hart 2009, 30). As a daily challenge to unlearn Euro-Western path-dependent social practices in "a complex renegotiation of values, knowledge, meaning, agency and power" (Porter 2010, 153), decolonization is also key to creating trust. As CLOUT's non-Indigenous research collaborators, we needed to follow the women's lead once they decided to make a film (LaRocque 2010; Davis and Shpuniarsky 2010; Hart 2009; Coulthard 2007; Alfred 2005), even as the nature of the project created many challenges for us. These decolonizing dynamics existed before the film began, and they developed further during the filming process. The reciprocity of our relationship was also key to our ability to speak up when Winnipeg's mayor and city council decided to fund the YFC project – a decision that defied the participatory approach of our collaborative research projects in the North End.

As Greenwood, Whyte, and Harkavy (1993) note, participatory research tends to produce new and creative solutions to problems. Conversely, it is common for conventional research methods to not address the complexity of everyday realities since they are narrowly focused and "often simplify problems to match them to the modest solutions they have at hand" (ibid., 189). This explains why conventional or orthodox research models tend to be ineffective when applied to Indigenous issues and people. In contrast, the film and the CBPR research projects that preceded it were effective because they were unorthodox. They also provided CLOUT members with time and space to envision creative new research approaches that made sense to them. In the end, the film project constituted a new solution to an ongoing problem for CLOUT, that of not being recognized beyond the inner city for its community development work.

Serendipity also played a role. In May 2010, when the political events that triggered the making of this film were unfolding, I started a summer internship at the CCPA–MB as a requirement for a master's degree in city planning. I was drawn to the centre because of its reputation for conducting CBPR in the inner city. I was also interested in exploring Aboriginal community development and working on research projects with Aboriginal community development practitioners. What I brought to the table was more than a decade of work as a filmmaker and reporter for the CBC. My arrival also coincided with the search by CLOUT and the CCPA–MB for a more visible and effective knowledge mobilization tool. Not only did my filmmaking experience enhance the local CBPR toolbox, but the project was important to me because it enabled me to try a new approach with film. I was especially grateful for the trust that already existed between the CCPA–MB and CLOUT members, because it meant that the latter trusted me as the filmmaker, solely on the recommendation of the CCPA–MB. This trust was key to our ability to work together, since we were all venturing into uncharted territory.

A Personal Story

The process of making this film and interacting with CLOUT members and hearing their stories enabled me to better understand the complex dynamics of decolonization, and led me to try to develop a decolonizing lens in editing, which would later create more personal questions about privilege and power. This learning process was prompted by a comment from a CLOUT member during filming. At the end of her interview, after the camera was turned off, she said, "You know, what we really need are translators." She was expressing her frustration about the need to continually explain the complexities of colonialism to funders or other potential partners. Her remark seemed self-evident to me, as I had reached a similar conclusion and felt that once I finished my degree my work as a community development practitioner would entail acting as a "translator." I was also reminded of LaRocque's (2010, 166) criticism of non-Indigenous academics who claim to use a decolonizing approach in writing about the views of Indigenous people while actually "blocking-out the Aboriginal voice." These comments cemented the decision I had already made – in the spirit of decolonization – to let CLOUT members' voices take centre stage in the film and keep narration to a minimum. I saw my role as translator/filmmaker as a process of consolidating CLOUT's message to make it clearer and therefore more accessible – a translation. After all, it was CLOUT's story we were telling. As Indigenous community development practitioners, CLOUT members were best positioned to witness the everyday in Winnipeg's inner city, and as Indigenous people they were also best positioned to interpret the consequences of current socio-economic policies for their lives. My role was to create a repository for their understanding of these systems as they affected them. I also took the position – in the spirit of reconciliation – that part of making things right meant trying to see what Indigenous people see and creating a structure that enabled viewers to see this as well.

There is no doubt that I achieved this simple translating goal to the satisfaction of the participants in the film. For instance, one CLOUT member said she appreciated my efforts to condense both CLOUT's views and her own, since she had a tendency to "ramble." She also liked the film's presentation of CLOUT's story and the clarity of its message. Another CLOUT member appreciated how the film allowed her to hear her colleagues speak about the same issues they all faced, albeit separately, in their own organizations. Similarly, another woman said she especially liked how the film allowed her to see CLOUT members together, as if speaking in the same place, since getting together was often a struggle for them. Given the pressures of their daily work, they rarely had the opportunity to gather and discuss these larger issues.

Being presented with a coherent big picture in the film, also made this CLOUT member realize that the coalition tended to take its raison d'être for granted. She praised the editing, which allowed the women's diverse personalities and styles of speech to shine through. She especially liked hearing the younger members of CLOUT express their views in language that differed from her own; listening to them speak about the experiences of their generation gave her hope for the future.

Naturally, I was pleased to hear these assessments, but the fact remains that I, a non-Indigenous researcher/filmmaker, had the power to make most, if not all, of the editing decisions. CLOUT members did not participate in the editing process: they did not choose which quotes to retain and which to discard, and did not determine the order in which images appeared. I was in charge of this task, an arrangement that the group had agreed upon (though I provided versions of the work-in-progress to the director of the CCPA–MB as the editing progressed). This freedom and hands-off work environment again reveals the extent of the trust in the research relationship. It also belies my privileged position on the project, one that, at best, allows me to state only that I translated the words of CLOUT members in a way that I believed other non-Indigenous people would understand. I cannot know that my translation is correct, since translation, much like colonialism, includes the power of the speaker to speak, a power that I possessed and that, in the spirit of decolonization, I could only try to mitigate.

Putting aside these questions, what I value about making *Together We Have CLOUT* is that it allowed me, for the first time, to express a growing decolonizing approach through the telling of a politicized story. I particularly like that the film disturbs existing discourses, in what hooks (2008, 5) describes as a practical engagement of crossing boundaries "defined as on the edge, as pushing the limits, disturbing the conventional, acceptable politics of representation," as well as a praxis of going "to take another look, to contest, to interrogate, and in some cases to recover and redeem." In my attempts at being political I also took to heart LaRocque's (2010) description of being Indigenous in a colonized world as being inside and outside at the same time – an unsettling position for Indigenous individuals, but which can also describe non-Indigenous people attempting to decolonize.

Another important outcome for me was that the film led to my thesis work on alliance building in planning – a field that is currently being challenged to decolonize, a tall order given planning's historical roots in colonialism. However, bright spots do exist in planning, as in Marcuse's (2012) call to planning activists to expose, propose, and politicize – an exhortation that also informed the film as an attempt to expose the complex lives of Indigenous Winnipeggers and then to present CLOUT's proposal for an alternative approach to social policy. Being widely accessible, the film itself also works well as a politicization tool. In the end, making the film operationalized and politicized CLOUT's desire to become more visible while also embracing a broader analysis of the dynamics that constrict its ability to build more capacity in the North End.

The Bigger Story

The CLOUT members who participated in the film project state that they benefitted from the experience – an outcome that aligns with CBPR. They add that the project remains useful and relevant to this day, years after its completion. They use it to educate existing and potential funders, at conference presentations to promote CLOUT's approach to community building, and to familiarize new staff and board members about the larger role that CLOUT plays in the North End. The film is also available through some CLOUT member websites.

Filmmaking is now part of CLOUT's toolbox as a strategy for community research, advocacy, and development. One woman told us that, had it not been for her positive experience of making *Together We Have CLOUT,* she would not have thought about making a film to promote an important community development project on which she was working. As she put it, "I am a firm believer in film now." For our part, as CLOUT's research partners, *Together We Have CLOUT* also led to a number of other film/research projects as knowledge mobilization tools to politicize stories about the North End and to break barriers and build bridges in Winnipeg (see Chapter 12 in this volume).

All these outcomes suggest that the film conforms to the usual outcomes of CBPR as an ongoing learning process, involving continual readjustments and change. It also aligns with the participatory action research features described by Greenwood, Whyte, and Harkavy (1993) since it integrated collaboration, local knowledge, diversity, and case orientation. And though its original purpose was to devise a new – and hopefully more effective – response to a frustrating local situation, it became an emergent process linking understanding and social action. And further, it solidified and expanded upon existing knowledge, achieving "important intellectual and practical results" due to its shift in focus "from internally-driven critique to real-world engagement, practice and critique, with all three components operating and interacting more or less simultaneously and continuously" (ibid., 187).

Linking understanding with social action via the film also strengthened relationships and deepened the trust between CLOUT and its community-based research partners. Creating this film made me a firm believer in CBPR.

Of all these outcomes, perhaps the most important is the suggestion that the film was a source of empowerment for all involved. To paraphrase Paulo Freire (2006), empowerment results from becoming aware of the political dynamics that surround you. And this is the spirit in which the film was made; it was an attempt by CLOUT's research partners to give something back to CLOUT and to create a space where its members could reflect on the colonial and neoliberal dynamics that constrict their everyday community development practice, culminating in a sense of power over these dynamics by defining them for oneself.

Perhaps the film's best feature was its ability to show the women's faces as they spoke in their own voice about their work. This was new to our efforts as research partners. The film also allowed audiences to see the "everyday" North End neighbourhood and some of the positive community-based activities that regularly occur there. CLOUT members especially valued being interviewed in the physical place they were talking about. That the film also presents ordinary activities that could occur in any Canadian town – community gatherings, locals enjoying hamburgers, and kids being treated to face painting and pony rides – contrasts with ongoing media images that depict the North End as a dangerous place, discouraging people from venturing into the area for fear of gangs and violence. Placing the women outdoors subverted these negative portrayals, while the everyday images of the North End normalize the neighbourhood in the eyes of non-Indigenous viewers. One CLOUT member commented,

> I see how people must see the inner city, how they see Aboriginal people and how they get a bad rap, you know. They don't see the joy and all the kids happy and cared for, and all the people in the inner city who are working and trying to make a life ... They want the same things that everybody wants. (Quoted in O'Brien 2011)

This statement is a powerful reminder that film can normalize the everyday needs and wants of Indigenous people in Winnipeg – something *Together We Have CLOUT* did successfully. As a CLOUT member noted, there may indeed be crime in the North End, but most of its residents are family-oriented and law abiding, which is what audiences saw in the film – people going about their everyday.

Ultimately, the film reveals the power of storytelling. The very ability to see and hear CLOUT members talk about the barriers to their community development challenges audiences to ask themselves why some stories are heard and others are not, who has the power to tell them, and how they are controlled by people in positions of power (Keil 2002). In giving voice to a different point of view and making North End stories visible to audiences, the film resists the hegemony of power. As one woman remarked, the ability to have conversations is ultimately the kind of power that CLOUT members want: "When you are going to have an impact on people, you need to hear those people ... Have that conversation with me ... I might just compromise with you ... I just want the opportunity to talk with you."

The amount of new clout the film created for CLOUT members, and for us as their research partners, cannot be quantified. But as a knowledge mobilization tool, it presents a compelling rationale for the need to decolonize and to effect transformative political change – the underlying goal of the film. We believe that community-based participatory research is inherently a political activity. To be effective, it cannot be objective or neutral. This is what we were trying to accomplish when we made *Together We Have CLOUT* – to develop a space for political dialogue and perhaps create some new clout in our ability to transform social processes in Winnipeg.

NOTE

1 For information about the Winnipeg branch of Youth for Christ, see its homepage at http://yfcwinnipeg.com/index.html.

REFERENCES

Alfred, Taiaiake. 2005. *Wasáse: Indigenous Pathways of Action and Freedom*. Toronto: University of Toronto Press.

Baikie, Gail. 2009. "Indigenous-Centred Social Work: Theorizing a Social Work Way-of-Being." In *Wicihitowin: Aboriginal Social Work in Canada*, ed. Raven Sinclair, Michael Anthony Hart, and Gord Bruyere, 42–61. Halifax: Fernwood.

Bishop, Anne. 2002. *Becoming an Ally: Breaking the Cycle of Oppression in People*. 2nd ed. Halifax: Fernwood.

Coulthard, Glen. 2007. "Subjects of Empire: Indigenous Peoples and the 'Politics of Recognition' in Canada." *Contemporary Political Theory* 6: 437–60.

Davis, Lynne, and Heather Shpuniarsky. 2010. "The Spirit of Relationships: What We Have Learned about Indigenous/Non-Indigenous Alliances and Coalitions." In *Alliances: Re/Envisioning Indigenous-non-Indigenous Relationships*, ed. Lynne Davis, 334–50. Toronto: University of Toronto Press.

Freire, Paulo. 2006. *Pedagogy of the Oppressed*. 30th anniversary ed. New York: Continuum.

Gough, Jamie. 2002. "Neoliberalism and Socialization in the Contemporary City: Opposites, Complements and Instabilities." In *Spaces of Neoliberalism: Urban Restructuring in North America and Western Europe*, ed. Neil Brenner and Nik Theodore, 58–79. Oxford: Blackwell.

Greenwood, Davydd J., William Foote Whyte, and Ira Harkavy. 1993. "Participatory Action Research as a Process and as a Goal." *Human Relations* 46 (2): 175–92.

Hart, Michael. 2009. "Anti-colonial Indigenous Social Work: Reflections on an Aboriginal Approach." In *Wicihitowin: Aboriginal Social Work in Canada*, ed. Raven Sinclair, Michael Anthony Hart, and Gord Bruyere, 25–41. Halifax: Fernwood.

Harvey, David. 1992. "Social Justice, Postmodernism and the City." *International Journal of Urban and Regional Research* 16: 588–601.

hooks, bell. 2008. *Outlaw Culture.* New York: Routledge.

Keil, Roger. 2002. "'Common-Sense' Neoliberalism: Progressive Conservative Urbanism in Toronto, Canada." In *Spaces of Neoliberalism: Urban Restructuring in North America and Western Europe,* ed. Neil Brenner and Nik Theodore, 58–79. Oxford: Blackwell.

LaRocque, Emma. 2010. *When the Other Is Me: Native Resistance Discourse, 1850-1990.* Winnipeg: University of Manitoba Press.

MacKinnon, Shauna, et al. 2008. *Is Participation Having an Impact? Measuring Progress in Winnipeg's Inner City through the Voices of Community-Based Program Participants.* Winnipeg: CCPA–MB.

Marcuse, Peter. 2012. "Whose Right(s) to What City?" In *Cities for People, Not Profit: Critical Urban Theory and the Right to the City,* ed. Neil Brenner, Peter Marcuse, and Margit Mayer, 24–41. New York: Routledge.

O'Brien, Carole, dir. 2011. *Together We Have CLOUT.* Winnipeg: CCPA–MB. https://www.youtube.com/watch?v=rSmn7X2-Glw.

–. 2013. "Having CLOUT: Becoming an Ally and Having the Power to Resist Colonialism and Neoliberalism in Winnipeg's Inner City." Master's thesis, University of Manitoba.

Porter, Libby. 2010. *Unlearning the Colonial Cultures of Planning.* Burlington: Ashgate.

Roussin, Diane, and Tammy Christensen. 2010. "Public Funds for Youth for Christ: Have Our Politicians Learned Nothing from Past Mistakes?" *Fast Facts* (CCPA–MB), February 23. https://www.policyalternatives.ca/publications/commentary/public-funds-youth-christ.

Smith, Linda Tuhiwai. 2008. *Decolonizing Methodologies: Research and Indigenous Peoples.* New York: Palgrave.

Storper, Michael. 1998. "Civil Society: Three Ways into a Problem." In *Cities for Citizens: Planning and the Rise of Civil Society in a Global Age,* ed. Mike Douglass and John Friedmann, 239–46. Toronto: John Wiley and Sons.

11

Preserving the History of Aboriginal Institutional Development in Winnipeg
Research Driven by the Community

JOHN LOXLEY and EVELYN PETERS

This chapter chronicles a research project titled Preserving the History of Aboriginal Institutional Development in Winnipeg.[1] Its purpose was to strengthen the archival record of Aboriginal activity in Winnipeg, as the numerous institutional initiatives by Aboriginal people were insufficiently recorded, and many faced the prospect of not being documented at all. The intent was to work with members of the Aboriginal community to identify initiatives where documents were not archived, gather whatever written records existed, and ensure that they would be housed in an appropriate archival institution or library. The original plan was to hire a member of the community to work with a student archivist and the authors to undertake the project and to interview key actors where written records either did not exist or were deficient.

For the authors, what motivated the project was earlier research that both had conducted on Aboriginal institutional development. John Loxley had done research for the Royal Commission on Aboriginal Peoples to document, analyze, and preserve Aboriginal approaches to economic development in Winnipeg (see Loxley et al. 1996; later published in modified form in Silver 2000). Looking at the institutional developments around these approaches and preserving their records seemed a logical and worthwhile extension of that work. Evelyn Peters has a long history of recording Aboriginal institutional development across Canada, especially in urban centres. Some of her work already encompassed important institutions in Winnipeg, such as the Indian and Metis Friendship Centre and Aboriginal women's initiatives (Peters 2000), so this project was a natural extension of her previous work.

The Evolution and Aboriginalization of the Project

The project commenced in 2008. During its early stages, a graduate student in the University of Manitoba's Archival Studies Program was hired to determine what relevant materials were already held in various Winnipeg libraries and archives. To achieve this, he examined books, academic and popular articles, newspapers and reports, as well as websites that referred to Aboriginal organizations and then tried to find materials for these institutions in archives and libraries to assess the level of "archival integration" (Stinnett 2008, 1). He identified more than forty Aboriginal organizations, almost all of which were still operating in 2008, briefly described their function, and supplied addresses and contact numbers for each. If the latter information was not available, he noted the text or texts that referred to the organization. However, the two main archives – the Archives of Manitoba and the University of Manitoba Archives – possessed virtually no material for these groups (ibid., 17). We approached the City of Winnipeg Archives for assistance, but it did not respond.

This research formed the foundation of the second phase of the project, in which records would be sought and actors interviewed. During this stage, it evolved from a university-based archival project undertaken by non-Aboriginal authors to a joint community-university endeavour with a majority Aboriginal input. A research advisory committee was formed, consisting of the two authors and three experienced Aboriginal activists, Kathy Mallett, Louise Chippeway, and Larry Morrissette. Each had a long history of building Aboriginal institutions in Winnipeg and would in any case have been interviewed for the project. Kathy Mallett had also worked in the Archives of Manitoba; Louise Chippeway was the managing editor of a report commemorating the twenty-five years of service of the Indian and Metis Friendship Centre of Winnipeg, honouring "the people who worked hard to make it a success" (Indian and Metis Friendship Centre 1983, 2). And Larry Morrissette had been heavily involved in the repatriation of Indian artifacts from institutions in Winnipeg to their home communities up north. This distinguished group brought many years of practical and organizational experience to the project and gave it a clear

Aboriginal direction. The committee met at least monthly and oversaw all critical decisions. These included selecting interviewees, drafting interview questions, hiring staff and student authors, choosing the repository for archival material, and planning the final celebratory feast. Real power resided with the committee and with its Aboriginal majority, but it was exercised in a collegial and consensual manner. This included the choice of people and institutions to be interviewed. An initial list of potential interviewees drawn up by the researcher at the start of the project was greatly expanded by the Aboriginal members of the committee. Draft interview questions were prepared by the authors and the Aboriginal interviewers but were edited and approved by the whole committee. The hiring of staff and student authors was approved by the committee. Where to deposit the archival material was entirely the decision of the Aboriginal committee members but was endorsed by the authors. Planning and organizing the feast was also a joint exercise.

The group hired Darrell Chippeway, a student and First Nation journalist who had been working with the CBC. Darrell then assumed the key role in advancing the project on the ground.

The Maturing of the Project

Darrell was instrumental in shifting the direction of the project toward digitally video recording key informants. Although collection of paper archives was under way, its progress was slow. Thus, we decided to focus on interviewing people who had built Aboriginal institutions. Darrell argued that video recording would be the best option, as it would give a richer view of interviewees, was relatively inexpensive due to advances in technology, and would generate a reasonably permanent end product. The committee agreed and then hired another young Aboriginal student, Crystal Greene, to do the video recording; she too had worked with the CBC. On her recommendation, appropriate equipment was purchased. Later in the project, Crystal was joined by Darryl Nepinak, an experienced Aboriginal videographer and filmmaker.

The advisory committee met several times to determine who should be interviewed. The focus was to be on Elders and on individuals who had worked extensively, though not exclusively, in Winnipeg. Thus, we decided to exclude non-Aboriginal people, even those who had significantly contributed to building Aboriginal institutions in Winnipeg. The list of interviewees developed organically from the committee, the staff, and from suggestions made by people whom we sought to interview. Fifty-one possible candidates were identified (twenty-seven women and twenty-four men). A secondary list of sixteen people was also compiled, to be drawn upon if time and money permitted.

An interview procedure was agreed upon, and lists of questions were constructed. Ethics approval had been obtained for the first phase of the project through the University of Manitoba Joint-Faculty Research Ethics Board, and this route was taken for subsequent stages, with indicative questions being submitted to the board for approval (see Appendix 1 on page 206).

Darrell approached each interviewee to request a pre-interview, and the notes from these were written up and submitted to the advisory committee for comment. Amended where required, these notes formed the basis of the interview itself. In this way, a structure was imposed on the video recording sessions for both interviewer and interviewees, though the latter were encouraged to be spontaneous and relaxed during the actual filming.

Early on, it became apparent that the interview process would be strengthened by the participation of one of the Aboriginal advisory committee members, who had more knowledge than the young interviewers of the historical, institutional, and political landscape of Winnipeg. Larry Morrissette undertook this task. He prepared an information letter, which was sent to potential interviewees. It emphasized that the project would preserve important aspects of Winnipeg's Aboriginal history for future generations, invited the recipients to participate in videotape interviews at the Manitoba Indigenous Cultural Education Centre, and requested that they deposit for safekeeping any written records they might have. A list of suggested questions was prepared for the interviewers (see Appendix 2 on page 207), some of which were included in Larry's letter. All interviewees were required to sign an informed consent form.

The Consent Form

The consent form invites involvement in a research project that "attempts to collect and safeguard the Aboriginal history of the Winnipeg community." Printed on notepaper with the logos of both universities, it gave the names and contact information of the principal investigators. It specified that Darrell and Larry would conduct the interviews and that Crystal would be the videographer, that interviews would last about an hour, and that participants would receive the questions beforehand. The consent form emphasized that "none of the questions should make you uncomfortable, but remember that you can decide not to answer a question and you can also withdraw from the interview at any time. You can ask to have your video and transcript destroyed at any time." It stated that the videotapes and transcripts would be deposited in the archives and made accessible to community members, students, and other authors, and that the two authors might draw on the materials to write papers "for academic or public policy purposes." Videos and transcripts would be made available to interviewees on request. The form noted that the University of Manitoba's Joint-Faculty Research Ethics Board had approved the project and should be contacted if participants had any concerns or complaints regarding it.

The Interview Questions

The suggested interview questions were developed by the advisory committee during several meetings. Participants were asked how they came to reside in Winnipeg and what relationships they maintained with their home community. They were questioned about their education and whether they had completed it in their youth or as adults. Particular attention was paid to the state of institutional supports for Aboriginal people when the interviewees came to Winnipeg. They were asked about their role in building institutions in the city and how these had performed. They assessed the strengths and weaknesses of the current institutional set-up from the perspective of Aboriginal people. They commented specifically on the role of women and on the principles underlying their activities. They outlined the alternative approaches to community economic development in which they were involved or had observed and commented on the contrast between the collectivist Neechi Principles and Stan Fulham's more private enterprise approach (see Loxley 2010; and Chapter 4 in this volume). Finally, people were asked how Winnipeg compared with what it was when they first arrived, what the experience of their children and grandchildren had been in the city, and what steps contemporary Aboriginal youth might take to improve their lives there.

Since draft questions were prepared for each interview, the standard questions could always be adjusted to more fully engage interviewees and to draw out their specific experiences. Also, the interviewers ensured that the encounters were not too tightly scripted.

Some of What Was Collected

It is not the purpose of this chapter to recount or analyze the forty-plus interviews collected in the videos (for a list of interviewees, see Appendix 3 on page 208). It can be said, however, that they blend together life stories, personal struggles, and achievements with institutional development as well as social commentary on colonialism and the racism to which Aboriginal people are routinely subjected. As Chippeway (2013, 1) argues, these are inseparable, and "the development of institutions and the growth of individuals are interrelated and connected." The following select summaries reproduced from Chippeway (ibid., 2–3) give a flavour of the richness of the interviews and the importance of their historical and institutional span:

- Reverend Stan McKay recounts his boyhood working at the Indian and Metis Friendship Centre (IMFC) with his mother, as early as 1958.
- Flora Zaharia talks about seeing the IMFC transition in the 1960s from a non-Aboriginal-run institution to being controlled and operated by Aboriginal people.
- George Munroe discusses being the first local Aboriginal executive director of the IMFC from 1969 to 1974.
- Cyril Keeper speaks about being the executive director at Native Family Life Counselling in the 1970s.
- Marileen Bartlett, executive director of the Centre for Aboriginal Human Resource Development, talks about how it evolved from Native Employment Services, a small group in the 1980s, to become an important urban Aboriginal organization today.
- Lucille Bruce discusses her nineteen-year tenure as executive director of the Native Women's Transition Centre of Winnipeg.

- Wayne Helgason recalls how the child welfare system was turned upside down in the early 1980s, which led to the development of the Ma Mawi Wi Chi Itata Centre. Helgason also explains that the Aboriginal Centre of Winnipeg came into being because a building owner wanted her rent early so she could pay the moorage fee for her yacht.
- Chief Jim Bear talks about being the first executive director of the Aboriginal Council of Winnipeg in the 1990s.
- Vern Morrissette discusses his role in the creation of Children of the Earth High School.
- Leslie Spillett speaks about the history of Aboriginal resistance and her experience as a trade union organizer and political activist.

This is merely a small sample, but it clearly demonstrates the central role played by interviewees in the development of Aboriginal institutions in Winnipeg.

In a radio interview with Robert Falcon-Ouellette (2013), Larry Morrissette and Darrell Chippeway discussed some of the issues raised in the project. Some of these are discussed in the following sections.

Choosing the Archives

An important issue from the outset was where to archive the materials collected by the project. Members of the advisory committee met with the provincial archivist, who was very supportive but who concluded that the Archives of Manitoba's restrictions regarding what it would accept precluded receiving the material. The problems were twofold: the archives would accept only original records, not copies, and once these had been donated under a certificate of gift, they became the property of the archives. The advisory committee felt that both provisions were unduly restrictive, especially the second one, and did not want to rule out the possibility that an Aboriginal archive might one day take possession of the material.

We also held discussions with the archivist at the new Canadian Museum for Human Rights, who was very supportive, but it was felt that the fledgling museum might not have the capacity to immediately handle the materials being generated by the project. The advisory committee then organized formal interviews with the archivists from the University of Winnipeg and the University of Manitoba. To that point, we had been favouring the University of Winnipeg Archives as the repository, for a number of reasons. First, its location in downtown Winnipeg was central and convenient. Second, the university had made Aboriginal issues a major priority and had built some important programs aimed at the Aboriginal community. (It offered a master's of arts in Indigenous government and a master's in development planning, as well as a bachelor of arts in urban and inner city studies.) Third, an increasingly large share of the capital for the project was being provided by Evelyn Peters's Canada Research Chair funding at the university. As it turned out, the interviews with the archivists seemed to suggest that the University of Manitoba was much better equipped than the University of Winnipeg in terms of space, technology, and above all, staff. They also revealed that the former's protocols for Aboriginal materials were more advanced, with an emphasis on steward-ship rather than ownership of materials. Furthermore, the close association of the university archive with the Archival Studies Program and its students seemed to offer a more integrated and comprehensive package of assistance to the project. Finally, the attraction of the University of Manitoba was heightened by the possibility (later confirmed) that the files of the Truth and Reconciliation Commission would be deposited there.

The Aboriginal members of the advisory committee were unanimous in choosing the University of Manitoba as the repository, and the two authors agreed with this decision. This is not to say that there are no residual issues of accessibility in this selection, and efforts must be made to ensure that inner-city people in particular will be informed of the records and given assistance to access them.

Once the location had been chosen, the project underwent another transformation, bringing in Shelley Sweeney, the University of Manitoba archivist. She was joined by Tom Nesmith and Greg Bak of the Archival Studies Program, who introduced two graduate archival studies students into the project: Jesse Boiteau was Metis, and Sarah Story had worked on archival matters as an intern at the Nelson Mandela Centre of Memory in Johannesburg, South Africa. These new additions considerably expanded the expertise available to the project, and the students, in particular, aug-mented the skilled labour available. Subsequently, Canada Works summer employment money was found through the efforts of Jim Sinclair of the Indian and Metis Friendship Centre, to hire two undergraduate Aboriginal students – Charlotte Nelson and Kerri Johnston – to work on the paper files of the IMFC. Yet another Aboriginal student, Chrystal Kakekagumick, assisted in processing files held by the Aboriginal Council of Winnipeg. So, by 2012 a project that started with one researcher and one student ended with a fifteen-person team with varying degrees of involvement, ten of whom were Aboriginal and seven of whom were students. The project is an excellent, if rare, example of co-curation and participatory archiving (Boiteau 2013).

The Letter of Understanding

Once materials began to flow, both digital and written, it was necessary to have a clear written agreement regarding the terms on which they would be held by the university. Notwithstanding the agreement between the archivist, Shelley Sweeney, and the advisory committee that the University of Manitoba would retain the records under stewardship, arriving at a mutually agreeable letter of understanding that those providing material could sign proved highly problematic. The standard deed of gift agreement used by the university was soon ruled out, as both inappropriate and too complex – three and half pages long, excluding space for signatures and the list of items donated, it was wordy and full of legalese that lay people would find difficult. It dealt with "property" and its valuation, as well as the charitable tax receipts that might flow to "donors" under the Income Tax Act. More importantly, it stated that "the Donor hereby gifts, assigns and transfers all of the Donor's right, title, and interest in and to the Property, to the University, for its own use absolutely, subject only to the terms of this Deed," which hardly suggested a collaborative arrangement.

In response to these concerns, the university drafted a letter of understanding, which was much shorter (half a page), more intelligible, and more accessible. "Donors" were replaced by "stewards." The university would become the new steward of the materials and would "respect Indigenous archival principles." In addition, it was not obligated to retain the materials indefinitely and could transfer them "according to standard archival principles" to another archive if it felt that "the records would be more appropriate to be housed at another facility." However, the advisory committee felt that this draft was deficient in a number of ways. For instance, it made no provision for consultation with the original stewards in the event that the university wished to transfer the records. Nor did it suggest that the transfer would be governed by Indigenous archival principles. It did not attempt to define "standard Indigenous archival principles." After much discussion, the committee eventually recommended that the transfer paragraph read as follows:

> The University may transfer or dispose of the Materials according to standard Indigenous archival principles such as the Society of American Archivists' Protocols for Native American Archival materials.[2] For example, after consulting with the steward(s), the University may transfer a portion or all of the Materials to another archive if they feel records would be more appropriate to be housed at the other facility.

Unfortunately, the lawyers for the university would not accept this wording, so it did not appear in the finalized letter of understanding. Even so, with its emphasis on stewardship and Indigenous archival principles, the final version represented a major step forward for the university (see Appendix 4 on page 209). According to Shelley Sweeney, it is probably unique in Canada.

The Wind-Up Feast

The advisory committee felt it was important to celebrate the completion of the project by inviting participants to a feast. The gathering was held on October 22, 2013, at Thunderbird House in Winnipeg, and the meal was catered by Neechi Foods, an Aboriginal workers' co-op. About a hundred invitations were sent, and some eighty people attended. In preparation for the meeting, Darryl Nepinak produced a film that drew on six of the interviews (those by Doris Young, George Munroe, Wayne Helgason, Kathy Mallett, Vern Morrissette, and Larry Morrissette). It also incorporates interviews of the principal investigators (the authors) and the chief archivist at the University of Manitoba, Shelley Sweeney. This short film (Nepinak 2013) was shown at the feast and was very well received. An archival display was prepared by Sarah Story, one of the graduate archival students, and representatives of both Aboriginal youth, male and female, and Aboriginal

Elders were invited to speak. The project, the feast, and the video were covered by the local press, which described interviewees as "Aboriginal trailblazers" (Story 2013, 9) and carried a photo of Chief Jim Bear (Brokenhead First Nation), Jim Sinclair (IMFC executive director), Lorne Keeper (First Nations Education Resource Centre executive director), and Dan Highway (Aboriginal activist, role model, and residential school survivor) at the gathering.

Kathy Mallett underscored the importance of both the project and the feast when she stated that "I wish we had more time to celebrate changing the system ... and to celebrate and acknowledge the people you are working with" (Nepinak 2013).

The Challenges of the Project

The main challenges of the project revolved around time and money. The advisory committee met regularly and was quite demanding of all members. Every meeting required that practical decisions be made, and the agendas were substantial: we selected interviewees, hired interviewers, listened to staff progress reports, read pre-video interviews and watched the videos themselves, planned the feast, and much more. The committee also handled the personal issues that arose with any employees. All of this made the project very demanding in terms of time, and although much of the work was done by the authors the whole advisory committee was heavily involved. Its work was not remunerated, and the Aboriginal members participated out of dedication to the project.

Conducting the interviews and contacting groups for their paper records also took time. Organizing and finalizing over forty videotaping sessions took much longer than originally anticipated, with the result that the payment to interviewers was also higher than expected. This heightened the second challenge, which was financial.

Initially, the money to hire authors was provided by grants from the Social Sciences and Humanities Research Council (SSHRC). This proved insufficient for the scale of the video interviews, so the project relied heavily on Evelyn Peters's Canada Research Chair funding, which covered most of the labour of the interviewers and the videographer. The University of Manitoba's Office of the Executive Lead, Indigenous Achievement, also funded one of the Aboriginal authors, and its Faculty of Graduate Studies generously subsidized one of the archival master's students. The feast was co-funded by the University of Manitoba, the University of Winnipeg, and the Community Education Development Association. So funding was a patchwork quilt, and keeping the project going was quite demanding.

Organizing the interviews was also challenging, given their sheer number and the various stages through which they and subsequent edits had to pass. Some interviewees no longer lived in Winnipeg, and meeting with them was complicated.

Finally, the project was quite successful in video recording Aboriginal institutional history but less so in safeguarding documentary history. Nonetheless, some notable successes occurred even here. The most important was in obtaining the historical records of the IMFC. Given the centrality and continuity of the IMFC in urban Aboriginal historical experience, this was extremely significant, although not all the records had survived. The extant documents were consolidated by Lena Friesen, who was the IMFC executive director in the early 1980s. Equally, if not more important, are the voluminous paper files of the Aboriginal Council of Winnipeg and of several other Indigenous organizations housed in its Aboriginal Centre, which might not have survived were it not for this project (Boiteau 2013). Larry Morrissette donated a history he had written of the Ma Mawi Wi Chi Itata Centre for a conference held in Albuquerque, New Mexico, in 1988, and Louise Chippeway donated an Aboriginal housing study she had written in 1971. Ivy Chaske submitted pictures from various urban Aboriginal conferences and gatherings from the 1980s (Chippeway 2013, 3). Increasing such acquisitions should be a focus of attention for future researchers. Collecting digital records, which was beyond the purview of our project, is also something that should be considered

Impressions of the Project

Our overwhelming impression is that the archives project is a source of great pride to the Aboriginal members of the advisory committee, to the interviewees, and to the Aboriginal community as a whole. Early Aboriginal institutions did not tend to archive their records, because no one thought to do it and the people involved were too busy to document their work (Chippeway 2013). Kathy Mallett put it best: "We didn't document things very well, we were so busy doing the work ... A lot of the work we were doing was organic and we didn't have a lot of funds to do it ... We were responding to the issues of the day" (quoted Sanders 2013, A6). Lucille Bruce makes exactly the same point (Chippeway 2013, 3). Many activists who played pivotal roles in Winnipeg's institutional development were female and were also "the ones raising the children and looking after the seniors. You've got to be responsible for your community" (Kathy Mallett, quoted in Sanders 2013). In that situation, the historical record takes a distinctly secondary place to the activism and to the challenges of daily life. In many cases, the events do go unrecorded or the paper trail disappears "in a dumpster" (ibid.). This project helps to preserve that record to some extent.

The interviews revealed the lack of supports for Aboriginal people when they came to Winnipeg in the early days and the creative ways in which they banded together to help with the transition to urban life. A myriad of formal institutions soon arose to meet their diverse and growing needs. The Indian and Metis Friendship Centre, founded in 1958, played a key role here and was also the breeding ground for several other important institutional developments, such as the Main Street Project, Aboriginal court translators, and hospital cultural interpreters (Sanders 2013). Our video interviews provide a fairly comprehensive account of subsequent institutional development in Winnipeg and the rich diversity of approaches in child welfare, women's issues, education, employment, training, and economic development.

The project recorded that by 2013 some two hundred Aboriginal organizations had existed or were currently active (Chippeway 2013, 1). As Evelyn Peters explains, this rich institutional development "is the success side and it really needs to be told because it's an important part of what is happening in Winnipeg today" (CBC News 2013). Furthermore, some of the challenges and accomplishments covered by the interviews have great relevance for contemporary struggles and could usefully be consulted with this in mind.

Conclusion

The Aboriginal archives project evolved over time and became a model example of how Aboriginal community authors and academics can cooperate in capturing and preserving urban Aboriginal history. It is, we feel, a testimony to the foresight of the SSHRC's shift toward recognizing the importance of joint community-academic research and facilitating it through grants. Without the SSHRC funding, the project would not have been possible. Nor would it have developed as it did without significant financial support from Evelyn Peters's Canada Research Chair. We were fortunate, therefore, in having these two flexible sources of finance available for the research.

Although much has been accomplished, more remains to be done. Some important Aboriginal path-breakers were not interviewed, mainly because they did not live in Winnipeg. New leaders and institution builders are emerging as every year goes by. And much more needs to be done to collect and preserve the paper records of Aboriginal institutions, as well as their digital records. The necessary authors and videographers are on the ground, and the archival arrangements are in place, but others, and especially more youthful leaders, should be encouraged to document their activities. There is scope, therefore, for a reprise of this project if funding could be obtained.

APPENDIX 1:
ETHICS APPROVAL DOCUMENT – INDICATIVE LIST OF QUESTIONS TO BE ASKED

Set A – for persons who might be knowledgeable about which institutions exist or existed
Please review this preliminary list of Aboriginal institutional initiatives in Winnipeg and comment on its completeness.

Are there any other institutions, which are not listed? If so, what are they?

What were the functions of those institutions and who were the key actors?

Do you have contact addresses for the key actors?

Do you know where written records of these institutions might be held and by whom?

Were there suggestions for Aboriginal institutions, which never materialized? If so, what were they and who were the key actors?

Do you foresee any problems in our contacting these key actors?

Set B – for people identified as key actors in institutions, which exist or existed
Please describe the nature of your involvement with the institution in question.

What was/is the nature of the institution and what are/were its goals?

Do you know the whereabouts of any documents relating to the formation, operation evaluation or, if it no longer exists, the closure of the institution?

These documents could include aims and objectives, legal documents, minutes of meetings, funding requests, ads for public meetings, presentations to government or other bodies, financial reports, contributions to public debate, record of accomplishments, etc.

Who else involved in the project might have kept records and how might they be reached?

Would there be any problems making these records available publicly?

If written records do not exist, or if they are deficient, would you be prepared to contribute orally to recreating or creating such records?

Set C – for key actors where written records are non-existent or deemed deficient
Please describe the nature, purpose and origin of the initiative.

What major issues was the initiative designed to address and why was it deemed necessary?

What problems did it face and how did it attempt to overcome them?

How was it funded?

Who was involved in the initiative? Were people paid or were they volunteers?

What was your role in the initiative?

What were the accomplishments of the initiative?

If it no longer exists, why is this?

Why were no records kept or, if they were, why were they deficient?

What is your evaluation of the contribution of this initiative to improving the lives of Aboriginal people in Winnipeg?

Do you wish to be quoted in any write-up on this initiative?

Are there other sources which might add to your recollection?

APPENDIX 2: SUGGESTED QUESTIONS FOR KEY ABORIGINAL CONTACTS

Could you please describe when you came to Winnipeg and under what circumstances?

Did coming to Winnipeg represent a clean break with your home community or have you remained in contact since? If you have remained in contact, please describe your relationship over the years with your home community.

Where did you do your schooling and, if you feel able and willing to share this, what is your assessment of your schooling experience?

Did you return to school in your adult years and if so, why, where and with what effect?

What facilities and supports were there for Aboriginal newcomers to Winnipeg when you and your family arrived?

Could you describe the organizations with which you have been involved since coming to Winnipeg, their purpose, funding sources and role in the community. Please describe the role(s) you played in developing these organizations. How would you assess the experience(s) and the performance and contribution of these organizations?

How do you see Aboriginal organizations which now exist in Winnipeg? Do they cater for the main needs of Aboriginal people? Are there any gaps?

What role have Aboriginal women played in developing Aboriginal organizations in Winnipeg?

How would you describe the principles which have governed your activities in the community?

In the Aboriginal community there appear to be quite diverse approaches to community economic development, for instance the collectivist approach of Neechi versus the more private enterprise oriented approach of Stan Fulham. What would be your views on these different approaches? Are there other approaches you would recommend?

How have your children and grandchildren fared in Winnipeg over the years?

Would you say that because of Aboriginal initiatives, Winnipeg is a better place for Aboriginal people to live than it was when you first arrived? If so, why and how? If not, why and how?

What would you recommend needs to be done by contemporary Aboriginal youth to improve the lives of Aboriginal people in Winnipeg?

APPENDIX 3: INTERVIEWEES

Bartlett, Marileen	Courchene, Mary	Hill, Josee
Bear, Jim	Cowan, Elaine	Jackson, Tom
Black, Darlene	Daniels, Dennis	Johnston, Damion
Bruce, Barbara	Fontaine, Janet	Keeper, Cyril
Bruce, Lucille	Fontaine, Phil	Keeper, Joe
Callahan, Ann	Friesen, Lena	Laramee, Myra
Champagne, Louise	Guilbault, Mary	Lavalle, Jackie
Chaske, Ivy	Helgason, Wayne	Lavallee, Margaret and Jules
Chippeway, Louise	Highway, Dan	Mallett, Kathy

McCloud, Albert

McKay, Stan

Mead, Thelma

Meadmore, Marion

Mercredi, Ovide

Monkman, Yvonne

Morrissette, Larry

Morrissette, Vern

Munroe, George

Murdock, Ruth

Nepinak, Clarence

Robertson, Don

Roesler, Francis

Schoffly, Art

Shed, Bill

Sinclair, Murray

Spillett, Leslie

Westasacoot, Jim

Young, Doris

Zaharia, Flora

APPENDIX 4: LETTER OF UNDERSTANDING

I/We _____ am/are the recognized steward(s) of the material to be transferred, or represent the steward(s), and have full authority to enter into this agreement. This transfer is not subject to the conditions of any other agreements, or to the consent of any other person or persons.

I/we agree to transfer and assign all rights to the outlined materials (see attached transfer schedule) (the "Materials") to the University of Manitoba Archives & Special Collections, (the "University") which will act as steward of these materials for the use absolutely of the larger community subject to this letter of understanding.

Any desired copyrights and/or access restrictions must be agreed upon between the person(s) transferring and the University of Manitoba Archives & Special Collections prior to the transfer.

It is the University's intention to archive and hold these Materials in order to preserve them, yet the University is not obligated to retain the Materials indefinitely. The University may transfer or dispose of the Materials according to standard archival principles. For example, the University may transfer a portion or all of the Materials to another archive if they feel the records would be more appropriate to be housed at the other facility.

The steward(s) will protect the University so that the University will not be held liable for any claims relating to the steward's/stewards' stewardship of the Materials and right to transfer the Materials to the University.

Steward's Name (please print):

_____

Address:

_____

Telephone _____

(Organisation) _____

Date _____   Signature _____

University of Manitoba

Per: _____

Schedule

Transfer agreement

From _____ to the University of

Manitoba

The following records are transferred to the University of Manitoba as of

(date): _____

   1.

   2.

   3.

   4.

   5.

   6.

   7.

   8.

   9.

  10.

_____

(Witness signature)

_____

(Steward's signature)

Steward's Name: _____

ACKNOWLEDGMENTS

The authors acknowledge the helpful comments received from Sarah Story.

NOTES

1 The project was sponsored by the Manitoba Research Alliance from 2008 to 2013. It also received funding through the Social Sciences and Humanities Research Council, Community University Research Alliance, and Partnership Grants provided through a Canada Research Chair grant.

2 Canada does not have a set of protocols for archiving Indigenous materials, which it badly needs. Shelley Sweeney has been developing an Indigenous archiving policy for the University of Manitoba based on the Aboriginal and Torres Strait Islander Data Archive Protocols of Australia, which are grounded in respect, trust, and

engagement. Aboriginal and Torres Strait Islander Data Archive, "Principles," http://www.atsida.edu.au/protocols/atsida/principles.

REFERENCES

Boiteau, Jesse. 2013. "Co-curation and Participatory Archives." Paper presented to "I Have Never Forgotten His Words ... Talking about Indigenous Archives," Institute for the Humanities, University of Manitoba, October 5.

CBC News. 2013. "Winnipeg's Urban Aboriginal History Being Pieced Together." March 4. Video. http://www.cbc.ca/news/canada/manitoba/winnipeg-s-urban-aboriginal-history-being-pieced-together-1.1398000.

Chippeway, Darrell. 2013. "A Report on Preserving the History of Aboriginal Institutional Development in Winnipeg Project." Manitoba Research Alliance, Winnipeg.

Falcon-Ouellette, Robert. 2013. Radio interview with Larry Morrissette and Darrell Chippeway on "Preserving the History of Aboriginal Institutional Development in Winnipeg Project." *At the Edge of Canada: Indigenous Research.* https://www.umfm.com/programming/programgrid/341/.

Indian and Metis Friendship Centre. 1983. "History of the Winnipeg Indian and Metis Friendship Centre, 1958–1983." Indian and Metis Friendship Centre, Winnipeg. http://imfcentre.net/static/documents/25-year-history.pdf.

Loxley, John. 2010. *Aboriginal, Northern and Community Economic Development: Papers and Retrospectives.* Winnipeg: ARP Books.

Loxley, John, Bernie Wood, Louise Champagne, E.J. Fontaine, and Charles Scribe. 1996. "Aboriginal People in the Winnipeg Economy: Case Study." Research study prepared for the Royal Commission on Aboriginal Peoples.

Nepinak, Darryl, dir. 2013. *Preserving the History of Aboriginal Institutional Development in Winnipeg.* October 21. https://www.youtube.com/watch?v=EJAs8-x8a1I.

Peters, Evelyn. 2000. "'The Two Major Living Realities': Urban Services Needs of First Nations Women in Canadian Cities." In *Gendering the City: Women, Boundaries and Visions of Urban Life,* ed. Kristine B. Miranne and Alma H. Young, 41–62. Lanham: Rowman and Littlefield.

Sanders, Carol. 2013. "Putting Together a Piece of History." *Winnipeg Free Press,* March 4. https://www.winnipegfreepress.com/local/putting-together-a-piece-of-history-194755711.html.

Silver, Jim, ed. 2000. *Solutions That Work: Fighting Poverty in Winnipeg.* Halifax/Winnipeg: Fernwood/Canadian Centre for Policy Alternatives–Manitoba.

Stinnett, Graham. 2008. "Urban Aboriginal Organizations." Report on research progress, prepared for the Preserving the History of Aboriginal Institutional Development in Winnipeg project, November 24, mimeo.

Story, Jared. 2013. "Video Project Tells Story of Trailblazers." *Winnipeg Free Press*, October 29. http://www.winnipegfreepress.com/our-communities/times/Video -project-tells-story-of-trailblazers-229724021.html.

12

Breaking Barriers, Building Bridges
Challenging Racial, Spatial, and Generational Divides in the City

SHAUNA MacKINNON, CLAIRE FRIESEN,
and CAROLE O'BRIEN

Our Divided City

In January 2015, *Maclean's* magazine published a damning indictment of Winnipeg as a divided and racist city (Macdonald 2015). The article came as no surprise to people who live and work in its inner city. Although most urban areas can be described as "divided" (Hall 2006), Winnipeg is socially fragmented in many ways, and its class, wealth, race, and ethnicity are segregated along geographical lines, making the divisions very visible. Inner-city neighbourhoods, especially the North End, have historically drawn working-class immigrants and lower-income households, whereas the South End has been the preferred destination of middle- and upper-income earners (Artibise 1977). More recently, the gulf has become even more pronounced between inner-city and non-inner-city areas: the former are far more likely to house low-income residents.

Winnipeg is a town with racialized and spatialized pockets of poverty (Fernandez, MacKinnon, and Silver 2015), and its most notable divide is that between Indigenous and non-Indigenous people. A survey conducted by Probe Research (2014) shows that 75 percent of Winnipeggers "believe there is a deep racial gulf between Aboriginal and non-Aboriginal citizens and that it is a serious problem in the city." Indigenous residents, particularly in the inner city, fare badly on a host of social and economic indicators, and are likely to be poor.

Winnipeg also has the highest number of Indigenous people in all the census metropolitan areas of Canada, a number that is expected to expand significantly (Statistics Canada 2011). The increase occurs in part because the Indigenous population is young and growing at a fast rate but also because of migration, as individuals and families relocate to Manitoba's largest city in search of better opportunities. Proportionally, the Indigenous population in the inner city is markedly larger than in Winnipeg more generally. In 2011, 20.9 percent of inner-city residents identified as Aboriginal, compared with 11.0 percent elsewhere in town (Statistics Canada 2011). In some inner-city districts, more than 50 percent of inhabitants identify as Aboriginal, and they are among the most disadvantaged residents of these areas (Fernandez, MacKinnon, and Silver 2015).

Although a few parts of the inner city have been gentrified, it has increasingly been stigmatized as a place of last resort – it's where you go when you can't afford to live anywhere else. We continually hear of people who are seeking to move away from it. The media have played a role here, contributing to the extreme perception of the inner city as dangerous and unappealing – and best avoided, even in daylight. However, the challenges of living in many of its neighbourhoods are quite real. There is much to celebrate in the inner city, but it is also true that its disadvantaged youth feel pressure to join gangs, are dropping out of school at high rates, and are all too often trapped in cycles of poverty that have dogged their families for generations. Unfortunately, the broader community, though concerned, responds by staying away from the area. Winnipeggers know that a problem exists but either don't see it as their responsibility or simply don't know what to do.

The Breadth of the Divide

As noted, the divide in Winnipeg has many layers, one of which occurs in educational attainment. Although education levels among Indigenous Winnipeggers have improved dramatically in recent years, they still lag far behind their non-Indigenous counterparts (MacKinnon 2015). Progress has been made, but more must be done to improve the educational outcomes of Indigenous and inner-city students. High school completion rates are lower in Manitoba than in Canada generally, but they are particularly low for Indigenous Manitobans, and high school attainment for inner-city youth is especially low in comparison to non-inner-city rates. For example, researchers at the Manitoba Centre for Health Policy assessed high school completion rates in Manitoba by following two cohorts of Grade 9 students for six years. Students who enrolled in Grade 9 in 1997–98 were followed until the 2002–03 school year; those who enrolled in 2000–01 were followed until the 2005–06 school year (Brownell et al. 2008, 241). The researchers found that completion rates for the province as a whole increased from 74.3 percent to 77.7 percent during these two periods. The rates also rose in most parts of Winnipeg, except for the inner city, where they remained significantly below the provincial and city average. For example, in one inner-city neighbourhood only 52.8 percent of the cohort graduated, compared with the Winnipeg average of approximately 79.0 percent.

Data for 2009–10 show that whereas more than 90 percent of students in suburban and higher-income Winnipeg neighbourhoods completed high school within six years of entering Grade 9, the comparable figure was 55 percent in the inner city and close to 25 percent in some North End areas (Brownell et al. 2012, 207).

The divide is also clearly evident in the overrepresentation of Indigenous people in the criminal justice and the child welfare systems. Fully 80 percent of those incarcerated in Manitoba identify as Indigenous, and more than 85 percent of children in care are Indigenous. Acknowledging the root causes of these disturbing statistics is essential to an improved societal response.

Yes, This Elephant Is Still in the Room

That colonization and systemic racism are the root causes of the difficulties experienced by many Indigenous people is well documented (TRC 2015). The work of the Truth and Reconciliation Commission of Canada (TRC) gives us new hope as it draws attention to the devastating legacy of residential schools and provides recommendations for a way forward. The TRC emphasizes the importance of revising the school curriculum to accurately present Canada's history. Winnipeg school divisions are slowly responding to this call by integrating topics such as residential schools into the high school curriculum. This important step toward decolonization will help to address what many Indigenous people describe as a negative educational experience (Huffman 2008; Silver 2006; TRC 2015). Residential schools left grandparents and/or parents psychologically and spiritually damaged, and they naturally passed their distrust of schools to their children. Furthermore, the continued use of Eurocentric content and teaching styles, the shortage of Indigenous teachers, and the lack of visible evidence that education equates with a better life prompts many Indigenous youth to drop out at an early age. The result has been low literacy levels, lack of hope for a better future, and a perpetuation of poverty.

Improving education and other outcomes for Indigenous people requires that Indigenous and non-Indigenous people alike embark on a process of decolonization to tackle the problem of deeply entrenched systemic racism. The school curriculum is a good place to begin this healing and reconciliation because real progress won't be made until Canadians fully understand how policies of forced assimilation and countless cases of physical, mental, and sexual abuse produced an intergenerational cycle of poverty, mental and spiritual anguish, cultural dislocation, and many related problems. Bridging the divide will require us not only to understand historical forces but also to measure the effectiveness (or ineffectiveness) of our response.

Building Bridges and Breaking through Barriers

As we do each year, representatives of community-based organizations and researchers met early in 2012 to discuss issues that we might explore through community-based participatory research (CBPR). Our research paradigm aligns with the Indigenous agenda described by Linda Tuhiwai Smith (1999, 116), which emphasizes the central importance of research as part of decolonization, healing, transformation, and mobilization. Our intent is to engage community members as active participants in research that aims for radical change in policies, programs, curriculums, and broader public attitudes and beliefs.

After much discussion, we chose a research project grounded in the idea that healing and reconciliation begin with an open and honest dialogue about racism. We decided to combine the wisdom of Elders with the experiences of youth to explore various ways to bridge the divide in our city. We intended to involve both inner-city Indigenous youth and youth who lived elsewhere in Winnipeg; the latter probably knew little about the inner city other than what they learned from mainstream media. We felt that the project would help to improve understanding across our divided city and would encourage the broader community to seek for solutions rather than look the other way. We also thought that it would introduce non-Indigenous people to the idea that they too have been affected by colonialism and are not immune to the pervasive and systemic racism that is its legacy.

We agreed that a growing number of young people were concerned about social and economic injustice and that we had neglected to fully tap into their experiences. In recent years, youth have led a number of important social events across the globe and are effecting change in ways that we have not seen for decades. These include the student-led struggle for democracy in oppressive states, the international Occupy Movement and its protest against extreme income inequality, the Quebec student movement's rallying cry against increases in postsecondary tuition, Idle No More's calls for respect of Indigenous rights, protests against gas and oil pipeline expansions, the Black Lives Matter movement, and the growing demand for action to protect Indigenous women and girls. It is increasingly clear that youth are aware that something is seriously amiss in our world and are eager to change it.

We also talked about the role of Indigenous Elders. As Loxley and Peters discuss in Chapter 11 of this volume, a vibrant Indigenous activist community emerged in Manitoba during the 1960s and 1970s. Many of its leaders are still involved and have much to teach a new generation of Indigenous leaders and their non-Indigenous allies. We saw youth as the best hope for breaking down barriers and building bridges but also felt that they could learn much from the Elders. Elders commonly hold a special place in Indigenous cultures, and youth are instinctively drawn to them as transmitters of knowledge and history. We hypothesized that engaging Indigenous, non-Indigenous, inner-city, and suburban youth in discussions with Elders could help bridge the divide, as they could learn from the Elders in a safe, non-judgmental, and welcoming environment. The following pages describe how we tested this hypothesis and what we learned.

We received funding from the Manitoba Research Alliance and the Social Sciences and Humanities Research Council, and we obtained ethics approval through the Senate Committee on Ethics in Human Research and Scholarship at the University of Winnipeg. Thus, we were able to organize a series of interviews, workshops, and sharing circles, and to document the project in both writing and film.

Talking to Elders

Our first step was to interview five Elders, asking them to share a message to youth that would inspire discussion. The Elders spoke about their experiences as young people, how they dealt with racism, and what prompted them to become involved in their communities. We videotaped their interviews, with the intent of showing the film to three groups of students in preparation for their meeting with the Elders themselves. This was a practical way of giving them a sense of with whom they would be interacting.

Talking to Youth

The youth who participated in the project consisted of twenty students from Collège Béliveau and Grant Park High School, each situated in relatively affluent, mainly non-Indigenous neighbourhoods, and eleven students from the inner-city after school program, CEDA Pathways to Education (see Chapter 3 in this volume). A total of five Collège Béliveau and Grant Park students identified as "Aboriginal" or "Métis." All but one of the Pathways students identified as "Aboriginal."

We held workshops at the two schools and at the CEDA Pathways program site, during which we showed the filmed interviews and asked students to share their opinions about the inner city and Indigenous people. They also discussed how others (media, parents) saw the inner city, Indigenous people, and teenagers in general. They identified the source of these perceptions. A few weeks later, we brought the youth and Elders together.

Not knowing what to expect, we planned to spend two hours with each group but were prepared to end the discussion after one hour. We were pleasantly surprised to find that we had no problem filling up the two hours. In fact, we could have used more time. We were extremely impressed with the honesty, openness, and thoughtfulness of students, who very respectfully shared their ideas and concerns. Interestingly, though there were a few notably different perceptions across the three groups, there were more similarities than we had anticipated.

Neighbourhood Perceptions

We also asked the students to tell us about their own neighbourhoods, an idea that came to us after our workshop at Collège Béliveau. All but one of the CEDA Pathways students didn't like their neighbourhood, whereas all but one of the Grant Park students did. Pathways students cited gangs and violence, whereas the Grant Park students mentioned the safety and peacefulness of their neighbourhood.

Students from all three groups noted that media portrayals of the inner city were highly negative, and they identified this as a major factor in creating their fear of the area. For the CEDA Pathways students, media played a role as well, but their fears were also based in personal exposure to violence and youth gangs.

Interestingly, the inner-city students from CEDA Pathways expressed more negative perceptions of the inner city than did the others. Although all three groups identified the area with violence, gangs, drugs, crime, and poverty, the Grant Park students also mentioned its positive aspects. This included organizations such as Art City and the West End Cultural Centre, as well as the abundance of music, good restaurants, culture, diversity, and interesting places.

Adult Perceptions of Teenagers

We asked students about adult perceptions of teenagers. All three groups responded with typical adolescent remarks about the negative attitudes of parents, who saw them as lazy, moody, and rebellious. Some said that their parents were generally very supportive and encouraging.

Barriers and Supports

Here too, the three groups made similar comments regarding the supports they needed and the barriers that might stop them from finishing high school. However, the CEDA Pathways students tended to focus on the support they received from the Pathways program, whereas the others concentrated on support from their parents. This speaks to the importance of community-based programs and supports for young people who have complicated lives, often associated with poverty.

Perceptions of Indigenous People

Finally, most students felt that racism toward Indigenous people had diminished, but they agreed that it remained endemic. Interestingly, the views of the Grant Park and Collège Béliveau students were more positive than those of CEDA Pathways students. The suburban non-Indigenous students seemed to understand that the disadvantages experienced by many Indigenous students were grounded in societal injustice, not personal failings. We found that encouraging.

The differing perceptions between Indigenous and non-Indigenous students were instructive for at least two reasons. First, they revealed that internalized oppression continued to run deep and that the media had perpetuated this by failing to contextualize the realities of the inner city and Indigenous people. As Freire (2006, 63) notes, "self-deprecation is a characteristic of the oppressed ... So often do they hear that they are good for nothing, know nothing, and are incapable of learning anything – that they are sick, lazy, and unproductive – that in the end they become convinced of their own unfitness." This pattern is well entrenched in the inner city, where youth come to accept the negative media portrayals of themselves and their communities. This contributes to their belief that nothing better is possible – that they are destined to fail – and this sometimes leads to poor, albeit not entirely irrational, choices.

Second, the differences in opinion reminded us that there is hope. The non-inner-city students were keenly interested in learning how they could make a difference. Due in large part to the work of the TRC, non-Indigenous students are beginning to learn about Canada's colonial history and the devastating impact of Indian residential schools and the Sixties Scoop. These students are the natural allies of the new generation of Indigenous inner-city leaders. Non-Indigenous youth are looking for ways to channel their social justice efforts, but they need some guidance to help them understand that their role is not to "save" through a charity approach, but to support and walk beside their Indigenous peers and advocate for change together.

We were somewhat surprised but also inspired by the fact that the non-inner-city students were fairly well informed about the inner city. They identified many of its negative aspects but were far less naive than we had expected. For example, they expressed much skepticism regarding media portrayals of the area and were very aware that the media focuses on its negative and sensational aspects, rarely reporting anything positive. One student astutely suggested that parents sometimes used the inner city as a scare tactic, inferring that young people who behaved badly and didn't do as they were told would end up "like them." Students seemed to understand that however well intentioned, this attitude simply exacerbated the problem by implying that bad things happen in the inner city because the people who live there are bad.

It was refreshing to see that the students were questioning what they heard about the inner city and Indigenous people. They understood that something more profound was going on, and they wanted to find out what it was and how to fix it. We were inspired to learn of their awareness, which was much greater than many thought. Although our sample size was small and therefore probably not representative of the diverse views of youth, it showed that leadership existed among Winnipeg students. We were optimistic about bringing the groups together and hoped that dialogue among themselves and with the Elders would be useful to them.

At Circle of Life Thunderbird House

On October 13, 2012, we brought the three groups of students together at Circle of Life Thunderbird House, where we were joined by their teachers, mentors, and four of the Indigenous Elders whom we had interviewed. Circle of Life Thunderbird House is an Indigenous education and cultural centre situated in the heart of Winnipeg's inner city. In spite of its striking physical beauty and its potential as a space to practise truth and reconciliation, a relatively small number of non-Indigenous Winnipeg residents visit Thunderbird House. The day began with participants gathered in a circle. Elder Clarence Neepinak opened the day welcoming students and explaining the history, design, and significance of Thunderbird House. He described the use of sage, the significance of the smudging ceremony, and the importance of tobacco. Elder Barbara Neepinak then explained and conducted the water ceremony, a sacred Indigenous rite traditionally led by women.

Claire Friesen, the mentor coordinator from CEDA Pathways then led some activities to break the ice by encouraging students to interact with those whom they did not already know. The group then returned to the circle and Elder Mark Hall introduced them to Dakota teachings and traditions, welcoming them with a song and a prayer. It was a powerful opening, with the Elder's strong voice filling the room, setting the tone for the day.

Kathy Mallett, director of CEDA, then spoke about the sharing circle in Indigenous cultures. The activities of the day would be structured around the sharing circle and not all students were familiar with the concept and protocols. She explained that a speaking stone would be passed to participants sitting in the circle. When passed the stone, the participant had an opportunity to speak while others listened. If participants didn't wish to speak, they were informed to simply pass the stone on to the next person. Students were told that the sharing circle is intended as a safe space to share thoughts and feelings in confidence and without judgement. Kathy opened the sharing circle. She talked about her life as an Indigenous woman growing up in Winnipeg during the 1960s and 1970s, mentioned the racism that she experienced, and expressed the sadness and anger that persisted. She introduced her colleague, Rebecca Blaikie, a non-Indigenous woman thirty years her junior. Rebecca spoke about her relationship with Kathy and her role as an ally – continually learning, taking the lead from her Indigenous colleague as they worked together to challenge racism and social and economic injustice.

Rebecca then led the sharing circle in a smudge ceremony, advising everyone that participation was voluntary. Ann Callahan shared her experiences as an Elder and encouraged the students to be the leaders of the future. For the next hour, a speaking stone was passed around the circle, enabling all to express their thoughts and tell the group why they chose to spend a Saturday afternoon with Elders and others at Thunderbird House. Many students had much to say, whereas others silently passed the stone along.

Some very powerful moments occurred in the circle, which won't be described in detail in respect for those involved. However, one example was especially powerful. One non-Indigenous boy from an affluent neighbourhood was visibly moved by the experience, so much so that he burst into tears when it was his turn to share. But more surprising to us was the response of two Indigenous boys from an inner-city neighbourhood. These brothers clapped their hands in genuine applause for the young boy who spoke so honestly about his privileged position and the injustice that his Indigenous peers experienced. When the circle broke up, the boys walked directly to him, shook his hand, and chatted with him. It was heartwarming and inspiring to witness this bridging of the divide. These boys would probably never forget what transpired that morning. And neither would we.

At the end of the lunch break, the group broke into four smaller circles, allowing students to spend more time with the Elders to learn about their experiences with racism and residential schools, and to hear what youth might do to carry on their work. Lively discussion ensued, filling up every bit of the final few hours of the day.

The Speaker's Booth

Throughout the day, students were encouraged to share their thoughts in a speaker's booth that was set up in a quiet, private room. There, they were filmed as they spoke about racism, social and economic injustice, and how they could combat these. The larger gathering at Thunderbird House was also being videotaped for use in a film titled *Breaking Barriers, Building Bridges* (O'Brien 2012). The students knew that it would include footage from the speaker's booth, with the permission of both their parents and themselves.

In the booth, several students spoke to the camera, providing insightful reflections about the divide in Winnipeg and their hopes for the future. They expressed appreciation for the time spent with the Elders. A non-Indigenous student said,

> One of my favourite parts was when – well most of it's been awesome, so I've really liked it – but specifically one of my favourite parts is when [Mark Hall] ... started speaking in his Aboriginal language. And I thought that was really cool that most of the people here have been speaking ... in their Aboriginal language and then talking to us. And he, he sang, and it was just so breathtaking ... It was beautiful. It was

breathtaking, but even though it was very nice, but it was more so like empowering and it ... just gave me shivers through my spine. It was very, very strong.

I'm glad I got to meet a lot of the Elders. I learnt a lot from them today. I've learnt some of their stories; they've been, like, open enough to share their stories, and I think that's really good and awesome because if we don't share our stories, we won't be able to learn from other's mistakes or our own mistakes. (CCPA 2012, 26)

Before ending the day, everyone returned to the larger circle to talk about how to move forward. At the request of Elder Ann Callahan, we held hands in expression of solidarity and commitment to work toward ending racism in our city and making it a good place for everyone to live. The students were told that they would be invited back to view the film and to participate in the release of a report that would further our efforts to build bridges across geographies and cultures.

Where to Go from Here

A young woman spoke to the need to build on the momentum that was started in this project:

This is an amazing experience. I'm so glad I came and it's just been phenomenal ... how often do you meet people ... and discover something about yourself? ... We had a sharing circle and almost every time someone said something I could relate to – at least a part of it. I think that's really awesome that we have the same values, and even if we come from different points of view or even if we have a couple of different values, we can still share something together. I think that's really important and I think that we should do that more with each other ... We'd learn how to help ourselves by helping others and that's really important because we need to learn how to respect others more than we do ... I find a lot of youth today don't respect people as much as they should ...

Activities like this help me figure out [how to]... stop racism ... We get together, we talk it out, we don't just judge each other and not say anything cause we really need to talk things out ... I'm glad that I came and I thank everyone who came today and all the Elders ... for sharing their stories and it was an amazing experience. Thank you. (CCPA 2012, 27)

At the end of the project, we decided that several things needed to happen if its momentum were to continue. These are:

1   The enthusiasm with which youth responded to this project shows that there is a real need to establish a forum for Indigenous and non-Indigenous youth, inner-city and suburban youth, to talk to and learn from one another. Dialogue is the first step toward breaking down barriers. We must enable students to engage in it.

2   Non-Indigenous and non-inner-city youth should be encouraged to identify their role in bridging the divide and be provided with support to take leadership. We need to supply them with tools so that they can detect social and economic injustice, question its origin, and criticize current approaches that rely far too much on charity as a remedy for ills. We must explain to them that social and economic difference is a societal problem, not an individual problem, and that disadvantaged youth want their respect, not their pity. We need to help them understand that solutions will come from working side by side to break down barriers, build relationships, and most importantly, to effect change at a societal level. This means speaking out and working to end poverty, racism, and their associated harms. Furnishing guidance and ongoing dialogue will help make this happen.

3   Inner-city and particularly Indigenous youth must have every possible opportunity to reclaim their pride – to embrace their identity. Their Elders and spiritual leaders can help them to discard the negative stereotypes of Indigenous people so that they can move forward "from a place of strength," as the Elders say in the film. Elders can help them retrieve their culture through traditional teachings.

4   Adults have an important role to play. Both Indigenous and non-Indigenous teachers and mentors can support and guide youth who are desperately looking for a way to make real change. They need and want our help to determine how to proceed.

5 The important role of Elders and of space and place must not be minimized. Most students who participated in our project had never been to Thunderbird House. Many had never met an Elder. The history and symbolism of Thunderbird House provide an evocative backdrop for events such as the one described in this chapter. For Indigenous youth, the gathering was powerful because it showcased a bit of their culture to their non-Indigenous peers. We did not anticipate their sense of pride, yet it made perfect sense. They were welcoming privileged non-Indigenous youth into *their* space, with *their* Elders. They were allowing the non-Indigenous students to experience the positive spirit of their culture, which too often goes unnoticed. Thus, Thunderbird House can be both a safe space and an important part of the learning process. Educators who teach students about Indigenous history and culture would be wise to bring them to Indigenous spaces such as Thunderbird House and to include Elders in the process.

6 And finally, we all have something to learn. Teachers from the two schools and program staff from CEDA Pathways also participated in the sharing circles and the speaker's booth. We all learned something that day. One teacher was particularly open and honest. We include his words because he inspires us all to be honest with ourselves about the racism that is so deeply engrained in our society and thus internalized within us all:

> Well I think one lesson I took home from today is that we're not that different after all. Sometimes we feel like we're different or you know.
>
> What I learned from the Elders today is to trust myself, to be honest and to not be scared to share and to share what I know, share my knowledge, share my, my wisdom. I kind of wish that I could be an Elder one day and hopefully I will be and I kind of am right now cause I'm a teacher so I have to, have to teach but I think the way they taught was very, well very good for me, for my learning style.
>
> What kind of world do I dream of living in as an adult? I think I live in a pretty good world but for my children I want them to live in

a world where they are proud of who they are but one that does not, it does not hold them back from being open to other cultures but being proud of their own culture and but still being open to others, but being proud of who they are and by being proud of who they are they're not scared to, to learn about others.

Another thing I learned today is not to be scared ... You get a feeling from the media that, that going downtown is dangerous and I walked here today and I have to admit I was scared at the moment, I even hid my earphones because I had an iPhone and I didn't want to get it stolen and it's kind of stupid and I feel guilty about feeling that way. But and not looking people in the eye like I was coming here and I would, I would refrain from looking at people in the eye and I think today that I should, I should not be scared of, of looking people in the eye.

Countering racism. Well I kind of realized today that I thought I wasn't racist but I still have some stereotypes in my head that I need to get rid of and I need to learn how to take away those barriers because you come with a cultural background and then you come in listening, reading in the media and looking at TV and movies etc. and we're taught and I teach my students to be open-minded and sometimes I'm not that open-minded as I think I am, so I need to really open up my mind and that's what today, that's what I learned today and I'm, I'm proud that I did and I still have lots of work to do and lots of wisdom to, to accumulate still and hopefully I can be one of these Elders one day.

Yeah and be in touch, I learned to, to be in touch with who I am and I think there's somebody inside that wants to get out and hopefully it will. I can learn to let that person out some day. (CCPA 2012, 28)

Concluding Thoughts and Progress Made

On every level, the gathering at Thunderbird House far exceeded our expectations, thanks to the commitment of the Elders, but especially to the young people who listened so intently and shared so openly, trusting in the power and safety of the circle.

Despite the overwhelming success, there were a few limitations of note. One individual observed that the students in his group tended to direct their thoughts to the Elder rather than to each other. This is not particularly surprising, but it is something to consider in future. We expect that students felt more comfortable speaking with the Elders, but the fact that they shared in the presence of other students was an important first step. The next step, as mentioned above, is to encourage greater dialogue among the students themselves.

Also, we were unable to spend much time discussing how the work of this project could be furthered. Herein lies an ongoing challenge. What began as a community-based research project, testing the hypothesis that engaging youth and Elders might help address the divide in Winnipeg, evolved into something of great potential. The issue, however, is how to move it forward from a group with very little capacity. We have encouraged the Winnipeg school division to take on this project but have not yet been successful. Nonetheless, we continue to use our film as an educational tool whenever the opportunity presents.

Despite the limitations, we are grateful for having had the chance to spend our Saturday with such an inspiring group of students and Elders. It was a transformative event in which dialogue with youth, Elders, teachers, and others reminded us that there is great hope.

Encouraged by its powerful impact, we hoped that a variation of this project would be incorporated into the school curriculum, perhaps as the Breaking Barriers, Building Bridges Program. However, progress was slow. The *Maclean's* article describing the racism in our city was published two years after the gathering at Thunderbird House. Then, in 2017, after many meetings with government curriculum developers, the Winnipeg School Division, and funding agencies, CEDA Pathways was able to move the project forward. A second cohort of suburban non-Indigenous students came into the inner city to learn with inner-city Indigenous youth and Elders at Circle of Life Thunderbird House. The aim is to host two of these events each year so as to slowly chip away at the racism that continues to plague our city. Winnipeg remains a divided city and racism persists. But through this project youth and Elders have shown us that change is possible.

REFERENCES

Artibise, Alan F.J. 1977. *Winnipeg: An Illustrated History.* Toronto: Lorimer.

Brownell, Marnie, Carolyn De Coster, Robert Penfold, Shelly Derksen, Wendy Au, Jennifer Schultz, and Matthew Dahl. 2008. *Manitoba Child Health Atlas Update.* Winnipeg: Manitoba Centre for Health Policy. http://mchp-appserv.cpe.umanitoba.ca/reference/Child_Health_Atlas_Update_Final.pdf.

Brownell, Marnie, Mariette Chartier, Rob Santos, Okechukwu Ekuma, Wendy Au, Joykrishna Sarkar, Leonard MacWilliam, Elaine Burland, Ina Koseva, and Wendy Guenette. 2012. *How Are Manitoba's Children Doing?* Winnipeg: Manitoba Centre for Health Policy. http://mchp-appserv.cpe.umanitoba.ca/reference//mb_kids_report_WEB.pdf.

CCPA (Canadian Centre for Policy Alternatives). 2012. "Fixing Our Divided City." In *Breaking Barriers, Building Bridges: State of the Inner City Report, 2012.* Winnipeg: CCPA–Manitoba.

Fernandez, Lynne, Shauna MacKinnon, and Jim Silver, eds. 2015. *The Social Determinants of Health in Manitoba.* 2nd ed. Winnipeg: Canadian Centre for Policy Alternatives–Manitoba.

Freire, Paulo. 2006. *Pedagogy of the Oppressed.* 30th anniversary edition. New York: Continuum.

Hall, Stuart. 2006. "Cosmopolitan Promises, Multicultural Realities." In *Divided Cities: The Oxford Amnesty Lectures 2003,* ed. Richard Scholar, 20–51. Oxford: Oxford University Press.

Huffman, Terry. 2008. *American Indian Higher Education Experiences: Cultural Visions and Personal Journeys.* New York: Peter Lang.

Macdonald, Nancy. 2015. "Welcome to Winnipeg: Where Canada's Racism Problem Is at Its Worst." *Maclean's,* January 22. http://www.macleans.ca/news/canada/welcome-to-winnipeg-where-canadas-racism-problem-is-at-its-worst/.

MacKinnon, Shauna. 2015. *Decolonizing Employment: Aboriginal Inclusion in Canada's Labour Market.* Winnipeg: University of Manitoba Press.

O'Brien, Carole, dir. 2012. *Breaking Barriers, Building Bridges.* Winnipeg: CCPA–MB. https://www.youtube.com/watch?v=NIMrk8sE5tA.

Probe Research. 2014. "Winnipeg Is a Divided City, Citizens Say." October 7. http://news.probe-research.com/2014/10/winnipeg-is-divided-city-citizens-say.html.

Silver, Jim. 2006. *In Their Own Voices: Building Urban Aboriginal Communities.* Halifax: Fernwood.

Smith, Linda Tuhiwai. 1999. *Decolonizing Methodologies: Research and Indigenous Peoples.* New York: Zed Books.

Statistics Canada. 2011. "Demographic Characteristics of Aboriginal People." NHS
    Focus on Geography Series. http://www12.statcan.gc.ca/nhs-enm/2011/as-sa/
    fogs-spg/Pages/FOG.cfm?lang=E&level=2&GeoCode=46.
TRC (Truth and Reconciliation Commission of Canada). 2015. *Honouring the Truth,
    Reconciling for the Future. Summary of the Final Report of the Truth and Recon-
    ciliation Commission of Canada.* http://www.trc.ca/websites/trcinstitution/File/
    2015/Honouring_the_Truth_Reconciling_for_the_Future_July_23_2015.pdf.

13

Reclaiming the Talk
Popular Theatre and Historical Testimonies as First Nation Women's Empowerment in Hollow Water, Manitoba

DORIS DIFARNECIO

Storytelling is commonly used in community-based participatory research (CBPR). It can be a particularly powerful means of gathering knowledge from individuals whose voices have been silenced, and the knowledge can be used in transformative ways. This chapter looks at diverse ways of approaching CBPR. As a director of popular theatre, I am invested in first-person narratives and the retelling of these narratives to encourage women to reconnect with their personal agency and to share this encounter with both their communities and the outside world. I have witnessed this process as profoundly transformative and life affirming for the women I direct, their communities, and myself. I am deeply implicated as a facilitator of this process. Thus, I see my role as walking *with* the women: I am not an expert who comes in with knowledge and power but rather a co-performer, a witness, and a friend. I have as much to learn from them as they do from me, if not more.

In this chapter, I recount my time with Shavon Sinclair and her eldest daughter, Mallory, as "walking with" on personal journeys toward agency in the face of neocolonial violence. Both Mallory and Shavon are Anishinaabe activists from Hollow Water First Nation, a small and remote Anishnaabe First Nation on Lake Winnipeg. Although Shavon did not attend a residential school, other family members did and she is a witness to their trauma and alcoholism as a result of the violence they experienced there. Using the methods of oral history performance (Pollock 2005) and popular theatre, "reclaiming the talk," I argue, is a way for First Nations women to reclaim voice, space, and agency.

Reclaiming voice has also been central to the Truth and Reconciliation Commission of Canada (TRC), which travelled the country between 2008 and 2015, hearing testimony related to residential schools. An important role of the TRC was to "gather statements from former students of the Indian Residential Schools and anyone else who feels they have been impacted by the schools and their legacy" (TRC n.d.). The TRC saw these statements as an important part of the healing process, which is necessary if Indigenous and non-Indigenous people are to achieve "reconciliation towards a new relationship" (ibid.) in Canada. Although reconciliation is a complex possibility, I believe that the TRC validated victims' lives by listening to their testimonies of traumatic experiences. Nonetheless, a great deal of work remains to be done in building social relationships and healing communities where the trauma of residential schools continues to be passed from generation to generation. Thus, I humbly propose oral history performance through popular theatre as an alternative, or perhaps supplemental, method of inquiry that can bring about transformative change. Knowledge transference is generated through ritual, poetry, dance, spirituality, and testimony to enable community building and healing. Popular theatre attempts to inspire the audience to think about community and real possibilities for change.

I was introduced to Shavon by Peter Kulchyski, head of the Department of Native Studies at the University of Manitoba, after he saw my work with a group of Indigenous actresses and writers in Chiapas, Mexico. Since our first meeting, we had talked about the possibility of visiting Hollow Water and meeting the women leaders in the community. The women of Hollow Water First Nation had moved forward in their storytelling through sheer determination to achieve long-term closure and healing for themselves and their community. I was drawn to Shavon's story and promised that I would visit Hollow Water. In February 2015, I went to Manitoba to work with her and her personal testimony, which is grounded in trauma and sexual violence stemming from residential schools.

In Mexico, where I presently live and continue to direct theatre and work as an activist for women's rights, I was the theatre director in-residence with a Mayan writers' collective in San Cristóbal de las Casas, Chiapas, from 1999 to 2012. This collective (FOMMA: Fortaleza de la Mujer Maya/ Strength of the Mayan Woman) is composed of performers, playwrights, and teachers whose theatrical work focuses on Indigenous women's rights, literacy, cultural survival, ecology, health, and education. Having worked as an actress, educator, and director in New York, I implemented theatre techniques and training in an intercultural exchange between Western theatre practices and Indigenous Mexican popular theatre to develop FOMMA's repertoire. Most FOMMA members lived through neocolonial violence within and outside of their communities of origin that included but were not limited to sexual and interpersonal violence and trauma, displacement, language barriers, government extortion, and health injustice. The central theme of my dramaturgical direction and their written and scenic work was empowering themselves, one another, and their communities to change their circumstances, with theatre as the vehicle.

As a working-class immigrant myself, born in Medellín, Colombia and raised largely in New York, I was drawn to the stories of interfamilial violence and trauma (particularly patriarchal violence) as a way to collectively find creative strategies out of these "destinies." With FOMMA, I toured to Tzeltal and Tzotzil Indigenous communities in the Highlands of Chiapas, Mexico (all FOMMA members are Tzeltal or Tzotil women). The success and accessibility of the work also took us to Mexico City, other parts of Mexico, Argentina, the United States, Brazil, Guatemala, Nicaragua, Spain, and Egypt. The political and cultural implications of this artistic collaboration continue to resonate in every area of my personal and professional life, affecting my artistic experiences and pursuits, as well as my scholarly endeavours.

With this experience, I arrived in Canada excited by the challenge of working in a different cultural context – that of First Nations women. Although their language, history, and regionally specific stories differed from those of the Mexican Indigenous women with whom I had worked, there were a number of parallels that gave me an understanding of and entrance into their world. The most marked of these were the legacies of colonial violence and their current repercussions, particularly sexual violence and abuse in Indigenous communities.

Residential Schools and the TRC

Canada's infamous residential school policies date from as early as the 1880s and continued as late as 1998, when the last school finally closed its doors (Rice 2011). First Nations children were removed from their families – and thus from parental involvement in their lives – and sent to government-funded and church-run institutions. The intent of the schools was to eliminate Indigenous languages, culture, identities, traditions, and practices, replacing them with Euro-Canadian Catholic/Protestant values and a rudimentary Western education. Under Canadian law, all Aboriginal children were required to attend residential schools, which became their legal guardians. The schools were run by the four major churches in partnership with the federal government (Rice 2011). The schools focused on cultural assimilation through forced labour and numerous types of violence. This formative experience left a legacy of rage and grief, which remains largely unresolved due to the ongoing violences of colonialism. Passed from generation to generation, this trauma has had a profoundly damaging impact on First Nations people and other Canadians, including future generations, who have become "bearers of a legacy." Survivors have passed on the pain to their children, who have inherited it as their own (Smith 2012).

Although the TRC was intended to address this history, it was not universally acclaimed. Particularly controversial was a restriction that prohibited survivors and school staff from naming or otherwise identifying individuals accused of wrongdoing or violent crimes (Rice 2011). In other words, the commission was a civil process, not a criminal court; it could not subpoena offenders, and they would not be subject to prosecution. Nonetheless, the TRC created a space that brought First Nations people to publicly share and denounce the violence they suffered through residential schools. Although this validated their lives and memories, the healing process does not end there. The performance of oral history can contribute to healing individuals and communities, and the knowledge that it produces can have profound implications for them and for policy makers. Oral history performance through popular theatre as a means of conducting research can empower people to think about their place in the world and their community. Sharing cultural and historic memories can lead to strong social relationships that are required to build community for the future.

Rehearsal Notes on Beginning the Process of Retelling

A member of the Anishinaabe First Nation's Bear Clan, Shavon Sinclair is presently entering an Indigenous studies master's program at the University of Manitoba. Peter Kulchyski, chair of Native Studies at the university, who had worked with her for a number of years, suggested we should meet and develop a theatrical performance based on the testimonies, oral history, and life stories of the women in Hollow Water. Shavon and I met in the summer of 2014, and she introduced me to her family members, friends, and the Elders of Hollow Water. I was fortunate to meet Berma, Shavon's mentor, a respected community organizer and political activist in Hollow Water. She was interested in oral history performance and emphasized the importance of family and the relationship one has to a place of origin, including with natural features such as trees, rivers, and mountains (the latter of which I have come to call the geography of memory). Berma felt strongly that shared histories could build community, connect families, and share values. She encouraged Shavon not to be fearful of exploring performance as a way to speak the truth about her life. I believe that Berma's support of Shavon allowed us to shift community-based research into a process that merged art and research.

During the second week of our rehearsal, Shavon decided to invite Mallory, her eldest daughter who was twenty years old, to attend. Since Shavon took the rehearsal process as a healing experience, she felt that Mallory's presence and involvement were crucial. We then commenced rehearsals as a collective.

Mallory's participation was fundamental to the creation of the play. Serious and committed, she became the stage manager, keeping the order and timing of our rehearsals. She also archived video footage and kept meticulous notes of our direction, later applying the notes to help her mother remember the scene work. In the beginning, the physical warm-up exercises were difficult to integrate, but bringing in popular culture such as hip hop and the music of First Nations bands such as A Tribe Called Red helped us to express ourselves with less inhibition. Mallory was determined to learn and observe every detail of the production. She became an indispensable part of the process, though that had not been our initial plan.

Before Mallory arrived, Shavon had written her life story, creating an autobiographical arc. In First Nations worldviews, the spine of an eagle feather represents the arc of one's life. Shavon began her eagle feather trajectory at her birth and proceeded to the present. As she recounted specific traumatic events throughout her life, Mallory listened intently and interwove her own experience into her mother's narrative.

The continuation of the rehearsal and creative process included the use of music videos, Audre Lorde's recorded reading of her essay "Uses of the Erotic: The Erotic as Power,"[1] and journal entries about personal journeys with trauma and violence in particular, as a result of colonial violences. Physical and vocal warm-ups were essential in releasing the tension and sorrow from the body, voice, and breath.

Oral History Performance and Finding Talk through Decolonization

During our rehearsal process, Shavon wrote the following poem:

> *i lost my talk*
>
> *i lost my talk ...*
> *the talk you took away*
> *when i was a little girl at hollow water school ...*
> *you ... snatched it away*
> *i speak like you ... i think like you ... i create like you*
> *the addicted words*
> *two ways i talk ...*
> *both ways i say*
> *your way is more powerful...*
> *so gently ... i offer my hand and ask ...*
> *let me have my talk ... so i can walk away*

This work is closely based on "I Lost My Talk," a poem written by Mi'kmaq residential school survivor Rita Joe (1988). We found it in a book of First Nations poetry, which was suggested to us by Roewan Crowe, a dear friend and a scholar in the Department of Women and Gender Studies at the University of Winnipeg. Shavon chose it because she felt connected to the political message of naming what had been taken: voice.

She wrote, "I was only a little girl and he told me he was going to show me how to become a woman ... I was just a little girl. He took my talk away."

Reading this poem aloud was a painful process of remembering not only her own trauma, but also her sister April's rape at the age of six. She begins to address this by relating her own daily decision to wear layers of clothing, symbolically protecting herself and covering her body from violence:

> *You know why I don't wear dresses?*
> *I've learned dresses get you into trouble.*
> *My sister and I ...*
> *my beautiful sister*
> *She was 6, I was 8*
> *She wore a pretty yellow shirt*
> *a beautiful white skirt*
> *she was so pretty ...*
> *light brown hair*
> *it was sunny outside*
> *white puffy clouds*
> *sky was blue*
> *I asked April to play hide and seek*
> *where are you April*
> *April!*
> *April*
> *where are you?*
> *I can't find her*
> *April?*
> *April ... where are you?*
> *I don't want to play this game no more*
> *I sit in silence ...*
> *She's being raped ...*
> *I wait ...*
> *she comes back*
> *I know what happened*
> *C'mon little sister, I'll hold this with you*
> *I'll take you to the clouds ...*

As Shavon noted, "the trauma of sexual abuse is a taboo to talk about with family and community." She adds, "We don't talk about these stories and we don't need these stories of abuse anymore, we need to release them, throw them away." She repeatedly told Mallory of the importance of letting go of oppressive silence:

> Working with my mother and daughter brought me to a place of pain, sorrow and lastly to a place of laughter. We cried together, we danced together and we would laugh together. Hearing our stories and telling my story was the hardest task to do. It was hard to hear the stories of my mother and daughter. It was especially hard to tell my story to my mother. My mother was strong and brave. She encouraged me to tell my story in order to heal my past memories. My mother wanted me to let go of the hurts I endured as a child, adolescent and a mother. She wanted me to tell my story raw and not lie to protect others. She said, "Let it go and know, I can take it, whatever your story is. I would tell my story raw."

Oral History

Shavon layered her narrative with metaphor to navigate the pain and sorrow of remembering. Her stories fit into the historical colonial context of First Nations people in Manitoba, and thus I see my video interviews with her as oral history rather than mere journalistic tellings.[2] Oral history involves recounting one's story in a controlled and trusting environment, always aware of the larger social structures and issues one is connected with. Pollock (2005, 2) suggests that oral history is a performance and relates it to memory making and transformation: "The performance of oral history is itself a transformational process. At the very least, it translates subjectively remembered events into embodied memory acts, moving memory into re-membering. That passage not only risks but endows the emerging history/narratives with change." Oral history is performed as much for the teller as for the listener. In this sense, Shavon performed her oral history testimonies for me, after which we considered how they could be re-performed. Shavon also emphasized the importance of including her mother in the process:

> I wanted to demonstrate the significance of storytelling and the impacts of the intergenerational abuse cycle. I wanted to attack the gloomy past

with grace and honesty. I wanted the world to know, Anishinabek culture complements the workings of performance art. I wanted to demonstrate the work in performance arts is in fact a methodology of healing. I wanted to demonstrate there is a way to include both performance art and methods of healing using concepts used in Anishinabek culture and traditions.

When she was a child, Shavon tried to escape sexual violence by hiding on a hill and looking at the sky. As an adult, she rewrote the experience poetically:

> When I was a little girl, granny's hill
> I'd go lay under the clouds ... Dream ... Escape
> I see grandpa, sitting on the porch ... Carving
> Carving bears, beavers, wolves, berries, fruit.

Speaking with the intention of being heard (as opposed to being silenced) creates emotional movement, so retelling is not necessarily painless. Early in the rehearsal process, Shavon sometimes felt physically weak and fragile. The recollections had visceral effects on her body. She struggled with words and the forms with which to talk about the past. Her determination to move forward and to work through her pain and anxiety helped her to express herself:

Together, we all worked on the story arc and then turned the story arc into a performance. I thought about turning my story arc into a performance for one major reason. I knew a portion of my life consisted of memories that were both positive and negative. I wanted to transform the negative into something beautiful and how else to achieve that ... well turn my memories into a beautiful performance that can help others to tell their stories. Memories live in everyone and memories will never leave you; however, it is the memories that entice you to either live in the negative or positive. I choose to turn my negative and positive into a story that will invoke others to turn their memories into something beautiful.

My own witnessing became political. What I saw was an individual and collective mourning that made visible a history of brutal colonization of a people. Shavon's written narrative and testimony emerged from the extreme margins of life in a First Nation afflicted by poverty, abandonment, and sexual violence. Like a thrown stone skipping across the surface of a lake, her talk spreads out and moves in and through us:

> *i place this rock here to close the circle to protect me and my daughter*
> *i place this rock here to close the circle to protect me and my daughter*
> *i place this rock here to close the circle to protect me and my daughter*
> *i place this rock here to close the circle to protect me and my daughter*

The ripples created by the stone as it touches the water are the ripples that Shavon's words have begun to make in her community. A single story is never just one story. It tells the history of a people and their desire to move beyond colonialism.

When oral history is performed as popular theatre, it communicates social issues and denounces injustice, with the intent of building community and moving away from colonial legacies. A narrative like Shavon's can become a radical positioning, a subversive act of confronting a colonizing power that is still very much present in Canada. As Linda Tuhiwai Smith (2012, 93) explains, "colonialism brought complete disorder to colonized peoples, disconnecting them from their histories, their landscapes, their languages, their social relations and their own ways of thinking, feeling and interacting with the world." Oral history performance connects and engages the teller with the listeners. When we reveal ourselves to others, we generate knowledge and become politically involved in the process. The creative process is one way to work toward decolonizing the self. The colonial past is embedded in our political discourses, our humour, poetry, music, storytelling, and other quotidian moments that take history's colonial burden for granted (Smith 2012).

In telling their stories and wrestling with a traumatic past, the women in Hollow Water occupy centre stage. This embodiment offers alternatives to combating social structures that marginalize and oppress them. Self-empowerment begins when they gain the confidence and ability to analyze

– and dream of changing – the social and economic challenges that they and their communities face. Mallory described it this way:

> In our performance we used ceremony to give us the strength and courage to be able to give these traumatic experiences a voice and prove that there is another way of healing and getting through it. Ever since I was a little girl I was always close with my grandmother and she taught me about my people and our ceremonies and had passed down some of our people's teachings.

A traditional healer burns sage in a smudging ceremony, prays to the four directions, honours the creator, and sprinkles water on the top of her head, all of which Shavon replicated in her performance. Afterward, when Shavon's parents asked her where she had learned these gestures, she replied, "I don't remember where I learned the movement – it's in my body, in my memory. It comes from my people." In and of itself, the performance was a process of reclaiming and of reclamation of body, of land, of territory, of community, and of story. It helped to publicly release pain and rage through the ritual of mourning. This was a moment in which the subject became empowered by reclamation in heightened and protected time – in performance.

In the re-performance of oral history narratives, embodied truths about racial discrimination, poverty, and sexual violence surface, making present the historical atrocities endured by First Nations people. Retelling evidences the complexities involved in a process of reconciliation through performative reclamation.

Remembering, writing, and speaking about past traumas introduces the mind, body, and spirit as tools of expression and restoration, uncovering an individual's innate ability to articulate the will to survive. The performance of oral history in the context of Canada's "collective amnesia" requires a radical repositioning by a subject to visibilize and bear witness to his or her *own* historical memory. Autobiographical remembering (an inherited legacy of Indigenous tradition and ritual) creates an emergent and politicized subject. The oppressed person localizes metaphorical language to engage historical witnessing through popular theatre and oral history performance. Engagement is key in the theatrical provocation of distancing oneself from the normalization of violence and patriarchal gender politics. This is a bold act of artistic resistance that confronts, head on, issues of race, gender, and economic inequality.

Popular theatre and the performance of oral history as intersecting methods of artistic practice are active counterpoints toward shifting hegemonic paradigms of cultural erasure. Testimony, as the transmission of knowledge, becomes a metaphor for historical survival. Witnessing becomes a political and *participatory* act, creating urgency by displacing the normalization of violence, which is typically accompanied by denial and impunity. Oral history itself bears witness to the spirit of survival and determination of First Nations people – creating a synergy between the teller and the listener, who then both exercise agency and engage each other's personhood.

When the quotidian is disrupted, the audience is invited into a representation of the conditions of extreme violence, performatively construed. The moment of ritual allows an entrance into what would otherwise be unbearable or difficult to consume as audience-witnesses, regardless of the violence of the original events. Shavon remembers a vision she had when she was struggling with addiction. The bear appeared to her giving her strength to withdraw from her addiction. In performance she ritualizes the vision with her daughter Mallory by smudging her with sage and repeating as she smudges her body, "I will take back the pain."

> *I will take back the pain, the hurt I gave you,*
> *so you will dance your own dance*
>
> *my head is hung low ...*
> *i see artifacts around me, in a circle ...*
> *then i can hear the bear ...*
> *i stand up ...*
> *i stand in fear ...*
> *i can feel it ...*
> *walking ...*
> *smelling ...*
> *breathing ...*

> *the bear is in me ...*
> *i am the bear.*
> *I am of the bear clan.*

Circling an eagle feather around her daughter's body, she cleanses the pain. In the same way, her poetry hails the symbol of the matriarchal Bear Clan. The bear surrounds her, walks by her, and enters her. It claims her and pulls her out of violence and addiction. The ritual enacts the power of First Nations women, the Bear Clan women, to make the ungraspable sorrow become a collective sense of being. The witnesses' consciousness, moral values, and ethics are brought to the forefront, forcing them to look at themselves and their silence regarding the social, political, and identitarian repercussions for a population that lost its lands and sovereignty to colonial violence.

The cartography of struggle – a remapping of one's life – contributes to the sustainability of Indigenous knowledge and spiritual and ethical connectivity. Smith (2012, 39) notes that "contested stories and multiple discourses about the past, by different communities, are closely linked to the politics of everyday contemporary indigenous life." The rise of a new political subject occurs in opposition to the marginalization that First Nations people continue to experience in Canada.

Performing oral history creates an emergent subject who is willing to decentralize the site of power through the performance. These performances function as insurgent movements. Responding to the violence of erasure and oppression, Shavon writes,

> *You said I had to work at it –*
> *YOU, made me ugly.*
> *YOU, made me weak*
> *You stole my story, used it as your own*
> *BITCH*
> *I grew up*
> *Time passes*
> *And you were wrong*
> *You will never tell my story again*

In her retelling, Shavon reclaims her talk. Crucial to the decolonization of First Nations people is the reclamation of telling, of story, and ultimately, of agency. Cultural erasure is overturned by oral history performance in popular theatre. Autobiographical visibility gives agency to the teller and listener, as historical specificities provide both symbolic and social transactions that challenge conventional frameworks of knowledge. Shavon tells us,

> The signing of the treaties was conducted in 1876 with Hollow Water First Nation. This is an important day as it recognized title to the traditional territories. Chief Thick foot was the signatory who signed the treaty for Hollow Water First Nation. Chief Thick foot would sign the treaty with an X. The X signed in the treaty is significant as it entails the oral history of the community. The X in the treaty, represents the four elements of Anishinabek cultural beliefs. The X was not used only because the Chief didn't know how to write, it was used to signify the covenant made between Anishinaabe people and the creator. My mother would include this teaching in the performance.

In a globalized world rife with political interests and territorial neocolonialism, accountability is implicit in the performance of oral history. It seeks to dismantle colonial powers and knowledges. Entrenched in neocolonialism is the contradiction and uncomfortable memory of those whose lands were stolen and colonized. Oral history bears witness to the colonized, naming the contradictions and violent repercussions that may be reconciled by the TRC. What I have offered here is oral history work and performance as *one* option to reconstitute and reclaim senses of community and self for First Nations women and their communities.

It seems clear to me that the TRC sought to learn from the mistakes of the past so as not to repeat them, but its work of gathering evidence through testimonies is now complete. It has opened a door for healing to begin, but the door must be opened more widely if a long-term process of community healing is to occur. Sharing through oral history and popular theatre has much to contribute to the process. Healing comes through being seen and engaging in full citizenship, within one's own community, free of state legitimization and the racial and cultural biases that continue to marginalize First Nations in Canada.

If genuine progress is to be achieved, state policies must recognize that remediating the trauma imposed by colonialism is a complicated process. Thus, the Canadian government must provide financial support for Indigenous ways of knowing, remembering, and making sense of historic trauma. Ottawa must also supply long-term funding for comprehensive, holistic supports that allow individuals and communities to heal mentally, physically, emotionally, and spiritually.

Situating oral narrative within the context of healing provides an opportunity to realize the broader objective of building and sustaining community by "making oral history understood as the recreation of storied experiences for the primary purpose of gaining social-historical perspective" (Pollock 2005). If the TRC vision of "reconciliation ... towards a new relationship" with Indigenous people is to be realized, it will require a broad societal understanding that the healing has just begun.

NOTES

1 Available at https://www.youtube.com/watch?v=xFHwg6aNKy0. See also Lorde (2007).
2 My 2015 interviews with Shavon Sinclair are quoted throughout this chapter.

REFERENCES

Joe, Rita 1988. "I Lost My Talk." In *Song of Eskasoni: More Poems of Rita Joe,* ed. Lee Maracle. Charlottetown: Ragweed Press.

Lorde, Audre. 2007. "Uses of the Erotic: The Erotic as Power." In *Sister Outsider: Essays and Speeches by Audre Lorde,* 53–59. Berkeley, CA: Crossing Press.

Pollock, Della, ed. 2005. *Remembering: Oral History Performance.* New York: Palgrave Macmillan.

Rice, Joanna. 2011. "Indian Residential School Truth and Reconciliation Commission of Canada." *Cultural Survival Quarterly Magazine,* March 1. https://www.cultural survival.org/publications/cultural-survival-quarterly/indian-residential-school -truth-and-reconciliation.

Smith, Linda Tuhiwai. 2012. *Decolonizing Methodologies: Research and Indigenous Peoples.* 2nd ed. New York: Zed Books.

TRC (Truth and Reconciliation Commission of Canada). N.d. http://www.trc.ca/ websites/trcinstitution/index.php?p=807.

Conclusion
Possibility, Promise, and Policy Change

SHAUNA MacKINNON

This collection of stories about community-based participatory research (CBPR) shows that research can have a transformative impact on the people who participate in it and the communities where they live and work. For the university academics who undertook the projects discussed here, CBPR has brought their research skills outside the ivory tower to collaborate with those working on the front lines to effect social change.

Many scholars have activist roots aligned with social justice, but the pressures and responsibilities of academic life all too often disengage them from the community. The demands of academia are increasingly such that faculty are deterred from public involvement. The university has become "more and more institutionalized, professionalized and commercialized" (Jacoby 1999, 115). Although universities promote excellence in teaching and service to community, professors are mainly rewarded for their research, the number of publications they produce, and the grants they receive. And though research-funding agencies increasingly look for university-community collaboration, institutional demands have made it difficult for academics to undertake such activities. As Cahill, Cerecer, and Bradley (2010, 412) explain, engaging in CBPR is challenging for university-based academics, who are required to "jump through academic hoops that sometimes celebrate, but mostly regulate, and often leave us feeling delegitimized as community-based participatory action researchers." Although these obstacles are very real, community-university alliances can provide a welcoming and creative environment for academics who wish to conduct research that is useful to non-academics who share their social justice aims.

CBPR enables activist-minded academics to rediscover a role as agents of social change. It allows us to explore new approaches that respond to the needs and desires of community partners who share our hopes for equity and justice. Gramsci (1971) envisioned the intellectual as strategist, leader, and educator, working side by side with the "subaltern," and the CBPR described in this book provides examples of researchers, students, activists, and community residents working together. Each brought unique skills, experiences, and expertise to examine lessons learned, explore what is possible, and use their collective knowledge and power to effect policy change.

For the students who contributed to this publication, CBPR furnished a transition from their university life into the "real world." Like their professors, students all too often become fixated on textbook knowledge and the demands of Western-defined scholarship. Of course, these forms of knowledge provide an extremely important base, but as students Agnieszka Pawlowska-Mainville, Rosa Evelia Sanchez Garcia, Maya Seshia, Sarah Cooper, and Carole O'Brien learned, a world of knowledge lies outside the classroom. CBPR provides a context where textbook knowledge can be applied but also where different forms of knowledge are learned. It allows researchers to apply what they know while also learning what they don't know. This can be a humbling and important lesson for seasoned researchers and students alike, as they step away from the protective walls of academia.

Involvement in CBPR can also come with great responsibility and self-awareness. Outsiders who undertake it owe much to their community partners for welcoming them into their world and trusting in them to do research differently. Although the outside researchers in this book are genuinely interested in non-hierarchical research that respects multiple ways of knowing, the realities of power and privilege cannot be denied. Indeed, tenured researchers who engage in post-research policy advocacy enjoy considerable privilege by virtue of their university ties, whereas many of their community partners remain vulnerable to the whims of governments and other funding agencies.

For the researchers and representatives of community-based organizations, involvement in CBPR provides an opportunity to demonstrate the depth and breadth of the knowledge they have garnered from their work on the front lines. These intellectuals play a central role in the CBPR described in this book. Typically, community partners have been the drivers of the research – it is they who decide what needs to be explored. Although researchers can offer a variety of methods and tools, community partners will select the ones that best suit their needs.

The projects with the greatest impact are those where researchers also assisted with advocacy for policy change. In these cases, the research contributed to real improvements. For example, Chapter 5 explains how an ongoing research-action relationship increased social and affordable housing in Manitoba.

As Chapter 4 reveals, research also helped to instigate many changes at the public-housing developments in Lord Selkirk Park. And the experiences that residents describe in Chapter 9 prompted policy makers to strengthen their commitment to make resources available to public-housing developments. This research also led to subsequent projects involving researchers and residents of public housing (Brandon and Silver 2015).

The project described in Chapter 12 put a spotlight on racism at a time when many Winnipeggers were reluctant to admit its prevalence. Since the release of the report titled "Fixing Our Divided City" (2012) and the accompanying film *Breaking Barriers, Building Bridges* (O'Brien, 2012), the discourse in Winnipeg has shifted significantly, with the result that this "elephant in the room" has been widely acknowledged, and solutions are more openly discussed. The ongoing policy advocacy related to this project demonstrates the importance of remaining politically attuned to opportunities that arise. However, Winnipeg remains a deeply racist city, as exposed in *Maclean's* magazine (Macdonald 2015). Both this fact and the awareness stemming from the Truth and Reconciliation Commission of Canada have prompted an interest in the policy recommendations outlined in the "Fixing Our Divided City" report and described in Chapter 12. We have recently begun to meet with government curriculum developers to establish a similar project in the high school curriculum. This shows the importance of aligning CBPR with policy advocacy. The former can produce important tools, but unless we put them to work and strike while the iron is hot, opportunities can be lost. More than four years have passed since "Fixing Our Divided City" was published and *Breaking Barriers, Building Bridges* was released. We have only recently been able to move this research to action. It is also fair to add that were it not for the passion and persistence of researchers who advocate for policy change, we wouldn't have made it this far.

The projects discussed above are examples of the power and possibility of community-based, community-led, policy-focused research. For the other projects examined in this book, the impact has been less clear, though we believe they have made an important contribution to the public discourse and/or the advocacy capacity of communities. For example, systemic violence in Winnipeg's street sex trade remains a serious problem, as discussed by Maya Seshia in Chapter 8. However, public awareness and dialogue have increased, which we hope will lead to a safer environment for sex workers. A potential improvement arose in 2013, when Winnipeg Police Services announced a new approach, "implementing a strategy that focuses squarely on those who are engaged in the exploitation of women in the sex trade including the 'exploiters,' human traffickers, pimps, and sexual predators that target these vulnerable persons on a regular basis" (MyToba n.d.). We cannot directly connect Seshia's research with this development, but it has helped strengthen activist efforts to draw public attention to violence against women in the sex trade.

The dialogue on how best to evaluate programs through an Indigenous lens is ongoing, and barriers do remain. However, funding agencies have become increasingly open to the possibility. University and community researchers continue to work with community-based organizations to develop evaluation models that better reflect their programs and the realities of their participants. We have a long way to go before evaluating programs via Indigenous models alone is fully accepted, but Indigenous community-based organizations and many others are increasingly demanding change in the way they are evaluated. They are using our research to make a case for different approaches.

The research conducted in Hollow Water First Nation (Chapter 6) and Poplar River First Nation (Chapter 7) has yet to achieve a measurable impact. However, it has armed these communities with material that may prove useful as they confront legal challenges. The researchers who spear-headed these projects have since completed their studies and are no longer working with these First Nations. So, though they walked beside the community and employed CBPR that left knowledge behind for later use, they have not had a role in subsequent policy advocacy. Nonetheless, many benefits were realized, including amplified local capacity for future re-search as well as the documentation of Indigenous knowledge that will be useful for generations to come. In the research described by Difarnecio in Chapter 13, transformation through one individual's performance of oral history is having ripple effects for a family and community ravaged by the trauma of colonial policies.

Perhaps the most important promise of CBPR is captured in the title of Chapter 1 – "It's All about Relationships." The projects with the most promising outcomes arose from ongoing relationships of trust between academics, community researchers, and front-line workers. At the time of writing, advocacy associated with the projects discussed in this book continued. Also, many new projects are under way, and there will be un-doubtedly many new stories to tell.

Although our stories focus on a specific region and context, with unique demographics, personalities, and experiences, the lessons we learned are transferable. The basic formula for conducting the CBPR described in this book – grounded in a desire for transformative social change – is universally applicable. It includes the fundamental belief that research must be driven by and embedded in communities; that though researchers have much to contribute, what others bring to the table is equally important; and that the work doesn't end when the final report is written. Transformative community-based participatory research requires shared vision and long-term commitment to the shaping of a more equitable world.

REFERENCES

Brandon, Josh, and Jim Silver. 2015. *Poor Housing: A Silent Crisis*. Halifax/Winnipeg: Fernwood/Canadian Centre for Policy Alternatives–Manitoba.

Cahill, Caitlin, David Cerecer, and Matt Bradley. 2010. "'Dreaming of ...': Reflections on Participatory Action Research as Feminist Praxis of Critical Hope." *Afillia: Journal of Women and Social Work* 25 (4): 406–16.

Gramsci, Antonio. 1971. *Selections from the Prison Notebooks of Antonio Gramsci*, ed. and trans. Q. Hoare and G.N. Smith. New York: International.

Jacoby, Russell. 1999. *The End of Utopia: Politics and Culture in an Age of Apathy*. New York: Basic Books.

Macdonald, Nancy. 2015. "Welcome to Winnipeg: Where Canada's Racism Problem Is at Its Worst." *Maclean's,* January 22. http://www.macleans.ca/news/canada/welcome-to-winnipeg-where-canadas-racism-problem-is-at-its-worst/.

MyToba. N.d. "New Sex Trade Strategy for Winnipeg Police." http://mytoba.ca/news/new-sex-trade-strategy-for-winnipeg-police/.

O'Brien, Carole, dir. 2012. *Breaking Barriers, Building Bridges.* Winnipeg: CCPA–MB. https://www.youtube.com/watch?v=NIMrk8sE5tA.

Appendix

MRA REPORTS AND RELATED PUBLICATION AND KNOWLEDGE MOBILIZATION TOOLS

Websites

Manitoba Research Alliance. http://mra-mb.ca/
Manitoba Right to Housing Coalition. http://righttohousing.ca/

MRA Publications and Student Theses

Canadian Centre for Policy Alternatives (CCPA). 2005. *The Promise of Investment in Community-Led Renewal: State of the Inner City Report, 2005 (Part I: Policy Considerations)*. http://www.policyalternatives.ca/sites/default/files/uploads/publications/Manitoba_Pubs/2005/State_of_Inner_City_2005_Part1.pdf.

–. 2005. *The Promise of Investment in Community-Led Renewal: State of the Inner City Report, 2005 (Part II: A View from the Neighbourhoods)*. https://www.policyalternatives.ca/sites/default/files/uploads/publications/Manitoba_Pubs/2005/State_of_Inner_City_2005_Part2.pdf.

–. 2006. *Inner-City Voices, Community-Based Solutions: State of the Inner City Report, 2006*. https://www.policyalternatives.ca/sites/default/files/uploads/publications/Manitoba_Pubs/2006/State_of_the_Inner_City_2006.pdf.

–. 2006. *Inner City Refugee Women: Lessons for Public Policy: State of the Inner City Report 2006*. Research for Communities Series. https://www.policyalternatives.ca/sites/default/files/uploads/publications/Manitoba_Pubs/2007/Research_for_Communities_Refugee_Women.pdf.

–. 2007. *Step by Step: Stories of Change in Winnipeg's Inner City: State of the Inner City Report, 2007*. https://www.policyalternatives.ca/sites/default/files/uploads/publications/Manitoba_Pubs/2007/State_of_the_Inner_City2007.pdf.

–. 2008. *Putting Our Housing in Order: State of the Inner City Report, 2008.* http://mra-mb.ca/wp-content/uploads/8-sic_report_2008.pdf.

–. 2009. *It Takes All Day to Be Poor: State of the Inner City Report, 2009.* https://www.policyalternatives.ca/sites/default/files/uploads/publications/reports/docs/SIC_2009_report_120909.pdf.

–. 2010. *We're in It for the Long Haul: State of the Inner City Report, 2010.* https://www.policyalternatives.ca/sites/default/files/uploads/publications/Manitoba%20Office/2010/12/2010%20SIC%20long%20haul.pdf.

–. 2011. *Neoliberalism: What a Difference a Theory Makes: State of the Inner City Report, 2011.* https://www.policyalternatives.ca/sites/default/files/uploads/publications/Manitoba%20Office/2011/12/SIC%202011%20Full%20Report.pdf.

–. 2012. *Breaking Barriers, Building Bridges: State of the Inner City Report, 2012.* https://www.policyalternatives.ca/sites/default/files/uploads/publications/Manitoba%20Office/2013/12/State_of_Inner_City2012.pdf.

–. 2013. *A Youth Lens on Poverty in Winnipeg: State of the Inner City Report, 2013.* https://www.policyalternatives.ca/sites/default/files/uploads/publications/Manitoba%20Office/2013/12/State_of_inner_city_report_2013.pdf.

–. 2014. *Community, Research and Social Change: State of the Inner City Report, 2014.* https://www.policyalternatives.ca/sites/default/files/uploads/publications/Manitoba%20Office/2014/12/Inner%20City%202014%20low-res.pdf.

–. 2015. *Drawing on Our Strengths: State of the Inner City Report, 2015.* https://www.policyalternatives.ca/sites/default/files/uploads/publications/Manitoba%20Office/2015/12/Inner%20City%202015%20WEB%202.pdf.

–. 2016. *Reconciliation Lives Here: State of the Inner City Report, 2016.* https://www.policyalternatives.ca/sites/default/files/uploads/publications/Manitoba%20Office/2016/12/State_of_Inner_City_Report_2016.pdf.

Chippeway, Darrell. 2013. "A Report on Preserving the History of Aboriginal Institutional Development in Winnipeg Project." Winnipeg, Manitoba Research Alliance.

Cooper, Sarah. 2012. *You Know You're Not Alone: Community Development in Public Housing.* http://www.policyalternatives.ca/sites/default/files/uploads/publications/Manitoba%20Office/2012/04/You%20Know%20You%27re%20Not%20Alone%202012.pdf.

Lottis, Jovan, and Molly McCracken, with Mary Burton, Isabel Jerez, and Art Ladd. 2014. *Rooming Houses to Rooming Homes.* Report. Winnipeg: Canadian Centre for Policy Alternatives–MB. https://www.policyalternatives.ca/sites/default/files/uploads/publications/Manitoba%20Office/2014/05/Rooming%20Houses%20to%20Homes%20final%20report.pdf.

MacKinnon, Shauna. 2005. "The Real Housing Shortage in Winnipeg." *Fast Facts* (CCPA–MB), March 3. https://www.policyalternatives.ca/sites/default/files/uploads/publications/Manitoba_Pubs/2005/FastFacts_March3_05.pdf.

–. 2005. "What's Happening to Low Income Rental Housing in Winnipeg's Inner City?" *Fast Facts* (CCPA–MB), March 2. https://www.policyalternatives.ca/sites/default/files/uploads/publications/Manitoba_Pubs/2005/FastFacts_March2_05.pdf.

–. 2007. "Housing: It's Time to Set Targets." *Fast Facts* (CCPA–MB), May 17. http://www.policyalternatives.ca/sites/default/files/uploads/publications/Manitoba_Pubs/2007/FastFacts_May17_07_Housing.pdf.

–. 2008. "Privatization of Public Housing: Who Really Benefits?" *Fast Facts* (CCPA–MB), December 22. https://www.policyalternatives.ca/publications/reports/fast-facts-privatization-public-housing.

–. 2008. "Rent Control in Manitoba: Challenging the Myths." *Fast Facts* (CCPA–MB), December 23. https://www.policyalternatives.ca/publications/reports/fast-facts-rent-control-manitoba-2.

–. 2009. "I Just Want to Have a Decent Home: 'Joe's' Story." *Fast Facts* (CCPA–MB), July 8. http://www.policyalternatives.ca/sites/default/files/uploads/publications/Manitoba_Pubs/2009/FF_A_decent_home_070809.pdf.

MacKinnon, Shauna, and Charlene Lafreniere. 2009. "The Housing Crisis in Thompson." *Fast Facts* (CCPA–MB), April 29. https://www.policyalternatives.ca/publications/reports/fast-facts-housing-crisis-thompson.

MacKinnon, Shauna, et al. 2008. *Is Participation Having an Impact? Measuring Progress in Winnipeg's Inner City through the Voices of Community-Based Program Participants*. Winnipeg: Canadian Centre for Policy Alternatives–MB. http://www.policyalternatives.ca/sites/default/files/uploads/publications/Manitoba_Pubs/2008/Is_Participation_Having_an_Impact.pdf.

O'Brien, Carole. 2013. "Having CLOUT: Becoming an Ally and Having the Power to Resist Colonialism and Neoliberalism in Winnipeg's Inner City." Master's thesis, University of Manitoba.

Pawlowska-Mainville, Agnieszka. 2014. "Escaping the 'Progress Trap': UNESCO World Heritage Site Nomination and Land Stewardship through Intangible Cultural Heritage in Asatiwisipe First Nation, Manitoba." PhD diss., University of Manitoba.

Roussin, Diane, and Tammy Christensen. 2010. "Public Funds for Youth for Christ: Have Our Politicians Learned Nothing from Past Mistakes?" *Fast Facts* (CCPA–MB), February 23. https://www.policyalternatives.ca/publications/commentary/public-funds-youth-christ.

Seshia, Maya. 2005. *The Unheard Speak Out: Street Sexual Exploitation in Winnipeg.* Report. Winnipeg: Canadian Centre for Policy Alternatives–MB. http://policy alternatives.ca/sites/default/files/uploads/publications/Manitoba_Pubs/2005/ The_Unheard_Speak_Out.pdf.

–. 2010. "Naming Systemic Violence in Winnipeg's Street Sex Trade." *Canadian Journal of Urban Research* 19 (1): 1–17.

Skelton, Ian, and Richard Mahé. 2009. *'We Got Evicted ... Did I Leave That Out?' Stories of Housing and Mental Health.* Report. Winnipeg: Canadian Centre for Policy Alternatives–MB. http://www.policyalternatives.ca/sites/default/files/ uploads/publications/Manitoba_Pubs/2009/stories_of_housing_and_mental_ health.pdf.

Skelton, Ian, Cheryl Selig, and Lawrence Deane. 2006. "Social Housing, Neighbour-hood Revitalization and Community Economic Development." June 28. Winnipeg: Canadian Centre for Policy Alternatives–MB. https://www.policyalternatives. ca/publications/reports/social-housing-neighbourhood-revitalization-and -community-economic-development.

Films

Nepinak, Darryl, dir. 2013. *Preserving the History of Aboriginal Institutional Development in Winnipeg.* Winnipeg: CCPA–MB. October 22. https://www.youtube.com/ watch?v=EJAs8-x8a1I.

O'Brien, Carole, dir. 2012. *Breaking Barriers, Building Bridges.* Winnipeg: CCPA–MB. https://www.youtube.com/watch?v=NIMrk8sE5tA.

–. 2011. *Together We Have CLOUT.* Winnipeg: CCPA–MB. https://www.youtube. com/watch?v=rSmn7X2-Glw.

Contributors

Maureen Barchyn is program director at Family Dynamics. She retired in 2016.

Clark Brownlee is a retired social worker. He is a founding member of the Right to Housing Coalition, where he volunteered as the coordinator from 2006 to 2017.

Sarah Cooper is a doctoral student in urban planning and policy at the University of Illinois–Chicago.

Doris Difarnecio is director of Centro Hemispherico (San Cristóbal de las Casas, Mexico, and New York).

Claire Friesen is an activity-based learning facilitator at CEDA Pathways to Education.

Janice Goodman is the community development director at the North End Community Renewal Corporation.

Cheyenne Henry is past project coordinator at the Lord Selkirk Park Resource Centre.

Josie Hill is past director of Ma Mawi Wi Chi Itata Centre and is currently executive director of Blue Thunderbird Family Care, Inc.

Darlene Klyne is program director at CEDA Pathways to Education.

John Loxley is a professor of economics at the University of Manitoba.

Shauna MacKinnon is an associate professor and chair in the Department of Urban and Inner City Studies at the University of Winnipeg.

Janet Nowatzki is a researcher at CEDA Pathways to Education.

Carole O'Brien has a master's degree in city planning and is a freelance researcher and filmmaker.

Agnieszka (Agnes) Pawlowska-Mainville is an assistant professor with the First Nations Studies Department at the University of Northern British Columbia and the co-director of the international Cross-Cultural Indigenous Exchange Program between UNBC and Te Whare Wānanga o Awanuiārangi in Aotearoa.

Evelyn Peters is a Canada Research Chair in Inner City Issues, Community Learning and Engagement, University of Winnipeg. She is also a professor in the Department of Urban and Inner City Studies.

Diane Roussin is past executive director of Ma Mawi Wi Chi Itata Centre and the project director at the Winnipeg Boldness Project.

Rosa Evelia Sanchez Garcia is an assistant professor in the Community Economic and Social Development Department at Algoma University.

Maya Seshia is completing her PhD in political science at the University of Alberta.

Jim Silver is a professor in the Department of Urban and Inner City Studies at the University of Winnipeg.

Carolyn Young is the director of the Manidoo Gi Miini Gonaan Child Care Centre at Lord Selkirk Park.

Index

232. *See also* film and video; Hollow
Water First Nation, popular theatre;
Together We Have CLOUT (film)
Strand, Kerry, 7
street sex trade workers. *See* sex trade
workers
Strength of the Mayan Woman
(FOMMA), 233
strength-based approaches: asset-based
approach in CD, 83–84; CBPR principles, 5, 76; evaluation, 65; Family
Dynamics resource centres, 164, 170
surveys: distrust in Indigenous communities, 67, 139; housing, 166, 168,
169; impersonality, 67; Life Factors
Survey, 67, 71–72; sex trade workers,
153, 156; trusting relationships, 67
Sweeney, Shelley, 200–201, 210n2
systemic oppression. *See* colonization
and oppression

theatre, popular: about, 231–33; decolonization, 231–32, 250; oral history
performance, 232, 235, 238–42;
physical and vocal warm-ups, 235–
36, 239. *See also* Hollow Water First
Nation, popular theatre
Thick foot, Chief, 244
Thomas, Clive, 75
Thunderbird House, 221, 226
Together We Have CLOUT (film): about,
34, 179–80, 188–91; audiences, 188;
behind the camera, 184–85; decolonization, 184–88, 190–91; MRA
and CLOUT collaboration, 34; news
media, 180–81; online access, 49n1;
resistance to mainstream, 182–84;
stories and voice, 186–90; trusting
relations, 179, 184–85. *See also*

CLOUT (Community Led Organizations United Together)
transformative evaluation framework,
58
transformative research, 7–8, 27–28.
See also CBPR (community-based
participatory research)
transgendered people: sex trade workers, 145, 146
TRC. *See* Truth and Reconciliation
Commission
Tri-Council Policy Statement: Ethical
Conduct for Research Involving
Humans, 39–40
"The Trouble with Housing for Low-
Income People" (MacKinnon and
Silver), 100
trusting relationships: about, 8–9, 47–
48, 250; CEDA pathways program,
67; CLOUT projects, 179–80, 184–
85, 189; decolonization, 184–85;
empowerment of informants, 136;
financial costs, 140; Hollow Water
research, 122; Indigenous archiving
policies, 210n2; interviews for Life
Factors Survey, 67; knowledge prod-
ucts, 9, 47–48; "let's have tea," 134–
37; Lord Selkirk Park, 76–79, 86–87;
oral history, 238; power and privilege, 9; qualitative evaluation, 67; recognition in research, 140; research
assistants, 47–48; sharing circles for
evaluation, 61–63; smudge ceremonies, 62; time needed to nurture, 8,
140; transformative research, 8; visiting and sharing food, 135. *See also*
power relations
Truth and Reconciliation Commission:
archives at U of Manitoba, 200; oral